CONTENTS

PRAISE FOR *WHAT'S GOOD*

"*What's Good* is, among a great many other things, a byproduct of joyful obsession and immersion into both language and sound, an intersection that offers a rich and expansive land upon which to play. I'm grateful for Levin Becker's mining of that land and the revelations found along the way, revelations which come to life in this book with a vivid and generous exuberance."
—Hanif Abdurraqib, author of *A Little Devil in America: Notes in Praise of Black Performance*

"For those of us who love rap, *What's Good* is a gift. The book offers a new set of eyes and ears through which to see and to hear the language of rap. Its brief and brilliant chapters are like the best kinds of freestyles: spontaneous and structured, startling and profound. Daniel Levin Becker flexes remarkable command of more than forty years of music, putting 2Pac in conversation with Young M.A, the Fearless Four with Tyler, the Creator. A remarkable achievement."
—Adam Bradley, author of *Book of Rhymes: The Poetics of Hip Hop*

"Could this be the rap equivalent of Lewis Hyde's *The Gift* or Marina Warner's *Once upon a Time*? Anyhow, it's an electrifying book, full of wild epiphanies and provocations, an exhibition of a critical mind in full and open contact with its subject at the highest level, with a winning streak of confessional intimacy as well. Frequent sharp amazed laughter and a crazed hunger for contact with the music in question, those were the result for me."
—Jonathan Lethem, author of *The Arrest: A Novel*

WHAT'S GOOD

WHAT'S GOOD

NOTES ON RAP AND LANGUAGE

DANIEL LEVIN BECKER

CITY LIGHTS BOOKS

Cover design: Jeff Mellin / www.jeffmellin.com

ISBN: 978-0-87286-876-2
eISBN: 978-0-87286-858-8

Library of Congress Cataloging-in-Publication Data

Names: Levin Becker, Daniel, author.
Title: What's good : notes on rap and language / Daniel Levin Becker.
Description: San Francisco : City Lights Books, 2022. | Includes
    bibliographical references.
Identifiers: LCCN 2021014176 | ISBN 9780872868762 (trade paperback)
Subjects: LCSH: Rap (Music)—History and criticism. | Rap
    (Music)—Analysis, appreciation. | Music and language.
Classification: LCC ML3531 .L45 2022 | DDC 782.421649/09--dc23
LC record available at https://lccn.loc.gov/2021014176

City Lights Books are published at the City Lights Bookstore
261 Columbus Avenue, San Francisco, CA 94133
www.citylights.com

PREFACE

• •

IF YOU'RE READING THIS, it's already too late. Rap has moved on. This book can't be held responsible for or looked to for comment on whoever is newly canonized or canceled or dearly departed, whoever's just been handed a jail sentence or an honorary Ivy League degree, how we're currently feeling about Kanye West. This book wishes those people the best in whatever awaits them, but it has no insight into the future, which is to say into your present. At most it has modest hopes and expectations—that words like *opp* and *drip* and *twelve* will sound as canonically worn-out to your ear as *sucker* and *floss* and *five-o* do to mine, that you have come to lionize Dreezy and Kash Doll and think Desiigner is a typo—but it doesn't know anything beyond its now. We can't move through time that way, this book and I, and I bring it up because one of the magical and confounding things about rap music is that somehow it can.

This book is, was destined all along to be, the product of a moment: an interval of joyous immersion and contemplation and study that lasted the better part of a decade but whose subject spills past its temporal bounds in both directions. My intent was less to write anything definitive or exhaustive than to propose a sort of interpretive mesh whose specific examples—sports references, vegetal euphemisms for marijuana, best practices for credit card scams—could be replaced intuitively, productively, by fresher

1

material. "Write like something you don't mean to be erased but one day know will," as Kevin Young puts it in *The Grey Album*: "then let them try." I wanted to highlight, in between the specifics I did manage to inventory, some things that seem to me to be timeless in rap, transcendent or unchanging or in permanent flux. I wanted to think out loud about why I can't get them out of my head, about how they work and what they mean about language, that amber in which timelessness is visible when you squint.

I finished fussing over the mesh sometime in 2018. The world continued to spin. I had written about the weird life some rap lyrics come to lead when commodified beyond context, and about Jay-Z's wanton borrowings from other people's raps, and then Jay sued an Australian company called The Little Homie over a book called *A B to Jay-Z*, which contained the line *If you're having alphabet problems I feel bad for you son, I got 99 problems but my ABCs ain't one.* (Craftily, The Little Homie pointed out that Jay-Z had appropriated those words from Ice-T. You probably know better than I do how the case ended.) I had written about the worrisome trend of criminal courts in America admitting rap lyrics as evidence, and then I learned that rappers in England were getting court orders amounting to five-year censorship sentences. At some point Donald Trump pulled some strings to get A$AP Rocky out of jail in Sweden; later his reelection campaign scored endorsements from Ice Cube and Kodak Black and Lil Wayne, who praised his criminal reform efforts. At some point Kanye, who appears here in a song glorifying the Grammy Awards, tweeted a video of himself peeing on one. At some point *opp* was an answer in a *Times* crossword. I could go on listing these screw-turns of complexity, these slippages of reality from where I left it, but my point is that eventually the list will just be this book itself. So it goes. I've expanded or nuanced or corrected some things, but even now what follows feels like a time capsule from a time remembered only distantly.

At the end of this book I wonder about the notion that we speak a common language in America, about whether we can really take it on faith that we do if "Black lives matter" is a controversial sentence and Eric Garner can say *I can't breathe* plainly, repeatedly, and still be choked to death by police. And then this year George Floyd was murdered in the same way, in spite of saying the same words. By then, and all the more since, rap had begun to seem like a smaller and smaller subplot in a story about the world. Has it always been irresponsible to conflate rap with the black experience in America? Is it frivolous to think it can help us learn to understand each other? Maybe, maybe not. But rap is always present, its language, its attitude, its technologies of storytelling and misdirection and economy, the way it dramatizes pleasure and sadness and anger and pain. It finds its way into everything. It's history telling itself in real time, a telescope and a megaphone. It's a loop, at least for me, that makes the present that much richer, that much more intelligible.

Floyd was a rapper too, for a time. He didn't make a career of it, but he made some moves in one of the most magnetic and strange rap scenes of the twentieth century, and if his talents were modest he still fit in perfectly there, sounded buoyant and airy and free even over the glacial grind of a DJ Screw beatscape. The thing is he still sounds that way now, however many years hence. His loss is senseless and tragic, and neither this book nor I need to see the future to know that will still be true at the moment you're reading this, no matter many new bad things have happened since. No matter how late it's gotten. But what a joyous, generous, weightless way for his voice to stay alive. What a place to spend forever.

DLB, DECEMBER 2020

& in the way nets cannot hold water, nor could I paint the sea
RICHARD FLANAGAN, *GOULD'S BOOK OF FISH*

INTRODUCTIONS

RHETORICAL QUESTIONS

I'm into having sex, I ain't into making love
So come give me a hug if you're into getting rubbed

50 Cent, "In Da Club" (2003)

• •

IS THERE ANY couplet in the English language that so concisely spans the dizzying sweep of poetic possibility, the subtle gradations of sense illuminated in a few short words and the abyss of nonsense toward which we are ever drawn by carelessness and entropy? You don't have to answer that. The answer is "yes, many." I was making a point.

You've probably heard the stately bounce of "In Da Club," at least ambiently. It was 50 Cent's mainstream breakout single, and he mostly spends it surveying the fixtures of his nightlife: drinks and drugs, cars and jewelry, prospective lovers and pissy haters. If we're meant to take anything away from the song, though, it's that 50 is 25 percent hedonist and 75 percent hustler. So he puts the song to work for him, makes it tell us what he's about, what he's been through, who his friends are, how he moves through the world. After fifteen years of career ups and downs, flops and feuds, fluctuating wealth and implausibly diverse investments, it remains an indelible sketch of 50 at his fiftiest.

If you watch how I move you'll mistake me for a player or pimp /
Been hit with a few shells but I don't walk with a limp

"In Da Club"

9

I try not to say nothing the DA
might want to play in court /
But I'll hunt a duck nigga down
like it's a sport

50 Cent, "What Up Gangsta"
(2001)

Now, generally speaking, 50 relies as much as any rapper does on similes, homophones, trick rhymes, and assorted other kinds of semantic misdirection. He once even described the name 50 Cent as "a metaphor for change." Yet when you look closely, "In Da Club" contains almost no wordplay, no figuration, no trickery. When he says you can find him in the club, he's not being evasive: if you're looking for him, that's probably where he'll be. When he offers you ecstasy—*I got the X if you're into taking drugs*—he's barely even using slang. It is, and fittingly for the calling card of a no-nonsense street magnate, a bracingly direct song. Except there's this one line, tucked memorably but unassumingly into the hook, a line you could in fact read as the very essence of 50's no-nonsenseness:

I'm into having sex, I ain't into making love

It's perfectly clear what he means by this: he doesn't have time for romance. He's not a player, he's a *hustler*. No nonsense, all grind. It's slippery, though, this little pinprick of character definition, how what it says sits at odds with the way it's expressed. The distinction between *having sex* and *making love* is negligible biologically but critical sentimentally, after all—and here's 50 using it to tell us how uninterested he is in sentimentality. Quietly but repeatedly, twice in each chorus of the song that introduced him to the global pop market as a hard-nosed hood kingpin, he's framing his identity through language and idiom and metaphor. And finally, beneath the mythologies of money and sex, the beef and bullet wounds, what defines a rapper more intimately than his or her relationship to those things?

And then there's this—

So come give me a hug if you're into getting rubbed

—which… woof. How do you follow such a pearl of rhetorical legerdemain as the sex/love line with *that*? This question haunts me.

"In Da Club"

Yo, Pep, I don't think they're
gonna play this on the radio. /
— And why not? Everybody has
sex. / I mean, everybody should
be makin' love.

Salt-n-Pepa, "Let's Talk About
Sex" (1991)

10

It's not wholly displeasing to the ear: the internal vowel rhyme is a nice touch, as is that third *into* binding the lines together. But what does *getting rubbed* mean? Does it mean being sexually serviced in crude, utilitarian fashion? Does it mean being murdered? Will 50 Cent kill anyone who touches him, or accept a tender embrace on the condition that it lead straight to intercourse? In either case, is the best word really *rubbed*, which is too mealy to sound threatening and too workmanlike to be sexy? What's that conjunctive *so* doing there? What does this thought say about the previous one? How come I've never heard *rubbed*—*rubbed out* and *rubbed off* and *rubbed on*, yes, but never just *rubbed*—anywhere else? What am I missing? How, a thousand times how, does the sly precision of the immediately preceding line wind us up at a ham-handed muddle like this?

No, *you're* reading too far into it.

The point I'm making is that rap lyrics, even ones from such a poetically trivial source as "In Da Club," contain multitudes of meaning, and also of nonsense, of possibility, of exquisite care and carelessness and carefreeness, sometimes all at once. If 50 Cent can be ingenious and metaphysical *and* clumsy and puerile in the space of twenty words, six seconds, just imagine what depths of inventiveness and complexity and contradiction abound within a lyrical tradition that will soon turn, well, fifty.

Yes, many.

This book's argument is that rap music serves, consistently, contagiously, sometimes in spite of its own claims to the contrary, as a delivery mechanism for the most exhilarating and crafty and inspiring use of language in contemporary American culture. I hold this to be true on a number of levels, from the political and the conceptual down to the phonological and the syntactic, but I'm concerned most of all, here, with the semantic: with the creation and control of sense. There are plenty of resources available that encourage us to decide or debate what rap lyrics mean from this

I'm into having sex, I ain't into making love / So come give me a hug if you're into getting rubbed

So come give me a hug

11

song to that; there are plenty more that argue, often compellingly, often not, about what rap means as a cultural totality. There is, inevitably, some of both in what follows. But what I want to engage with above any of that is *how* rap means—how it can say both less and more than it appears to, depending on the way we listen; how it compels and challenges us to follow along; how it forges these vital, beguiling grooves of imagination and reality that lodge and blossom in our memory, personal and historical, even as the record keeps spinning.

REWINDING

• •

THE RECORD DOES not, of course, actually spin. If you're just joining us from the distant future, the vinyl LP has joined the ranks of the corded telephone handset and the stamped envelope as metaphors—*skeuomorphs* being the technical term—for processes that happen mostly in electronic independence of the devices that symbolize them. The 12" and the needle will always be part of hip-hop lore, as will the activities that accompany them: mixing, beat-matching, scratch breaks, picking through milk crates full of feathered cardboard sleeves in search of snippets to sample. But the majority of rap production and playback is done today with software, some of which is designed, functionally or metaphorically, to resemble the interface of turntable and record.

By the same token, *rewind* rarely still means to literally wind back. My copy of the Atmosphere mixtape containing "Higher

Living" was an actual tape, one I used to play in the cassette deck of a sky-blue Mercury whose chunky rewind and fast-forward buttons I miss with an almost tactile nostalgia. If you mashed both buttons at the same time the tape would flip over—another metaphor, since all it actually did was rotate the heads and reverse the direction of the motor. Still, there was a tiny bit of mechanical effort involved. *Push* really was the verb.

Odds are poor that it would break the top twenty all-time commonplace tropes of rapper self-aggrandizement, but tune in long enough and someone will eventually invoke what Slug does here: the power to turn the listener into a captive re-listener. An acolyte, a reverent exegete. It's not just rappers who rap about rapping who aspire to this power; it pops up all along the spectrum from gun-toting gangster to backpack-strapped indie lyricist. Slug does it, but so does 50 Cent. In a way it's the perfect rap boast, equal parts hyperbolic mind-control swagger and utterly attainable ambition: to be the man on the mic is to be *the man*, period, for as long as you're saying something people enjoy hearing. (I concede that most rewind boasts are not themselves particularly rewind-worthy.) And it's a pleasure verging on the narcotic when the thing it describes happens, when you find yourself caught up in the insular moment of a run or a riff or a rhyme, playing it back, held inside an almost literal loop of words.

• •

One evening in October 2009 the New Jersey producer Just Blaze went on the radio to debut "Exhibit C," a song he had made with the New Orleans rapper Jay Electronica. If you happen to have been listening, or to have downloaded the radio-rip mp3 that circulated for a few weeks before the CD-quality version dropped, you may recall a sickly, stringy spooling sound midway through the third verse while he spun the track back—on a vinyl emulation setup, I assume—muttering *hold up I gotta rewind I gotta rewind I*

To be the man that made you push rewind

Press rewind if I haven't blown your mind
Redman, "Blow Your Mind" (1992)

I crush 'em every time, punching with every line / I'm fucking with they mind, I make 'em press rewind
50 Cent, "Wanksta" (2002)

14

gotta rewind hoooold up. Then the song skidded to a stop and the verse started again:

> They call me Jay Electronica
> Fuck that: call me Jay Elec-Hanukkah, Jay Elec-yarmulke
> Jay Elect-Ramadan Muhammad asalaamica
> Rasoul Allah subhanahu wa ta'ala through your monitor
> My Uzi still weigh a ton, check the barometer
> I'm hotter than the motherfucking sun, check the thermometer

(2009)

Just Blaze was right. He still is, every time I play that mp3. You have to hear it twice, at least. Its density, its weightlessness. The way it glides over the ecstatic throb of the beat, piling up slant rhymes, blending pure phonetics and imagistic logic, slipping from English into Yiddish into Arabic back into English. The on-air rewind takes about four seconds, and in that space I hear triumph and bewilderment, a gestural acknowledgment that there's more in those bars than can be captured in a single encounter, perhaps in years of repeated plays. By the time I first saw Jay Electronica perform a few years later, you could go online and buy a T-shirt with some of this passage on it, and even the guy in the audience wearing that T-shirt couldn't quite keep up as he rapped along.

There's a reason the word *rewind* has stuck around so persistently despite the vanishing rarity of literal rewinding, and I don't think it's just that *progress bar* and *high-speed scrubbing* sound way lamer. It's that, to *rewind,* the listener has to make a choice. Causing someone to do it isn't just an accomplishment because it prolongs their passive consumption; it's worth bragging about because it demands and receives effort, mechanical or cognitive, forges a connection with someone who hears your words and decides to let them in, to hear them again, maybe once more, maybe twice, maybe on and off for so many years that some of those words start to mean new things. The

They call me Jay Electronica / Fuck that: call me Jay Elec-Hanukkah, Jay Elec-yarmulke / Jay Elect-Ramadan Muhammad asalaamica / Rasoul Allah subhanahu wa ta'ala through your monitor / My Uzi still weigh a ton, check the barometer / I'm hotter than the motherfucking sun, check the thermometer

*Baby girl you're so damn fine
though / I'm tryna know if I can
hit it from behind though / I'm
sippin' on you like some fine wine
though / And when it's over I
press rewind though*

Fetty Wap, "679" (2015)

rewind boast is anachronistic, but also utopian: it speaks to the faith that words can literally stop time, can bridge the past to the present, person to person, people to people.

I spend a lot of time thinking about these loops. I'm happy there. The best rationale I can give for this book is the extraordinary joy I find in exploring and revisiting them, my fascination with the way that spark travels from the mic to the tape to my mind, and with what happens to it as time passes. How the words become part of hip-hop history and American history and the history of the English language, and at the same time part of me. What goes on inside and outside of my head as I rewind this or that verse or couplet or one-liner, over and over, until my mental tape ribbon begins to fray and shear and other sounds, other words, start creeping in.

I know just printing the words here doesn't capture the full effect. It's not meant to. Rap is, in case it needs to be said outright, so much more than just words: it's rhythm and melody, cadence and accent, timbre and noise, tic and texture, attitude and memory and race and strife and struggle and squalor and opulence, vinyl scratches and tape splices and this one synthesized clang that's supposedly a cowbell but always sounds, to me, skeuomorphic at best. It's the riveting musicianship of producers and arrangers and DJs and hype men. All of these people and things are crucial to making rap what it is, but they're not the point of this book. This book is about rappers, who play language like an instrument, the best of them and the worst alike. This book is about language itself, which is already its own complex instrument, an unparalleled tool of manipulation and progress and power. And yet as I hear them, these rewindable moments only push further the limits of what language can do, realize its potential without exhausting it. They make something grow. My aim here is to present a selection of them with my commentary, from the molecular level outward to the grandiose, from individual words to the kinds of friction and fire they build together, in the hopes that even pressed

16

between the pages of a book they'll bloom in your eyes and ears and brain. Take them up slowly, if you have the time. Listen along, rewind and listen again, but also read them closely, say them out loud, tinker with them, challenge them, rearrange and be challenged and rearranged by them. Then hit play again, leave the loop, carry it with you as you move on.

ON COOL

The statements we make may be conceited and grim
But what's normal to us is an illusion to them

The Fearless Four, "It's Magic" (1982)

• •

FOR A TIME, near where I used to live in Paris, there was an always-parked truck whose sides were covered in an obscurely celestial blue and orange mural advertising someone named Mr. Agaz. Under his name was the legend MON CONCEPT VIENT D'AILLEURS: my concept comes from elsewhere. On aesthetic cues alone, I figured Mr. Agaz was an impressionist painter or an interior decorator or a voodoo priest, but as it turns out he's a rapper from Nice. His music sounds like mid-aughts outer-borough New York knucklehead rap, except in French, and in every photo I have seen of him he is scowling behind a neoprene face mask. *Mon concept vient d'ailleurs* is the name of one of his albums; its cover shows him scowling behind a neoprene face mask and under a bowler hat, wearing a T-shirt bearing a different photo of him scowling behind a neoprene face mask.

Before I knew any of this, there was only the slogan. Five words—four and a half, really. The way they came to live in my head is the way rap lyrics and other bits of language often do, mantras endlessly unfolding, and at some point I realized I was drawn to the way these words seemed to simultaneously describe and exemplify *cool*. Cool is unaccountable, evasive, inevitable. Cool comes from somewhere else and has another somewhere else to be in a minute—another *ailleurs*—but has touched down momentarily, effortlessly, to grace and unsettle you with its presence.

Mon concept vient d'ailleurs makes great sense as a rap lyric, since the fundamental purpose of most rap lyrics is to model coolness. Not always as directly as "It's Magic," whose central conceit is that the Fearless Four's rap skills are supernatural, literally enchanting, but as a kind of thematic default: absent a specific narrative subject, a rap's go-to move is to declare some superlative prowess, some mind-bending flyness, privileged access to some next next level that the rest of us won't even glimpse for months. ("What the fuck am I supposed to do, motherfucker?" Miles Davis, birth father of the cool, once asked a critic who called his latest work inaccessible. "Wait for you to get there?") Reflexively, even the most conventional, paint-by-numbers turn on the mic takes pride in its uniqueness, its beyondness. Even the squarest rap listener—so I've been told—feels the vicarious thrill of watching its orbit from back on Earth.

The vicariousness sometimes gives me pause. To spend too much time fixated on rap's otherworldly appeal is, I think, to risk treating it as a more comprehensive kind of elsewhere, to cordon it off as distant, exotic, *picturesque* in the Victorian sense: a place to visit with guidebook in hand. Now and then I've found myself, reading old notes, sounding like an excitable pith-helmeted explorer writing home to rhapsodize about the rugged beauty and mysterious majesty of this strange land where I've chanced to arrive—the wild-growing idioms! the unspoiled prosodies!—and I understand that this is wrong, spiritually and factually. I know that, for all its hereditary ties to the blues and the dozens and toasting and capping and *plena*

I packed my bags, I said goodbye / I kissed my woman and started to fly / I came to Earth via meteorite / To rock you all on the mic

Kurtis Blow, "Rappin' Blow, Pt. 2" (1980)

Not like any other ordinary MC / Who say how mystical and magical they may be / First we'll sock a groove to ya, then we'll prove to ya / That only our magic is the kind that will move ya

"It's Magic"

Here's that other shit that y'all ain't discovered yet / Yes I'm running it, like the government / Hint hint, Eric B nominated me for president

Senim Silla, in Binary Star, "New Hip Hop" (2000)

So you should pump this shit like they do in the future

Camu Tao, "When You're Going Down" (2010)

and *rumba* and other points along the diasporic continuum of what Cornel West calls "kinetic orality," rap is now the signal artistic idiom of contemporary Western culture. (Beyond, too, but I limit my focus here to American rap, all due respect to Mr. Agaz.) I know that, for all its inventions and truncations and intimacy with black vernacular, its language is still a blood relative of the language I'm writing in here. I know that, for all its roots in the pride and trauma of certain marginalized communities—for all the ways it is indeed **conceited and grim**—it's still the product of American life as a whole: American streets and schools, American codes and contradictions, American restrictions and innovations and resources and resource-fulness. I am aware that to think of rap's mystifying gifts as sorcery or voodoo, as superhuman black magic, is to risk losing touch with the deeper sense in which it's here, now, us.

Or—at least in some ways it is. Being simultaneously here and elsewhere, of this world and not, is part of what magic is. It's also part of a black rhetorical tradition of witticism and evasion and resistance to outside appropriation called *signifying*—or *signifyin'*, or *signifyin(g)*, depending on the commentator—of which rap can be readily read as a world-beatingly popular modern incarnation. Signifying encompasses a lot of the rhetorical power moves discussed in this book: the way rap lyrics exploit the play of difference under the guise of similarity, the way they create novelty by mining and commenting on the past, the way they pull in and push away with the same gesture. To be signified on—as by Esu-Elegbara, the trick-ster deity of Yoruba mythology, troped in black folklore as the shit-talking "signifying monkey"—is to be misdirected, unbalanced, dis-abused. It's to have your certainty undermined about who's talking and what they're saying and where they're coming from.

But this slipperiness doesn't happen by magic or accident either: it's the work and the play of real people. In rap, I think, signifying is all of the tricks and traps above, all of the defiance and joy, but also something much simpler: to signify is also just to *mean* really hard, to back up what you say with intention and thought, to build significance and sense through speech. Often impiously and subversively, sure; often to the confusion and sometimes even humiliation of the listener. But above all by dint of ingenuity and focus and care that, if acknowledged and respected as such, can maybe help bring together disparate and estranged understandings of what's normal and what's illusory. Zoomed out far enough, an elsewhere always becomes a here.

ON ME

I heard the beat and I ain't know what to write

Nas, in Kanye West, "We Major" (2005)

• •

A WORD, THOUGH, about my immediate here: where I'm coming from, what I'm about, what I mean when I say *normal* and *history* and *us*. "I love hip-hop, the noun," writes Jason Tanz in *Other People's Property*, an incisive and right-minded book about being a white rap fan, "but I am not hip-hop, the adjective." Same here. I'm white, middle-class, educated, risk-averse, law-abiding with the usual exceptions that are fine for middle-class white people. I'm the son of a doctor and a composer and the youngest of five brothers and sisters, all brilliant and accomplished in their respective white-collar fields. I can do a Sunday *New York Times* crossword in twenty minutes and have no idea how a car engine works. I care deeply about language and, like most of the things I care deeply about, my engagement is rooted more in fascination, in faith, than in dire need or worldly urgency. Nobody challenges the legitimacy of the way I speak or my right to do so. Nobody conspires to censor or silence me. I'm just the kind of person who routinely has, and enjoys having, lyrics and slogans and names and things unsaid stuck in his head like popcorn shards between teeth. The kind of person who knows "mental floss" would be an appropriate pun right here, but doesn't care to use it, but cares enough to let you know he doesn't care to. Complex, ornately. Like Nas, above, when he drops by for a cameo on "We Major" and spends the first line thinking out loud about how to use the first line. Actually, it's the first eight lines:

> I heard the beat and I ain't know what to write
> First line, should it be about the hoes or the ice?
> .44s or black Christ? Both flows'd be nice
> Rap about big paper or the black man plight
> At the studio console, asked my man to the right
> What this verse sound like, should I freestyle or write?
> He said "Nas, what the fans want is Illmatic, still"
> Looked at the pad and pencil and jotted what I feel

I will go to my grave wishing my self-conscious rhetorical throat-clearings could sound so cool. What Nas seems to toss off here is not just a very efficient overview of the themes he's spent his career elaborating—decadence, gunplay, activism, divinity—but also a rare window onto his composition process, his creative deliberations, the whole inner monologue around medium and message that is at once so tantalizing in a rapper and so often viewed as beside the point. Most of all, though, what I hear in it is a true statement about what it's like to speak on something so much bigger than yourself, so much more expansive than the present, something inexhaustible and infinite that is also *right here*. It's what it feels like, for me, to put words to a way with words that so often leaves me, before the rest colors itself in, speechless.

• •

I grew up in Hyde Park, on the south side of Chicago, home to the University of and described by waggish locals as bordered on the east by Lake Michigan and the three other sides by ghetto. Nobody said *ghetto*, except the usual exceptions that are fine for academics and their kids. Hyde Park has Farrakhan's mansion and a Milton Friedman Institute and a lovely lakeside promontory just past the Museum of Science and Industry. The Obamas lived in Kenwood, which shares our youth baseball league and college radio call sign. A public intellectual used to take me on walks around campus to look for exotic license plates. I played four square with the children of Nobelists, usually lost. William Upski Wimsatt, author of *Bomb the Suburbs*, a scrappier and more engagé book about being a white rap fan, babysat my friends. Hip-hop was always ambiently there, in graffiti murals and inscrutable flyers and low-stakes freestyle battles, but I came around to it late, somewhere in high school. Before then it was less that I was intimidated by it—though I am as scared today of the cover of Public Enemy's *Muse Sick-N-Hour Mess Age* as when I saw it on a poster at Rose Records on 53rd at age nine—and more that I assumed it wasn't for me. When it clicked, it didn't feel like rebellion, except maybe against the genteel drudgery of life as the studiously approval-seeking baby of a comfortable and supportive family. It was new fascination. Curiosity, more excitable and more insatiable as time went on, about all these new words and new uses of old words and plays on words that were unusually active somehow, unusually *alive*, all of it wrapped in a package that sounded irresistible and was, apparently, indirectly, dangerous. For neither the first time nor the last, my fascination turned into love.

Another line that rattles around in my head sometimes is the needling chorus of a song called "How I Could Just Kill a Man," by Los Angeles weed aficionados Cypress Hill. (I'm pretty sure I heard the Rage Against the Machine cover first.) The original is from 1991, back when there was still more to Cypress Hill's brand than "weed aficionados," and beneath its trebly hubbub is an undertow of chilling menace:

I always wanted to be the voice of the streets / But my father was a rabbi and my mother made / Beats / I mean / Books

Why?, "Cold Lunch (Albert Brown Mortuary Dumpster Dive Remix)" (2003)

Here is something you can't understand
How I could just kill a man

At the chorus, an ululating Jimi Hendrix guitar sample joins the fray, sounding not unlike a police siren; alongside it is a voice asking *What does it all mean?* (It's from a radio broadcast by Fiorello La Guardia, whom I once played in a musical at summer camp.) More than anything else—more than the murder, certainly—*that* snippet crystallizes why the song sticks with me. The chorus is just those two lines, taunting and rhythmically lopsided, proudly evasive yet also weirdly open and generous: you won't get it, it says, but *here it is.* "To me," Tanz writes, "the song represented a challenge—such as getting into college—that I knew I could pass. I could understand! I was smart, and I was sensitive, and I was trying so very very hard."

Again, same. I got into some colleges and went to Yale, where my sister had gone and my brother before her and my mother before them. I studied English and French and at one point, for some reason, forensic entomology. I learned to be a critic: I developed better and smarter ways of asking questions of the texts around me, and the attendant habit of treating most things around me like texts. Rap wasn't explicitly included in this, but it never made sense to me to exclude it either. I graduated before Yale published its 920-page *Anthology of Rap*, but I was classmates with the founders of Rap Genius, of which I was an enthusiastically contributing editor for a time, and the two guys who rewrote Dr. Dre's "Housewife" to be about how hard it was to get into the dining hall that had just gone fully organic. Honestly, I prefer it to the original. Hip-hop was ambiently there too, and thinking about it in private or in conversation or in writing brought me a deep and instructive satisfaction, the pleasure of dots connected and rules subverted and questions answered with other questions.

I mostly ate late from a thin paper plate / Eating Kraft Mac & Cheese, please, this shit ain't got no taste

Furyus (& Fitzgeezus), "BK2Night" (2004)

In the years since, in the various ways I've embraced language as a means and an end—as a critic, an editor, a translator, a scholar of people who write with such facility that they set themselves absurd constraints to keep things interesting—it has occurred to me more than occasionally to wonder what I have to offer hip-hop in return. Whether it cares what I have to say, whether my presence in the conversation is edging out someone else, whether I'm "lounging at tables marked *Reserved*," as Adam Mansbach puts it in *Angry Black White Boy*, a satirical novel about being a white rap fan that reads less and less like satire each passing year. For better or worse, my response to this line of inquiry has never been to step away or to give up, only to think about it more, to try harder to understand what I've been told I can't.

All of this is to say I come from places where a particular kind of intelligence is valued and rewarded and, past a certain point, presumed. Deliberation, curiosity, science and industry. Whether that's a kind of intelligence valued by rap, much less one it cares to claim for itself, is a persistent question in what follows. Curiosity for curiosity's sake, like art for art's, is a bourgeois extravagance, a closed loop: it's the opposite of Common, who was born in Hyde Park, saying *I ain't have time to think about what I believe in.* I've had my whole life to think about it, and I'm still thinking. *What does it all mean?* I spend a lot of this book thinking out loud about rap as process and as product and as language, wondering rather than finding out, being fascinated. That's where I'm from, who I am. I'm more interested in questions than I am in answers, and that may well explain the nature of my privilege better than anything else I can say.

"Kingdom" (2014)

SERIOUS RAP

Now what you hear is not a test
I'm rappin' to the beat
And me, the groove, and my friends
Are gonna try to move your feet

Wonder Mike, in Sugarhill Gang, "Rapper's Delight" (1979)

• •

"RAPPER'S DELIGHT" WASN'T the first rap to be recorded, but it was the first one to flash a glimpse of how wildly captivating and lucrative a hit rap song could be. At the time rappers were mostly pattering sidemen to DJs, keeping the crowd engaged, popping in here and there for syncopated station identification, and you can hear that legacy plainly in Wonder Mike's iconic skittering scat over the song's opening bars. But as soon as he starts rhyming in sentences, as it were, he tells us that this kind of rapping—*to* the beat, not in its margins—is the real thing. It's that next-level vision, that captivating magic, not some stray chatter picked up by a vocal mic someone left on while a band played some disco breaks. ("I've got these kids who are going to talk real fast over it," Sylvia Robinson, the studio owner who midwifed the recording of "Rapper's Delight," told the session musicians who played

27

the instrumental. "That's the best way I can describe it.") Mike's introduction is modest in its ambitions: he's going to use his rap as part of a collective effort to keep the dancers moving. But it's also a clever repurposing of the emergency broadcast system refrain, ubiquitous in the nuclear era: *This is not a test.*

That duality, of party ambiance and urgent announcement, has permeated rap ever since. "Rappers interpret and articulate the fears, pleasures and promises of young black women and men whose voices have been relegated to the silent margins of public discourse," wrote Tricia Rose in 1990. "The point is we enjoy it," wrote David Foster Wallace the same year: "Plus we've developed some theses about why serious rap is important, both as art-for-own-sake and as a kind of metaphor-with-larynx for a subbed-culture unique in its distillation of the energy and horror of the urban American present." Three decades later, during which interval rap has made plain both how much has evolved and how cyclical that evolution is, this notion of *serious rap* is still operational, still influential. Nobody paying attention today, nobody worth paying attention to, needs to be convinced of hip-hop's cultural and commercial importance. But the valuation of that importance, the degree to which we take it seriously and with what kind of indulgence, remains unevenly distributed.

Seriousness is, needless to say, in the eye of the beholder: the social critic's *serious* is different from the social worker's and the rap critic's, the hip-hop head's from the hip-hop scholar's, the black parent's from the white's. Depending on whom you ask, serious rap is the music you hear about on the news, or the music you hear at protest marches, or the music that will never ever slip its underground moorings and succumb to the rapacious whims of capitalism. It's **Mitch caught a body 'bout a week ago** or it's **We gon' be alright** or it's **Earth people, I was born on Jupiter.** It's the music that can be cited in defense of rap as high art, or cited as evidence of rap being the excrescence of a blighted culture of gang violence and sagging pants. It is, in a pinch, whatever the beholder doesn't think is wack.

You can find the Abstract listening to hip-hop / My pops used to say it reminded him of bebop / I said well Daddy don't you know that things go in cycles / The way that Bobby Brown is just ampin' like Michael

Q-Tip, in A Tribe Called Quest, "Excursions" (1991)

Bobby Shmurda, "Hot Nigga" (2014)
Kendrick Lamar, "Alright" (2015)
Dr. Octagon, "Earth People" (1995)

Me, I think all rap is inherently serious *and* inherently frivolous. I think entertainment and emergency are present equally in its DNA. Read that, if you will, as a disclaimer: not only that the lyrics I dwell on in this book are in no way a comprehensive representation of rap as a genre or as a tradition, but also that they're not restricted to rap with an explicit social conscience or an explicit lack thereof, rap with values that can be neatly embraced or neatly rejected. You'll find here a lot of what you might call acutely frivolous rap, whose themes and worldview are not uplifting or constructive or compatible with any mainstream moral agenda: rap about getting rich by selling drugs in your community, or robbing people for the hell of it, or surrounding yourself with luxury items and loveless dalliances and sleeping with a gun at your bedside. Rap that doesn't embrace the communitarian values of hip-hop or the decorum and pedigree of poetry, rap that's not a net positive in society and couldn't possibly give fewer fucks. Whether or not you call these things *serious*, I think, has a lot to do with what you want and what you expect from rap.

I ain't hungry, nigga, I'm greedy
Lil Wayne, "Hot Boy" (2015)

A couple decades in myself, I'm still figuring out what I want and expect from rap. I listen to be entertained and to be educated, and I believe this acute frivolity, this slyly skillful and irresistibly antisocial brand of ghetto storytelling, does both. But is it serious? Well, here's a way to look at it: it's not a test. It's happening, here and now or close enough, and if the message it bears isn't one we want to hear maybe it's still one we need to. As the modern American art form par excellence—and almost every good book I've ever read about hip-hop contains some version of this sentence—its ills are our ills, but its wonders are its own. What you hear being rapped to the beat is the pulse of the country and the world we live in: the fears and pleasures and promises, the energy and the horror. The fact that it brings in billions of dollars each year by challenging the mainstream moral agenda, and that those dollars come from listeners who look nothing like me and from listeners who look a whole lot like me, is also probably worth learning something from.

I been selling crack since like the fifth grade
"Hot Nigga"

More importantly, though, I *like* it too. It moves my brain and my heart and my feet, in that order. I believe it has a lot to teach about struggle and power, resilience and reinvention, about how language works without the artificial barriers of class and education and propriety; I also love it when it teaches me nothing. I love how easy rap can make it to pretend for a few minutes that the real world doesn't exist, that gravity floats and there is no America, just an echo chamber of excellence and freedom and joy. I don't think it's fair—I don't think it's *worth it*—to look at one side of the music without the other. If this book has an antagonist to tilt at, it's less the hysterical rap-is-evil discourse that punctuated my cultural coming of age, more whatever in us as a commentariat insists on instrumentalizing rap as a vector of sociopolitical insight without also reveling and rejoicing in its vital sense of play.

This isn't to say the ugly stuff doesn't get heavy after a while. It's not to say that the glorification of practices that tear communities apart doesn't feel gratuitous, that women and queer people aren't almost systematically disrespected, that the idea of black death doesn't come to seem awfully cheap. It's not to say I love every rap song or want to try to defend its merits, only to say that each time I think I've developed a thesis about what's important and serious and what's not, rap finds a new way to prove me wrong. It's to say that rap is always a few steps ahead of me yet always teaching me how to keep up, showing me the things that are stubborn and intractable and terrible in the world, and things that are incredible too.

Miley, what's good?

Nicki Minaj at the MTV Video Music Awards (2015)

In hip-hop parlance *What's good* is a salutation, but also a challenge, a confrontation, a way of testing someone. But it's not only a test: it's a real question too. What is goodness and what constitutes it and how does it map to seriousness and to frivolity? How do you

Melle Mel, in Grandmaster Flash & The Furious Five, "The Message" (1982)

Lil' Kim, "Queen Bitch" (1996)

compare **Don't push me 'cause I'm close to the edge** with **Got buffoons eating my pussy while I watch cartoons** when one is obviously serious and one is stridently not but both are so evidently *good*? These questions have weight beyond rap, but rap is one of the places I care most about asking from. Loving it is something I'm happy to share with so many people, including those whose lives are nothing like mine. It's the thing that makes me most consistently proud to be American: our best export, the purest contribution we've made to the world in my lifetime. For all my anxiety about appropriation and belonging and whom I'm speaking to and for and over, it remains indivisibly a plurality to which I'm delighted and grateful to belong: this music, this language, these strangers, my friends, the groove, and me.

That's the anthem get your damn hands up

Jay-Z, "Izzo (H.O.V.A.)" (2001)

WHAT'S GOOD

WORD MACHINES

Coke like a caterpillar, I make butter fly

Cam'ron, in Clipse, "Popular Demand (Popeyes)" (2009)

• •

As promised, we'll start small. Poetry, said Mallarmé, is made of words, not ideas; so too is it with rap. I know I said there was so much more to rap than words, but that was *pages* ago. We've all grown so much since then.

Lots of the lyrics that commandeer my rewind button are what you'd call *one-liners*: they're self-contained thoughts, single servings of imagery and wit rather than subordinate parts of a larger rhetorical proposition. Lots of great rap songs, in fact, are sprawling assemblages of essentially unrelated one-liners. **Coke like a caterpillar, I make butter fly** is a good example; **I'm coming after you like the letter V** is another, one that in fact so fully assumes its one-linerness that I've forgotten the line it rhymes with. I know it comes toward the end of a seven-minute Midwest-rap posse cut, but I've retained little else, and in a way that's exactly what I'm talking about: one line from a rap song may be a single brick in an entire wall, but one brick can be the reason we take note of the

OneManArmy in Binary Star, "The KGB" (2000)

35

wall in the first place, remember it when we don't even remember what rhymed with **letter V.**

The funny thing about one-liners—funnier, at times, than the one-liners themselves—is that as a rule they take several lines of explanation to unpack with any precision or utility. They're mechanisms that require more energy to assemble than to release. **I'm coming after you like the letter V** is not a particularly elaborate construction, meaning-wise: the pronoun *you* sounds like the letter *U*, which the letter V *comes after* in the Roman alphabet, much as one might vengefully *come after* an enemy, that enemy being *you*, the pronoun, and voilà, sentence diagrammed, joke autopsied, springloaded snake stuffed back into novelty can of mixed nuts. There is all the same a deliberate functionality to it, a specific sequence in which the words, few as they are, have to hit. The ironic part is how many more words you have to throw at it afterwards just to put it back together.

I don't owe you like two vowels

Lil Wayne, "A Milli" (2008)

Same, then, with Cam'ron on coke and caterpillars. One line, eight words—you're supposed to hear seven, but this particular mechanism doesn't engage until you parse apart the last two. By my count, there are three simultaneous meanings in the second half alone, distinct but overlapping:

(a) I sell crack (*butter*) so quickly it appears to fly away;

(b) I make crack fashionable (*fly*);

(c) I turn the ugly act of selling crack into a thing of beauty (a *butterfly*).

I'm already getting ahead of myself. How did we get to *(a)*? What makes *butter* crack? What makes crack *butter*? Why not give equal consideration to an interpretive scenario where Cam whiles away a slow day by making macramé butterflies or flinging pats of Land O' Lakes at passersby?

In a word, context. I happen to know that Cam'ron is the capo of the Harlem crack-rap syndicate The Diplomats, and that this line

36

concludes his guest verse on a record by the Virginia crack-rap duo Clipse. (*Crack-rap* is in no way a dig at either group, by the way, both of which rose to fame and greatness by rapping with tirelessly inventive gusto about selling crack, one convention of doing which is that you almost always call it something else, such as *rock* or *krills* or *yams* or *butter*.) If you have some inkling of these connections—and it's not like Cam keeps them a secret in the rest of his verse—you may also surmise that *caterpillar* pertains in some oblique way to the drug trade, that indeed any unexpected word in a crack-rap lyric will probably bend toward drugs, connotatively speaking, like a flower toward the sun. If you don't, not to worry: that's what the word *coke* is for.

So you rewind the thought, turning it over, looking for the seams. How do the two halves of the lyric fit together? Coke is **like a caterpillar**, and caterpillars become butterflies, so what does coke become? Why would Cam say **I make butterfly** rather than *I make butterflies* or *I make a butterfly*? This is the mechanism starting to work, defamiliarizing the thought in its constituent parts, raising questions you would never think to ask of the individual words by themselves. You know perfectly well what a garden-variety word like *butterfly* means until suddenly you don't—until you see it reacting strangely to the words around it, bending at odd angles, splitting apart, somehow making *butter* fly while the rest gives chase.

Some rappers enjoy unpacking their lyrics at the craft level, or at least oblige when asked to, but I've never heard Cam'ron break down any of the perfectly polished gems he drops with impossible regularity. The differential between talking and doing crops up a lot in hip-hop, and being able to create an immaculate little word machine like this isn't the same as being able to explain it, much less wanting to explain it. But that's the final beauty of a confection like **Coke like a caterpillar**, a riddle and its resolution contained in eight words: in spite of its clockwork construction, its elaborate internal contingencies, it asks little besides patience and experimentation to teach you to make sense of it.

I know your moms well! Tell your mother hi / I'm the other guy that got your mother high

"*Popular Demand (Popeyes)*"

Drug dealer, been that nigga half my life / Mongoose bicycle, I was stuffing junkie pipes

Pusha T, in Re-Up Gang, "*Dey Know Yayo*" (2008)

SLANG EVOLUTION

Speakin' my language if you talkin' 'bout tilapia
Say you want this money, nigga, so what the hell is stoppin' ya

Young Jeezy, in U.S.D.A., "Black Dreams" (2009)

• •

I ONCE GOT about a third of the way into what I thought was a marijuana purchase before I realized I was buying cocaine. The misunderstanding had nothing to do with the word *tilapia*, but it might as well have. Patience and experimentation alone won't get me to the bottom of what Young Jeezy is telling me here. If someone in a dark alley whispered *tilapia* at me, I'm sure I wouldn't know whether I was being offered food or offered drugs or insulted or incited to a sex act. The first thing any dictionary will tell you about tilapia is that it's a freshwater cichlid fish, which is also the last thing I'd expect to be discussing in an alley, or for that matter in a Young Jeezy song.

Because, once again, context. I'll go ahead and assume Jeezy is talking about drugs here, since, like Clipse and The Diplomats, he built his whole career on a remarkably steadfast foundation of talking about drugs. There have been times, though, when I've heard *tilapia* in a rap—happens more often than you'd think—and

Still smell the blow on my clothes / Like Krispy Kreme I was cookin' them Os / Like horseshoes I was tossin' them Os

Young Jeezy, "Go Crazy" (2005)

38

context suggests it *does* refer to the freshwater fish, or to a meal made of same, or to a woman. (Maybe she has pursed lips or beady eyes? I don't know what her deal is.) Sometimes it could plausibly be any of the above: **We get respected in the streets like the mafia / Young Future in the cut with tilapia.**

In principle, there's nothing weird about this. We use the same word to mean different things in different circumstances; if we didn't, the English lexicon would number in the millions of words rather than the hundreds of thousands. The operative meaning of *ride* depends on whether you're standing in an amusement park or a parking lot. Ditto *park*, for that matter. But it *is* a little weird to discover that I can't account for all the things *tilapia* means, even though if you'd asked me I would have said I knew how to define it. It's a funny feeling, to know a word perfectly well until suddenly you don't. Here I've been talking about tilapia for three paragraphs, and I still can't say with confidence that I'm speaking Jeezy's language.

In principle again, it would be hard to imagine a better example of a word that exists to name a particular thing. A tilapia is a fish; that fish is a tilapia. But the world is a complex three-dimensional space, and language works overtime to keep up. There are actually multiple species of fish that share the name, some of which aren't even in the genus *tilapia*, some that spend their lives swimming around in the south of Africa and some, rather unluckier, that get caught and eaten in any number of preparations. We use the same word for all of these—individuals and groups alike, too, because at some point someone decided to make fish words in English both countable and uncountable—which means that in practice, within this one apparently specific word, there are multiple senses, multiple *tilapia*, between which new *tilapias* sometimes sprout like semantic moss. Something that has an anonymously fishy look or smell? Close enough. A drug? A beady-eyed woman? A nonce rhyme for *mafia*? Sure, if you can make it sound good. The word has its set

I'm off that water water layin' up with some tilapia / She bad and she yella and I'm very proud of her

Future, in Young Thug, "My Everything" (2011)

Future, "4 My People" (2011)

We eat so many shrimp I got iodine poisonin'

Pimp C, in Three 6 Mafia, "Sippin on Some Sizzurp" (2000)

number of stable, attested meanings, but the intermediate values between them, like the fractions between zero and one, are theoretically infinite.

This is just how languages grow. Words extrude new facets all the time, getting more particular or more general through invention or co-optation or corruption, and one of the truly enthralling things about language is that the old ones don't disappear; they just recede into these deep pockets of ancillary signification, distinct from one another but held in place by ghostly affinities. Why does *rare* mean bloody? Why is the *quick* part of a fingernail? Did you know *picturesque* had a Victorian sense? *Ho* used to be unisex; *cock* meant vagina in some places until the middle of the twentieth century. A *dude* was a dandy, a fop, a city slicker, an East Coaster; now it can be as general as "male person" or as precise as "you're being very un-Dude" depending on how you inflect it. *Swag* has eighteen senses (plus two draft definitions) over four entries in the *Oxford English Dictionary*, spanning 1303 to 2002, from "a bulging bag" to "bold self-assurance in style and manner." *Rock and roll* doesn't refer to fucking anymore, but you can see why it used to if you think about it for a minute.

Sometimes two wholly unrelated ships come to dock in the same phonemic port—like *bat* or *fluke* or *doge*, which is both a sixteenth-century Venetian magistrate and a Shiba Inu surrounded by captions like *very excite* and *such delishus*—but most often the senses connect across time, through back channels forged by metaphor or memory or accident, a whole network of tunnels under the surface of contemporary spoken English. The most modern usages of *viral* and *tweet* and *drone* would be unintelligible to a person born in 1900, but once you showed them what those words mean now (along with an apologetic recap of late-capitalist techno-utopianism, I imagine) they could probably trace a path from past to present.

And so my best guess for *tilapia* is that it's fallen under the gravitational pull of *fish scale*, which has become common rap slang for high-purity cocaine due to the shiny flakes it contains in uncut form. Someone pointed out the resemblance once, someone else riffed on it, then it happened a few more times, and before long the semantic bridge between fish and drugs was sturdy enough to support a whole piscine menagerie: tilapia, sea bass, snapper. *Shorty sniffing haddock in the attic.* Likewise, because the dime novelist Ned Buntline used *cheese* to mean money way back in 1850, we have no trouble now putting two and two together when Dr. Dre calls himself *young black Rockefeller, hella Swiss and mozzarella. Touch my cheddar, feel my Beretta*, warns the Notorious B.I.G. *Real mannish with my Spanish*, says E-40: *If it ain't about no gouda, partna, you can vanish.*

None of this is unique to hip-hop vernacular; all words in all registers are fair game for semantic repurposing by hooligans and druggies and marketers and soulless app developers. But rap is restless and easily bored. It abhors linguistic stasis. So the symbolic placeholder for "money" shapeshifts from cheeses to quiches to curds—*He's in this for the quiche / You might as well not ask him for no free shit, capisce?*—even as it wanders into other associative chains based on its color, on the form factor of its protuberance (*You know it ain't nothing to drop a couple stacks on you; Can't wear skinny jeans 'cause my knots don't fit*), on the number of commas required to write out the full amount, on the white guy depicted on the bill (*It's all about the Benjamins; Pocket full of ivy and you know the faces blue*).

I still wanna sell kilos / Searching for the fish scale like I'm tryna find Nemo
Pusha T, "I Still Wanna" (2011)

Action Bronson, "Midget Cough" (2012)

"Been There, Done That" (1997)
"Warning" (1994)
in Snoop Dogg, "Candy (Drippin' Like Water)" (2006)

Lettuce and cabbage and broccoli / I'm cooking up catfish, tilapia / And I got flounders, got your bitch fucking on camera
Takeoff, in Migos, "YRH" (2014)

MF DOOM, in Madvillain, "Rhinestone Cowboy" (2004)

T.I., "Whatever You Like" (2008)
Jay-Z, in T.I., "Swagger Like Us" (2008)
Puff Daddy & the Family, "It's All About the Benjamins" (1997)
Denzel Curry, "ZUU" (2019)

(Eric B. &) Rakim, "Paid in Full" (1987)

I dig into my pocket, all my money's spent
So I dig deeper, but still coming up with lint
So I start my mission, leave my residence
Thinking how could I get some dead presidents?

Cam'ron, "Killa Cam" (2004)

AZ, "Doe or Die" (1995)

I only fuck with bitches for that toupee
Rich Homie Quan, "Flex (Ooh, Ooh, Ooh)" (2015)

in T.I., "Front Back" (2006)

Guns get distilled to make (Uzi, Glock, Desert Eagle) or material (chrome, steel, stainless) or metaphorical function (**Not toes or MC when I say "hammer time"**; **Keeping my toaster in a shoulder holster**). Oral sex has been *head* since the forties, hence *face* and *neck* and *top* and *skull*. Hence Pimp C: **I don't really wanna hit you with this hot thang / I just want to get some brain in the turning lane.** Hence *dome*, which was already slang for *head* in its nonsexual sense.

A$AP, get like me
Never met a motherfucker fresh like me
All these motherfuckers wanna dress like me
But the chrome to your dome make you sweat like Keith

A$AP Rocky, "F**kin' Problems" (2013)

Too many black bodies in the hospital housin' / So at 10 p.m. I was Audi 5000
Ice Cube, "Alive on Arrival" (1991)

The Notorious B.I.G., in 2Pac, "Runnin' from tha Police" (1995)

Hit 'em twice in a row / Hit a flight and I'm ghost
Bas, "Lit" (2013)

Once upon a time *I'm leaving* forked off into parallel chains: *I'm out* became *I'm outie* became *I'm Audi*, and *I'm gone* became *I'm a ghost* became *I'm ghost*, thereby opening the way to all things spectral, including a nod to the movie *Ghost*. **That's why I bust back, it don't faze me / When he drop, grab his Glock and I'm Swayze.** (The path from rappers' use of this construction almost exclusively to brag about peacing out right after sex to the contemporary sense of *ghosting*—abruptly severing communications with no explanation—is a great example of two distinct inflections that have more in common than they appear to at first glance.)

Tear down the rafters, venereals couldn't clap us
You need practice; hit chicks then I'm Casper

Punchline, in A Tribe Called Quest, "Rock Rock Y'all" (1998)

The Notorious B.I.G., "Machine Gun Funk" (2001)

Yellow Lamborghini, same color my butter Timbs
Gucci Mane, "Trap Boomin" (2012)

in The Alchemist, "All for It" (2016)

We know *butter* means crack, but it also stands in for luxury— **For the bread and butter I leave niggas in the gutter**—and smoothness, for anything yellow—sometimes more than one at once. Not long ago I heard Roc Marciano refer to the drug hustle as **weighing grams of Land O' Lakes** and then, a verse later, threaten to **butter your slut up like a waffle**. That is, we also use the same words —or

42

nearly—to mean different things at the same time. It's chaos and it's beautiful.

This is, again, how languages grow: constantly, digging ever deeper into the pocket and finding new intermediate values and metaphors and substitutions, expanding degree by degree of separation. I like to string together these clusters of near-synonyms and consider the connoted concept at the center—*heater, burner, toaster, biscuit; bail, bounce, dip, duck, jet*—and listen to what they say about the difference between knowing words and understanding things. This feels a bit like growing constantly too.

Wanna spend all night in your nine lives

Vince Staples, "Loca" (2015)

SLANG AND SLIPPERINESS

Keep searching all you want and try your local library
You'll never find a rhyme like this in any dictionary

EMD, *in* UTFO, *"Roxanne, Roxanne" (1984)*

• •

"THE SLANG WE be sayin', G, it could mean whatever at that time," Ghostface Killah of the Wu-Tang Clan told *The Source* in 2000. Take the word *lobsterhead*, which he uses in the song "Wildflower": "If a nigga fit that type of category, then he a lobsterhead. It's just that—slang. It's real, but it's what it means at that time."

Ghostface, whose fifth solo album is called *Fishscale*, calls to mind Humpty Dumpty, in *Through the Looking-Glass*, when he explains "in rather a scornful tone" that when he uses a word "it means just what I choose it to mean—neither more nor less." This sounds good but is mostly not actually true, slang tending to be both more *and* less than what the speaker intends, depending on the interpreter. More when we connect with it—I don't know any lobsterheads personally, but maybe you do and didn't know it until right now?—and less when we don't even register it as nonstandard.

Lobsterhead isn't particularly challenging as slang goes, but it's as handy a case study as any on how well Humpty's argument from mastery comes to life when exemplified by Ghostface and the rest of the Clan, who bend the English phrase to their will in a way that's almost always accessible without being altogether *clear*. Wu-Tang's resolute, practically reckless inventiveness with language earned them an entry all to themselves in Alonzo Westbrook's *Hip Hoptionary*, under "Wu-bonics": "the commingling of words that sound good but don't always make clear sense, i.e., using the name 'lobster head' to make a rhyme." *Lobsterhead* doesn't actually rhyme with anything in "Wildflower"—Ghost just calls a dude **this lobsterhead-ass nigga**—but how do you hear that and not want to know more? And once you want to know, where, besides through the looking glass, do you go to find out?

• •

"I heard they had a hip-hop slang book," says Method Man, also of the Wu-Tang Clan, beaming ecstatically in a scene from the 1997 rap documentary *Rhyme & Reason*. "And they had words in there like *b-boy*, *b-girl*, *fresh*, *chill*… we ain't used them shits since we was like nine years old out this motherfucker, man." He turns to dap a guy sitting on a couch behind him whose face is obscured by an off-white balaclava. "We don't even be saying *cool* anymore," Meth continues, back still to the camera. My best guess is that he's referring not to *Hip Hoptionary*, which didn't come out until 2002, but to Lois Stavsky's and Isaac Mozeson's 1995 *A 2 Z: The Book of Rap & Hip-Hop Slang*—but the identity of the book isn't really important. It should be obvious why rap's constantly expanding vernacular is a descriptivist lexicographer's dream, and also why the hope of ever doing the job authoritatively or comprehensively is insane. *A 2 Z* is out of print, as are most of the other glossaries that bubbled up around the end of the twentieth century. Ironically, a lot of the hip-hop slang books I know of are available *only* at my local library.

I bomb atomically, / Socrates philosophies and hypotheses / Can't define how I be dropping these mockeries / Lyrically perform armed robbery

Inspectah Deck, in Wu-Tang Clan, "Triumph" (1997)

I used to be in love with this guy named Sam / I don't know why 'cause he had a head like that of a clam

MC Lyte, "I Cram to Understand U" (1988)

And your shorty think I'm super cool / She want some shit, I sent that bitch home in a UberPool

Meyhem Lauren, "Bebop & Rocksteady" (2017)

Slang is insular and fleeting by nature and purpose, committed to and energized by its own novelty and indecipherability to all but a select in-group of outsiders. Nonstandard words for nonstandard people, as Paul Beatty puts it. Rap has the wiry restlessness of any vernacular art form and the don't-call-it-a-corpus unruliness of any slang corpus, but that's not all. There's another wrinkle of richness and resistance in signifying, which anthropologist Claudia Mitchell-Kernan says "incorporates essentially a folk notion that dictionary entries for words are not always sufficient for interpreting meanings or messages." Plus subcultures need antagonists, and the norms of "standard" English have always been white ones, which means we've got a pretty sound straw man in *the dictionary*. "The words given the special Black semantic slant tend to lose their linguistic currency in the black community," wrote Geneva Smitherman in 1977, "if or when they move into the white mainstream." Per John Russell and Russell John Rickford, the language is "forever morphing" by design, "constantly reinventing itself, bumping off words that were considered tony just the other day (but that have now been mainstreamed and co-opted by Madison Avenue to hawk everything from cereal to soda pop)."

The idea of a dictionary of hip-hop slang, then, is as necessary to some as it is invasive to others. But the longstanding paradox of black escape is how reliably it attracts and enchants the white mainstream. "Already entrenched in the teen-age vocabulary are superlatives like 'def' (the best)," the *New York Times* reported in 1988. "Words like 'stupid' (terrific) and 'wack' (awful) are now established in both the urban and suburban teen-age lexicon irrespective of class or color."

Rap keeps it moving. What else is there to do? It concerns itself only occasionally with policing usages or reclaiming *wack* and *cool* from overeager lobsterheads like myself; mostly it just goes on steepening its semantic slant, slinging new slang faster than *the dictionary* can keep up. Some rappers sound a little scornful when they talk about this, like Method Man; some are triumphal. "Everything that hip-hop touches is transformed by the encounter," Jay-Z writes, "especially things like language and brands, which leave themselves open to constant redefinition. With language, rappers have raided the dictionary and written in new entries to every definition—words with one or two meanings now have twelve." And some rappers, maybe most, come across as merely unconcerned, the hare's obliviousness to the tortoise plodding along in its dust.

• •

The internet turbocharged the tortoise, of course, good news for those of us on the invading side. If it was far-fetched to think in 1984 that EMD's rhyme would eventually wind up printed in a book—which it was, for the first time to my knowledge in Lawrence Stanley's 1992 *Rap: The Lyrics: The Words to Rap's Greatest Hits*—today it's hard to imagine *not* being able to call up a song's lyrics, or at least a rudimentary approximation, and likely some discussion of what they mean. The internet was built for this shit, hypertext for a hyper literature. None of that manual cross-referencing, that fabrication lag, that latency that made it so by the time you could look up a bit of slang in a print diction-ary it would have ceased to be, ah, *fresh*. Between the moderated annotation platform Genius, which offers interpretive glosses and close readings that are usually enlightening and sometimes fantas-tically far-fetched, and Urban Dictionary, where you can visualize the historical baggage of the English language as reconstructed by a horde of clever if psychosexually stunted twelve-year-olds, you can probably put together your own gloss of whatever song you want. I use both all the time; I happen to like the taste of the grain of salt with which it's necessary to take them. At best they double as everyone's local library, a lightweight amalgam of glos-sary and archive and oral history and rewind button, expanding

You'll never find a rhyme like this in any dictionary

in real time and curated, in Genius's case, by community editors and savant hip-hop heads and barely lucid lunatics and sometimes rappers themselves.

On paper, as it were, all participants in this collective effort love rap and speak its English, or are at least making a good-faith effort to learn. Perhaps inevitably, though, not everyone is wild about so much frictionless assimilation and dissection. You see intimations of appropriation and establishmentarianism; you see plausible accusations of shady practices, like Genius lifting a few thousand early transcriptions from Matt Jost's Original Hip-Hop Lyrics Archive without attribution; you see reminders, more or less eloquently stated, that foiling this exact kind of intellectual materialism is what signifying is for in the first place. *Rap Genius dot com is white devil sophistry*, argued Kool A.D. of Das Racist in 2011; *Urban Dictionary is for demons with college degrees.*

"Middle of the Cake" (2011)

For my part, I like to imagine that a productive relationship is possible between slang's semantic slant and these technologies of documentation and decipherment. It pleases me, however naively, to picture more popular attention begetting more mischief and subversion, every list of known euphemisms for money or marijuana or fellatio driving the discovery and coinage of further uncharted ones. I was taught never to say *the dictionary*, lexicography being as alive and multiple and necessarily unfinished as language itself—but while we've got the definite-article version on hand, why not let it represent a formal challenge to keep coming up with figurations so novel, so unique, so unaccountably fly as to resist mainstream cooptation forever?

• •

An early contender for Rap Genius's slogan—it ultimately lost to Biggie's *If you don't know, now you know*—was *Pay attention and listen real closely how I break this slang shit down.* That's the introductory patter to Big L's 2001 hit "Ebonics (Criminal Slang),"

"Juicy" (1994)

a song brassily framed as a rhyming glossary that defines about six dozen terms, many of which were new to me the first time I heard it:

> *Your bankroll is your poke, a chokehold is a yoke*
> *A kite is a note, a con is a okey-doke*

"Ebonics" is a terrific song, though you could argue, to take Geneva Smitherman at her word, that what makes its conceit so appealing to a novice listener is also what makes it kind of a seditious gesture. If slang is actively exhausted by being made accessible, unencrypted, to the white mainstream—"This song is like the OG Rap Genius," an early annotation of "Ebonics" says: "It explains rap music slang for anthropologists and Orientalists"—then aren't we just watching the song short-circuit the words it contains by pinning them down, revoking their status and potency as slang, leaving them as toothless and commonplace as *head* or *chill* or *fresh*? Two decades later, isn't learning these meanings just watching old news, navigating by the light of stars that burned out centuries ago?

Sure, maybe, if you take the short view. Rap can always forge new nonstandards, after all, always will. But the song also poses a more provocative question: what does it mean, when you're inventorying and glossing criminal slang, if some of the words are deep drug jargon but some of them are moderately jaunty *Times* crossword answers? Doesn't that come to say more about how you define criminality than anything else? Big L's greater genius here, so to speak, is to include under the banner of "criminal slang" not only rap lingo that scanned as relatively esoteric at the time, and arguably still does—I've never heard *poke* or *vine* or *bull scare* used anywhere else the way the song defines them—but also words and phrases that would be familiar to any anglophone alive during the twentieth century:

Your apartment is your pad, your old man is your dad
The studio is the lab and heated is mad

That is, it's one thing to find out that *krills* means crack, and a very different thing to be told that *cocaine is nose candy* or *movies is flicks*. For both to happen in the same song, for the recherché to coexist with the corny in this way, casts into sudden relief just how much of the vernacular we accept today as mainstream, sometimes so much so that it's quaint, itself originated as slang. No doubt people who call their heart their *ticker* and their father their *old man* are by now the ones who most need something like Rap Genius to keep up, whether or not they choose to use it. But it's instructive to imagine, if only for the sake of imagining it, that at one point they were the nonstandards, the scofflaws, the speakers of an embattled language, who most needed something like rap.

ON RHYME

Let a nigga try me, try me
I'ma get his whole motherfuckin' family
And I ain't playin' with nobody
Fuck around and I'ma catch a body

Dej Loaf, "Try Me" (2014)

• •

TRY ME, AS Dej Loaf says it on the hook to the song of the same name, sounds to my ear like it rhymes with *Charlie*. So do *family*, which is accordingly something more like *fahmly*, and *nobody*, which I hear as pretty much standard. Once the verse starts, the first four rhymes are *forty*, *macaroni*, *on it*, and *recording*. There's only one conventionally perfect rhyme in the song's whole three and a half minutes—*scoring* with *boring*—unless you count *nobody* with *catch a body*, which is a remarkably flippant way to refer to murdering someone. There are slant rhymes and then there are sheer drops. It's not that Dej Loaf can't rhyme; anyone can *rhyme*. It's that she gets more mileage here out of deciding not to.

With apologies to Tolstoy, all perfect rhymes are alike, each imperfect rhyme imperfect in its own way. Perfect rhyme tells us about a relationship between words that never changes; that

Mitch caught a body 'bout a week ago
Bobby Shmurda, "Hot Nigga" (2014)

The flow so Tolstoy, Fyodor Dostoy
/ Half oyster, half shrimp, fully dressed po' boy
Jay Electronica, "The Ghost of Christopher Wallace" (2010)

51

scoring with *boring* is a rhyme you *can* find in a dictionary is useful but also, not to put too fine a point on it, boring. But rhyming *family* with *body*—that's *interesting*. How does she do it? *Why* does she do it? Imperfect rhyme—slant rhyme, off-rhyme, near-rhyme, half-rhyme, lazy rhyme, deferred rhyme, overzealous compound rhyme, corrugated rhyme, what have you—illuminates something about the person creating it, about their ear and their mind and what they're willing to bend for the sake of sound. It tells us what they believe they can get away with through sheer force of will, like

"Beamer, Benz, or Bentley (Remix)" (2010)

how Fabolous rhymes **Beamer Benz or Bentley** with **team be spending centuries** and **penis evidently** just because he knows he can. Or:

> I'm ridin' through the metropolitan, everybody hollerin'
> Me I'm just acknowledgin' with this million-dollar grin
> Shine like a halogen, cool as the island wind
> I don't judge myself but if I do I'd give my style a ten

Fabolous, "From Nothin' to Somethin' Intro" (2007)

That last line isn't particularly memorable by itself, but as the culmination of a chain of rhymes that drift in and out of alignment with *metropolitan*, it's riveting—all the more so because he ends it by awarding himself a perfect score for style rather than precision. Style is how he gets away with spending two bars repeating the same vowel sound—at least as I say those words—and then abandoning it altogether. Confidence is how he gets *halogen* to rhyme with *island wind*.

I'm ridin' through the Metropolitan, everybody hollerin' / Me I'm just acknowledgin' with this million-dollar grin

In a similar way, imperfect rhyme tells us how much effort a rapper is willing to appear to put in, whether it's a little—

> I'm in the bucket, paid two hundred for it
> My lil' niggas thuggin', even got me paranoid
> I'm gettin' money, that's in any nigga category
> Double M, I got Gs out in California

Rick Ross, "Stay Schemin'" (2012)

—or so much—

What you doin' in the club on a Thursday?
She said she only here for her girl birthday
They ordered champagne but still look thirstay
Kanye West, "Bound 2" (2013)   **Rock Forever 21 but just turned thirtay**

The former is from the Miami rapper Rick Ross, whose manicured southern drawl—he says his last name as *Rauwss* and rhymes it almost exclusively with *boss*—goes only part of the way toward explaining how any of those end words could be aurally comparable. The latter is Kanye West, for whom obstinacy is as much an aesthetic principle as it is a personal liability. Both rappers are unusually fond of rhyming words with themselves, but for what scan to me as opposite reasons: Ross out of a sort of plutocratic lethargy, West out of pure insistence. Adam Bradley, who calls forced cases like *birthday* and *thirstay* "transformative rhymes," describes Kanye's willingness to distort pronunciation on stylistic grounds as "the poetic equivalent of Jimi Hendrix using his amp's feedback in his solo." One pictures him standing before a perfect rhyme, stroking his chin, considering how best to *perfect* it by fucking it up.

Hey, you remember when we first met? / Okay, I don't remember when we first met / But hey, admittin' is the first step / Ay ay, you know ain't nobody perfeck

"Bound 2"

• •

Rhyme is the most powerful, least cerebral way I know to tap into that strange attraction words in close proximity exert on one another, what David Caplan calls language's need to couple. By its form it sets up an expectation which, depending on how and when it's met, can relieve you or surprise you, pull you forward in time or hold you in place: imagine if the last line of "Happy Birthday" had to rhyme with the birthday person's name. Its internalized call-and-response dynamic gives it a sense of gravity, of purpose. It's rhetorically means-justifying, so much so that researchers have documented a cognitive bias known as the rhyme-as-reason effect, according to which statements that rhyme are easier to pass off as true than ones that don't. (See a 2000 *Psychological Science* report called "Birds of a Feather Flock Conjointly (?).")

Which accounts, perhaps, for what I've come to think of as slant idioms: single-use figurations based on imperfect rhymes that are as oddly compelling semantically as slant rhymes are aurally. What I have in mind is actually quite similar to Westbrook's definition of *Wu-bonics*—"the commingling of words that sound good but don't always make clear sense"—except these are cases where someone shoehorns words together because they sound good and the result makes *exceptionally* clear sense. Take the Notorious B.I.G., for instance—who rhymed *birthday* with *thirstay* two decades before Kanye did—and who, while cautioning inexperienced drug dealers to avoid consignment arrangements, finds time to compact that old Postal Service credo ("neither snow nor rain or heat nor gloom of night") into a crystalline synonym for *no matter what*:

*Birthdays was the worst days /
Now we sip champagne when we thirstay*
"Juicy" (1994)

If you ain't got the clientele, say hell no
'Cause they gon' want their money rain sleet hail snow   *"Ten Crack Commandments" (1997)*

Or take Jay Electronica capping off a happily-ever-after snapshot with a two-word distillation of a wedding send-off:

Life is like a dice game
One roll could land you in jail or cutting cake, blowing kisses in the rice rain
"Exhibit A (Transformations)" (2009)

and the Chicago rapper Vakill tap-dancing around *dead*:

Some niggas claimin' that they can drop me, serve me
Got it topsy-turvy, so fuck around and wind up autopsy-worthy
in The Molemen, "Keep the Fame (Remix '01)" (2001)

These coinages don't just sound good, don't just make plausible sense: I find them seductively self-evident, dazzling in their novelty and sublime in their perishability. In the seconds between call and response, they create and immediately fill a space in the language. You can't explain the difference between *thirsty* and *thirstay*, I don't think, but you can hear it.

And who's to say this isn't proof of a deeper semantic magnetism that rhyme allows us to tap into? Not the rhyme-as-reason of *If it doesn't fit, you must acquit* or *He who smelt it dealt it*, but the rhyme-as-redemption of 2Pac reassuring his mother

Four years ago couldn't go to a show / I was standing on the corner selling dope for dough / Now I no longer hope I blow, smoke my 'dro / On a yacht, nigga, fuck a boat that row

Ma$e, "Do You Wanna Get $?" (1997)

"Dear Mama" (1995)
**And even as a crack fiend, mama
You always was a black queen, mama**

—which I hear as its own kind of transformative rhyme: one that acts, that performs, the way *I confess* and *I now pronounce you man and wife* are more than just statements. It's not that perfect rhymes can't accomplish the same thing, just that the imperfection is what makes it feel purposeful, personal, human when it happens. It's in surmounting perfection, or ignoring it, that you show what you're capable of and what you refuse to be told you can't do, even if it's just rhyming *family* with *nobody* and *nobody* with *body*. It shows what *you* hold to be equivalent and thus, in a sense, true.

"People say that the word *orange* doesn't rhyme with anything, and that kind of pisses me off, because I can think of a lot of things that rhyme with *orange*," Eminem tells Anderson Cooper in a 2010 interview. "If you're taking the word at face value, and you just say *orange*, nothing is going to rhyme with it exactly," he says. "If you enunciate it and you make it, like, more than one syllable—*aw-rindge*—you could say, like, uh: *I put my orange four-inch door hinge in storage and ate porridge with Georidge.*" (A bemused chuckle from Cooper.) This is just it: taking words at face value is what good rappers almost militantly don't do. They find the blind

55

angles, the shortcuts, the secret overlaps, and use them, some-times, to build stunning models of invention and entente, spaces where small discords combine into larger resolutions and we see, hear, how boring it would be to live in a perfect world where like belongs only with like.

ON REGISTER

Bitch I'm morose and lugubrious
I'ma let the Uzi spit, turn his face into gooey shit

Lil Ugly Mane, "Bitch I'm Lugubrious" (2012)

• •

ARE THERE UNRAPPABLE WORDS? Not words that can't be gerrymandered into rhyme, but words so ungainly, so unwieldy, so unhip, so unhip-*hop*, as to definitively resist rap's tractor-beam powers of assimilation. Do such words exist? No! says the wide-eyed idealist in me. I mean, probably, says the grizzled skeptic, who doubts I'll hear *pulchritude* or *amortize* or *hoarfrost* or *chilblains* dropped over a beat before I die. But then there was a time not so long ago when I would have put *lugubrious* on that list, and now here we are. Lil Ugly Mane, a producer from Virginia with a gothically bug-eyed rapping style and at least a dozen different stage names, rhymes it with a run of propositions like **flyer than a stewardess** and **been sick since the uterus**, so I'm certainly not complaining.

"Before this point," writes Jelani Cobb of the seven-minute B-side version of LL Cool J's "Rock the Bells"—the version that has bells in it—"it would have been highly unlikely that a rapper

Fuck choosing a word, use /
Every one you've ever heard

Qwel, in Typical Cats, "Intro"
(2001)

57

would use the words connoisseur, tympanic, impresario, pestilence, plateau, subpoena, conjecture, cranium, plagiarism, metabolism, auditory, eradicate, adversary, membrane, jugular, manuscript, and virtuoso in a single song." Today, as we all know, it's practically mandatory for a rapper to use all of these words within a single song. (Kidding! That would be an intolerable world.) Today that density of five-dollar words remains as rare as it was in 1985, but surely no more so than finding those seventeen words in twenty pages of a novel or an episode of, I don't know, a medical malpractice drama about a vindictive librettist. LL was showing off for sport, stunting on the dictionary and just being obnoxious in that singularly charming way he used to have of being obnoxious. Nobody needed the *Macbeth* reference. Nobody needed to hear him say *I initiate gyrating*.

Still, Cobb has a point. This was one of those gestures that historically carved out a little more space in hip-hop for wordiness for wordiness's sake, from the experimental verbosities of Bahamadia or Busdriver or Milo to the Bulfinch-toting Ritalin oratory of Aesop Rock, who led the pack by miles in a 2014 token analysis of rapper vocabulary sizes; from the Sondheimian toniness of Lin-Manuel Miranda's *Hamilton* to this one tongue-in-retainer microgenre called nerdcore, where dudes put on exaggerated nasal voices to rhyme about Pentium chips and graphing calculators. LL wasn't the begetter of any of these things, but he's irrefutable evidence of precedent.

I'm not talking about wordiness for wordiness's sake, though. I'm talking about styles of rap where five-dollar words seem intuitively as out of place as four-part harmonies or terza rima. I'm talking about the clash of registers I can't help but perceive when I hear a word like *lugubrious* in a crusty rhyme about shooting someone in the face; I'm talking about how Wu-Tang claimed six of the top twenty-five spots in that token vocabulary analysis but my ears and eyebrows still perk up to hear RZA talk about fallopian tubes or Inspectah Deck about computer software. Is that odd? Should I be surprised? Does Kevin Gates have any less of a right to say *hind-quarters*, or Lil' Kim to say *buffoonery*, or Mannie Fresh to say *microwave oven* or Cam'ron to say *Fancy Feast*, or Nicki Minaj to say *tax bracket* or Ras Kass to say *fuck tithing*, or Guru to say *slacks* or Andre 3000 to say *exfoliating*, than—well, me?

There's an appealingly simple sociolinguistic view, one my grizzled skeptic appears to have embraced, whereby words function as vectors of status: where vocabulary and diction map faithfully to acculturation and lifestyle, where every social stratum has its vernacular and every vernacular its social stratum. If rappers, at least of the styles at issue here, dwell more on sex and criminality and intoxication than they do on education or science or dental hygiene, wouldn't they be better off sticking to a slang calibrated to those things, rather than to the distinct jargons of people who spend a lot of time talking about informatics or critical theory or electron microscopy? If we know Cam'ron to be a guy who raps about selling crack, isn't it naturally going to be hard to picture him feeding a housecat?

Well, no and no. The trouble with this sociolinguistic view is that it's not just simple but simplistic: for one thing, it fails to account for the omnidirectional inter-register slippage already underway at a time where you're as likely to hear Gucci Mane quoted by an MSNBC anchor or a tech VC as you are to hear Raekwon rhyme about escrow. For another, and more perniciously, it holds words themselves, and their corresponding concepts, as a kind of property delimited by milieu, which is to say by class. I might wonder innocently, naively, whether it's *appropriate* for Nef the Pharaoh to say *infrastructure* or Lady of Rage *botulinum toxin*, but that puts me only a few steps away from arguing that there are some places where rap and rappers don't belong.

Which is wrong, intuitively and philosophically. Say what you will about its morals and manners, rap long ago became the music of the overclass as much as the underclass, and its reliable preoccupation with having nice things—boastfully or covetously—is a

So I'm cruising in the car with this bougie broad / She said, "Jigga man, you rich, take the durag off"

Jay-Z, "So Ghetto" (1999)

We ain't graduate from school, nigga (Dumb it down) / Them big words ain't cool, nigga (Dumb it down)

Lupe Fiasco, "Dumb It Down" (2007)

Rich niggas don't lollygag

Juicy J, in A$AP Rocky, "Wavybone" (2015)

Cats had better change they Brita filters

Aesop Rock (& Homeboy Sandman), "Katz" (2015)

Compose a fly rap with an 18-karat Meisterstuck

Meyhem Lauren, in Action Bronson, "Expensive Pens" (2012)

(2015)

I'm on a stool getting brain from a tall dame [...] / 'Cause I'm 5'8", shorty like 6'2" [...] / I was born to rep, you fucking with a hornet's nest / Old shooters in the corner like Hornacek

Action Bronson, in Ghostface Killah, "Meteor Hammer" (2011)

Was the degree of the economy that do the sovereignty / Regarded as a prodigy, leery in sociology / Let the Wallabees always conceal my gynecology / Rhyming pathologically, that's how it gotta be!

Jane Doe, in A Tribe Called Quest, "Rock Rock Y'all" (1998)

supremely organic and democratic way for signifiers to flow across artificial barriers of diction. That's the best way I can find to read the Queens MCs Action Bronson and Meyhem Lauren, whose pious devotion to imported meats and expensive pens breezes through wealth-signaling, nods at showy precision, and comes to rest in a thrilling kind of mundanity. *Don't try to put me in a box like a tissue / 'Cause I'll put you in a box with a pink suit / Then fuck around and have some squid ink soup, bitch*, Bronson shouts in a song called "Falconry." He has an album called *Rare Chandeliers*; Lauren has one called *Mandatory Brunch Meetings*, plus song titles like "Fingerless Driving Gloves" and "Beautiful Areolas" and "Pan Seared Tilapia." I could go on. By cutting the bombastic opulence of Rick Ross with the highbrow materialism of Frasier Crane, and still leaving room for weird sex boasts and nods to vintage basketball players, they're not so much testing the boundaries of word rappability as flouting them altogether.

And who's to say that's not the future LL wanted? That no register has a monopoly on lived or imagined experience is the whole point of the language arts. The point of rap, among others, is the pleasure of finding words that aren't just transparently informative but challenging to use, surprising to hear, satisfying to say. (Seriously, say *lugubrious* out loud.) To draw on words of diverse origin in unpredictable succession, to code-switch within the same thought between the sumptuous pomposity of *lugubrious* and the blunt animism of *I'ma let the Uzi spit*, is not to be inconsistent, much less to trespass, but to preserve the same resourcefulness that's been core to hip-hop since DJ Kool Herc jacked electricity from the lampposts in Cedar Park to power his open-air dance parties. Unlike most of the things they describe—unlike electricity—words can't be bought or sold, which means they can't be stolen, which means they can only *appear* to be vectors of milieu and money and class and all the bullshit those things are supposed to distinguish. What words really are is a renewable resource whose possession and usage will not be regulated.

HAUNTED ROOTS

I'm just with my niggas hangin'
Hangin'

Mick Jenkins, "Martyrs" (2015)

• •

THERE'S ONLY ONE verse in "Martyrs," and as he raps it Mick Jenkins sounds both deliberate and breathless, his basso wry and spiteful as it double-time lopes to a loop of curdled guitar. At the chorus, though, a deadpan litany of ignorant hood-goon aspirations—*I'ma buy all this shit, I'ma fuck so many hoes*—he starts to leave some space around the words. They seem to get lighter and stiffer at once, like they're dangling in the breeze. A rattlesnake whisper of Carmen McRae's voice drifts in: *ssssummmer treeeeees*.

   Hangin' on for dear life, Mick says, eventually.

   The track is built around samples from McRae's 1962 recording of "Strange Fruit," a 1937 protest poem by Abel Meeropol about lynchings in the South that became popular a few years later when Billie Holiday began performing it as a song:

> *Southern trees bear strange fruit*
> *Blood on the leaves and blood at the root*

Black bodies swinging in the summer breeze
Strange fruit hanging from the poplar trees

Between the chorus of "Martyrs" and the snippets the track weaves together, it's almost possible to hear that third line about black bodies, even though it's missing from the song itself. Hanging from what? Swinging on what rope? Is it hemp or jute or sex or drugs or empty materialism or the murderous aimlessness of a hot summer on the south side of Chicago? Is it keeping Mick and his friends alive or slowly asphyxiating them, or somehow both? In the space between words, I think, you're meant to wonder.

Two years before "Martyrs" came out, Kanye West, who's also from the south side of Chicago, spun Nina Simone's rendition of "Strange Fruit" into a song called "Blood on the Leaves." In spite of the title's direct quotation from the poem, and the track's ample use of Simone singing it, it's not a song that seems to want you to wonder about such things. Instead, it's a brooding meditation on extramarital dalliances and designer drugs that would require a truly herculean interpretive effort to tie back to America's history of lynching black bodies. This will be no surprise to anyone acquainted with Kanye's comet tail of more or less galling political

And just imagine how my girl feel, on the plane / Scared as hell that her guy look like Emmett Till

"Through the Wire" (2004)

"On Sight" (2013)

"I'm In It" (2013)

insensitivities, like the time he compared himself to Emmett Till in a song about falling asleep and crashing his Lexus. At one point in "Blood on the Leaves" he likens the pressures of keeping wife and mistress from finding out about one another to Apartheid; he also says *Your titties, let 'em out: free at last* and *I put my fist in her like a civil rights sign* elsewhere on the same album, which is called *Yeezus*.

So sure, where "Martyrs" uses "Strange Fruit" to frame Mick as a scowling prophet, "Blood on the Leaves" makes Kanye sound like a guy who's solipsistic and vulgar enough to marshal the accumulated weight of American anti-black violence to complain that a tryst with a groupie didn't pan out so well. But Kanye's not doing this by accident. When you look closely—when you set aside his increasingly dispiriting thought-leader antics and just focus on the way he writes—he's always had this remarkable self-conscious knack for spinning grave historical blemishes into slyly righteous insights. The theme of "New Slaves," for instance, also from *Yeezus*, is how little has truly changed since

> *the era when*
> *Clean water was only served to the fairer skin*
> *Doing clothes you would have thought I had help*
> *But they wasn't satisfied unless I picked the cotton myself*

(2013)

Again, it's not in the greatest taste that he's pointing this out while simultaneously telegraphing his indignation that Fendi won't let him manufacture a line of leather jogging pants. But "New Slaves" is a raw and trenchant rundown of the ways slavery and segregation persist today under other guises, from predatory consumerism to for-profit prisons to the impenetrable legalese of record deals. His outrage is genuine and not misplaced. When he revisits and distills the cotton image a few years later, describing himself in a song called "Feedback" as a *rich slave in the fabric store picking cotton*, the read gets a little more precise: for all his wealth and sociopolitical capital, which allow him to do things unthinkable for a black man in America mere decades ago, he still feels no freer than a slave.

Y'all throwin' contracts at me? /
You know that niggas can't read
"New Slaves"

(2016)

As wordplay, this operates almost exactly the way Cam'ron's *Coke like a caterpillar, I make butter fly* does. The second part pulls together the seemingly incongruous elements of the first, multiplying their individual resonances: the paradox *rich slave* shows us two polar extremes of *picking cotton*, field hands cultivating crops and consumers (or designers) blithely selecting textiles. It collapses the centuries passed in between, indicts as empty the supposed gains made from the former to the latter. And even if Kanye's not the most credible signatory for such an indictment, he's doing something necessary by pitting the phrase's distinct senses against each other, exposing the poisoned roots they share.

I'm presenting all of this like it's self-evident, but it took me a while to pick up on what both Mick and Kanye were doing. That delay surely speaks to how abstract my own experience of oppression is, but also to how innocuous certain words and phrases have become in popular usage despite their contaminated legacies. To wit, when, and how, did the American English face value of *hanging* turn into something so casual, so carefree, so *safe*?

• •

Americanness, writes Hua Hsu, "is a sponge, not an ethnicity; normalization is a key part of how it works. It resides in the way that we speak, in the ideas that get refined and reworked and encoded in ordinary words until they seem harmless enough." Once you pull the thread, though, it's hard to unsee how many ordinary words are houses divided, how many of the trees that shade and shelter our everyday conversations have blood on their leaves. And it's hard, in turn, to unhear how present they are in hip-hop vernacular, where a necklace is a *rope* or a *chain*, where a car is a *whip*, where units of friends and colleagues are *mobs* or *gangs* or *crews* or *clans*. Where a song's original recording—of which all published versions are licensed copies, and which is usually owned by the label rather than the artist—is its *master*, where a *drum* is the clip of an assault rifle, at least among New York rappers who wear puffy winter coats year-round. Where *dope* is a term of pride and a drug to peddle, *crack* too, where *yams* is drugs and also power, where *work* is a prosecutable quantity of drugs for transport or distribution and the house where they're cooked or sold is a *trap*. Where money is *ends* and *means*, as far as I know, is nothing. Where a *hood* is a neighborhood and a truncation of *hoodlum* and part of a car and part of a sweatshirt and part of the iconic Ku Klux Klan getup.

Chillin' out, maxin', relaxin' all cool

(DJ Jazzy Jeff &) The Fresh Prince, "Yo Home to Bel Air" (1990)

Four hundred years later we buyin' our own chains

Kanye West, "Saint Pablo" (2016)

This whip can parallel park itself

Kevin Gates, "Just Ride" (2013)

Bitch-ass nigga, I ain't got no masters / Rich-ass nigga, I got all my masters

Lil Wayne, "President" (2007)

—What's the yams? / The yam is the power that be / You can smell it when I'm walkin' down the street

Kendrick Lamar, "King Kunta" (2015)

I ain't in the Klan but I brought my hood with me

Kanye West, "We Major" (2005)

Four doors, leather and wood
Ride like I got a horse stable under my hood
And I keep a chrome .45 under my hood
So if I die, nigga, bury me under my hood

The Game, "Too Much" (2006)

After seventeen-year-old Trayvon Martin was shot and killed by the neighborhood watch coordinator of a gated community in Florida, conservative mustache Geraldo Rivera maintained that his hooded sweatshirt was as responsible for the murder as the shooter was. "I am urging the parents of black and Latino youngsters particularly to *not let their children go out wearing hoodies*," he said on television. The cover of Claudia Rankine's *Citizen*, an elegy to black self-determination in an age of unpunished police brutality and everyday microaggressions, shows a sculpture by David Hammons: the disembodied empty hood of a dark gray hoodie, mounted on a gallery wall like a tribal mask. "It's called 'In the Hood,'" writes Dan Chiasson in the *New Yorker*, "and it suggests that racism passes freely among homonyms: the white imagination turns hoods into hoods."

What to make of all these haunted senses hanging around and over hip-hop? Is the music normalizing them in ignorance of their older connotations or defiantly reusing them, reclaiming them, tempering them with new intent? This is volatile work, not light and airy language play, which in a way is Kanye's point: that the progress separating this whip from that one is precarious, that on a long enough timeline throwing your hands in the air and waving them around like you just don't care is indistinguishable from throwing them in the air out of habit when you've been the victim of systemic institutional brutality for centuries.

Maybe carrying on like you just don't care is the best recourse in a world where actually not caring is impossible. Maybe there's real power in owning an expensive symbolic totem of the whips and chains that kept your people owned just a few generations before.

Overseer, overseer, overseer, overseer / Officerofficerofficerofficer / Yeah, officer from overseer / You need a little clarity? Check the similarity!

KRS-One, "Sound of da Police" (1993)

Hands up, we just doing what the cops taught us / Hands up, hands up, then the cops shot us

"Feedback"

65

Far be it from me to say W. E. B. Du Bois's double consciousness—the burden of seeing yourself through the eyes and values of a contemptuous and oppressive majority—can't coexist with celebration, can't sweeten the performance of forgetting the past. But even as people forget, even as countries seem to forget, words don't forget. Dictionaries can change but the past can't. Language is its own independent witness, its own record of triumphs and abuses, and its deepest scars are always there, hanging in the breeze, waiting for the next bitter wind. No reclamation is possible without this awareness, even if it's the very same awareness that the carefree modern sense of *hanging out* is predicated on the privilege of ignoring.

CODE AND CONTRABAND

I got twenty-five lighters on the dresser, yessir

DJ DMD, "25 Lighters" (1998)

• •

SNACKS AND SHIT, defunct since late 2011, was a collectively
authored blog that specialized in doggedly literal readings of what
it described as "ridiculous rap lyrics," *ridiculous* usually meaning "containing figurative language." Its exegeses almost always
sounded the same punchline: that the rapper who said the lyric
in question doesn't know how to talk, or give advice, or do sex,
or do life. There are plenty of slow clap–worthy assertions in the
annals of rap—Guru's **Lemonade was a popular drink and it still is** is   *in Gang Starr, "DWYCK" (1994)*
a time-honored one, Scarface's **If I die then my child will be a bastard**   *in Geto Boys, "Mind Playing*
another—but these bloggers were especially committed to their   *Tricks" (1991)*
indiscriminateness. To A$AP Rocky's line **Got a condo out in space,**   *"Goldie" (2013)*
for instance, the commentary is "I highly doubt that." It was all
meant in good fun, I'm sure, but it's hard not to read in its archive,
some years hence, the same implacable bullying energy as Donald
Trump's toxic haters-and-losers shtick. (Sample tags at the bottom
of a post: *depressing, so lonely, so sad, Tyga.*)

One of the blog's primary interpretive moves could be summed up as incomprehension, feigned or genuine—reactions like "What? Why?" or "Oh cool. WHO GIVES A SHIT????" or "No."—and that's the spirit in which the above lyric was given a close reading in late 2012. The line under examination wasn't from the DJ DMD song, a Texan rap classic with the memorable singsong hook *I got twenty-five lighters on the dresser, yessir / I gots to get paid*, nor is it from the 1995 8Ball & MJG track in which the line first appears; it was the iteration quoted in Kendrick Lamar's irresistible "Backseat Freestyle," which finds him playing a callow, braggadocious teen-age version of himself quoting DJ DMD quoting MJG. All of this contextual information is absent from the Snacks and Shit annotation, the entirety of which reads "COOL!!!!!!!!!"

I got twenty-five lighter on my dresser, yessir / Put fire to that ass, body cast on a stretcher / And her body got that ass that a ruler couldn't measure / And it make me come fast but I never get embarrassed

(2012)

True enough, at face value, any more than two or three lighters is a lot to have in one place, and it's certainly not obvious why you'd go bragging about having twenty-five. But rap has taught me over time to be wary of details that don't quite sit flush with the narrative but don't quite sound like hyperbole or metaphor either, of these quiet little bubbles in the rhetorical wallpaper. When Rick Ross mentions, apropos of nothing in particular, that he's driving a rental car, does that signal a lapse in his luxury car–collecting high life, or is he perhaps nodding to a best practice for drug capos monitoring out-of-state work handoffs? When Raekwon of Wu-Tang says *We usually take all niggas' garments*, is he talking about actually robbing people of their clothes—no question, the Clan got up to some rowdy shit—or are we meant to pay attention to certain less declarative qualities of the statement? (More on Five Percenter acronymy anon.) There are places, is my point, where a little bit of curiosity goes a long way. Rap Genius's origin story is that the site was born when one founder-to-be thought to ask another what Cam'ron meant by *Eighty holes in your shirt: there, your own Jamaican clothes.*

Following fundamentals, I'm following in a rental / I love a nasty girl who swallow what's on the menu

"Aston Martin Music" (2010)

"Wu-Tang: 7th Chamber" (1993)

"Family Ties" (2004)

So what can Genius—or, if you prefer, one of those here's-how-your-kids-are-probably-getting-high pamphlets for hysterical parents—tell us about MJG and DMD and Kendrick and their strangely cluttered dressers? Aha: that they're referring to the practice of using hollowed-out cigarette lighters as cheap and innocuous transport vials for crack. How strange! A slightly askew detail that separates the savvy from the dull-witted. By design, it's easy to miss: unless you think to stop to wonder and ask, you'll always just see a bunch of Bics on a dresser. Rather wonderfully, this is a lyric about smuggling that itself contains hidden contraband.

Or consider the even plainer-sight case in Jay-Z's inescapable New York City anthem "Empire State of Mind," a song I liked until I was trapped on a bus from Philadelphia to New York next to a kid listening to it on repeat, on poorly insulated headphones, from the moment the Manhattan skyline came into view until we reached Midtown. At one point—once again apropos of nothing in particular—Jay tells us *If Jeezy paying Lebron, I'm paying Dwyane Wade.* Why *(2009)* would he bring this up? Why would he be paying Dwyane Wade at all—why especially in 2009, when Jay was still a partial owner of the Brooklyn Nets and Wade still a shooting guard on the Miami Heat? So glad you asked. Young Jeezy, it turns out, released a song earlier that year called "24-23," a strident hustlers' anthem whose conceit is that Jeezy once got his cocaine wholesale at $24,000 a kilo but has since managed to knock that figure down to $23,000. Instead of saying as much outright, though, he says that he *used to pay Kobe, but now I pay Lebron.* Kobe Bryant's jersey number was *(2009)* 24, Lebron James's is 23. Jeezy undermines this inspired encryption later in the song by spelling it out explicitly, but then Jeezy's never been all that interested in subtlety.

Dwyane Wade's jersey number is 3.

Whether Jay is claiming to have used his business acumen and powers of persuasion to secure an 800 percent markdown or calling bullshit on Jeezy—*yeah right, and I'm the Duchess of Kent*—he's double-encoding his point, first by using an elaborate pro-sports substitution cipher and then by *hiding the key in someone else's*

Close shop then I do my count / Hide the rest of the yams in my auntie house

Young Jeezy, "And Then What" (2005)

song. That he does this in a monster hit single where he also freely reveals some verifiable specifics about his old illicit practices is pure signifying: classic misdirection swagger, the informed baiting the ignorant. *If you know, you know,* as Pusha T puts it. If not, well, you can always blog about it.

• •

Nowhere is this idea—that rap contains not just obscure slang but actively coded language—expressed quite as succinctly as in the title of Jay's annotated memoir, *Decoded,* published the same year as "Empire State of Mind." This isn't a fanciful thought. Scrutiny by an inquisitive public, law enforcement, and the tongue-clucking conservative factions that Tricia Rose calls "ideological dogcatchers" is nothing new for black American artists, as Erik Nielson explains:

The heavily coded lyrics of the earliest slave spirituals, and centuries later the blues, are a testament to the musicians' constant awareness of a hostile society watching their every move. To varying degrees, all of these musics became what they were because of it, adapting and responding in numerous ways, but none so profoundly as rap, which, in the face of unprecedented visibility, has internalized this public gaze so deeply that it has become part of its musical DNA.

(Nielson intimates in the same paper that the ingrained expectation of wiretapping accounts for the curious preponderance of skits on nineties rap albums framed as phone conversations and voicemail messages, which was as thrilling a revelation for me as learning what the lighters were for.)

"Saying one thing to mean something quite other has been basic to black survival in oppressive Western cultures," writes Henry Louis Gates, Jr. "This sort of metaphorical literacy, the learning to decipher complex codes, is just about the blackest aspect of the black tradition." Per Geneva Smitherman, "the

I used to cop in Harlem, hola my Dominicanos / Right there up on Broadway, brought me back to that McDonald's / Took it to my stash spot, 560 State Street / Catch me in the kitchen like a Simmons whipping Pastry

"Empire State of Mind"

Holler at me on the low, I take care of that / And feds buy mixtapes, yeah, I'm aware of that

Lil Wayne, "New Orleans" (2005)

Good day officer what's the problem? / They looking for answers I ain't got none

Curren$y, in Lil Wayne, "President" (2007)

historical realities of servitude and white oppression explain why this aspect of Black Semantics"—the use of coded dialect as a "register of exclusion"—"changes so rapidly, for once a word gains widespread usage in the White American mainstream, a new term must be coined; after all, a code is no longer a code if the enemy is hip to it."

I would share the definition of ballin' *with you white folks*, says 2Pac, voice pitch-shifted into the nether frequencies, in the intro to a song called "Str8 Ballin'," *but no. The game is to be sold and not told, so, uh, fuck you.*

in Thug Life, "Str8 Ballin'" (1994)

"I would keep the merciless slaveholder profoundly ignorant of the means of flight adapted by the slave," writes Frederick Douglass, explaining why his *Narrative* is so vague on the details of his own escape. "Let him be left to feel his way in the dark."

If you can't be free, writes Rita Dove in a poem about Billie Holiday, *be a mystery.*

And yet. Think again of what Big L was up to in "Ebonics." How long can code remain encoded? Does anyone *still* smuggle crack in hollowed-out lighters? Is the Hot Boy$ song "Tuesday and Thursday," a PSA about block-monitoring by government task forces, still useful intelligence, or did the narcs just switch up their schedule? Did YG really have to call his late-2016 anthem "FDT" when the acronym is unpacked right there in the hook?

On Tuesdays and Thursdays you better watch for the sweep / Look, them people gon' act a ass if you get caught in the street
(1999)

Fuck Donald Trump / Fuck Donald Trump / Yeah, nigga, fuck Donald Trump / Yeah yeah, fuck Donald Trump, yeah

Coding as a means of escape, as a practice of solidarity against haters and dogcatchers, is beautiful and humbling to behold on a spiritual level. But I have to wonder how well it can work in an age when rap's communications are massively public, its ciphers laid bare in print and online and pored over by thousands of chattering exegetes. How long can *be a mystery* coexist with **gots to get paid**? And if metaphorical literacy is coded as black, then what are my curiosity and I working so hard to accomplish? Am I telling the game or selling it or giving it away? What and whom am I resisting?

INTELLIGENCES

Lick you down to your belly button, I ain't frontin'
They don't call me Big for nuttin'
All of a sudden

The Notorious B.I.G., "One More Chance" (1994)

• •

It's the first time together and I'm feeling kinda horny / Conventional methods of making love kinda bore me

LL Cool J, "Doin' It" (1995)

Then you roll your tongue from the crack back to the front / Then you suck it all 'til I shake and cum, nigga / Make sure I keep bustin' nuts, nigga / All over your face and stuff

Khia, "My Neck, My Back (Lick It)" (2002)

She get to shakin' ass, she get to shakin' titties / She make that ass clap clap clap for a rack / But I bet you can't do that with a dick in it

Ty Dolla $ign, "I Bet" (2013)

EVEN BY TODAY'S standards, the standards of a world whose shock barrier has retreated steadily in slow creeps and sudden filthy lurches, a world in which it is the birthright, nay the imperative, of rappers of all genders and orientations to enumerate and commentate freaky sex acts in lurid detail, "One More Chance" is racy as fuck. It's so racy that it's actually even kind of quaint in its singleness of focus on its central theme, namely the unyielding excellence of Biggie's dick. Incredibly, the song's graphic nature doesn't cramp his *lyrical gift* (a term that is, per below, in sort of a gray area vis-à-vis whether or not it also means his penis): instead, the dexterity works in concert with the TMI. Biggie was the all-time champion of making rhythm itself semantic, and when he says *They don't call me Big* here he stretches the adjective out for a full quarter bar, making space, taking space, to evoke the amplitude of its bigness. Earlier in the song he does just the opposite, quickening his delivery as he crams an overlong line into the remaining quarter bar:

> *Whether it's stiff tongue or stiff dick,*
> *Biggie squeeze it to make shit fit, nowcheckthisshit:*
> *I got the pack of Rough Riders in the Pathfinder*
> *You know the epilogue by James Todd*
> *Smith, I get swift with the lyrical gift*
> *Hit you with a dick, make your kidney shift*
> *[untranscribable rapid intake of breath through gritted teeth]*

"One More Chance"

After that big *Big* at the end, the ensuing *all of a sudden* seems like filler, a glorified throat-clearing like *yo* or *come on* or *that's right*, an errant bit of patter no more meaningful than *nowcheckthisshit*. But suppose you're curious. Suppose you press the point—*all of a sudden* what, exactly?—and lock onto some intel you learned from Big L in "Ebonics," and all of a sudden the word directly preceding *all of a sudden* is not *nothing* but in fact *nutting*, which is to say ejaculating, and—well! In one swift motion, a moment's pause and rewind, the line at the very end of the song goes from *Not for nothing do they call me Big*—which is admittedly the song's central thesis—to *I certainly didn't get this nickname due to a problem with premature ejaculation.* Quite the opposite, *big* as in long, long as in the way he's just said the word *Big.* It wasn't a throwaway at all but an ingenious verbal victory lap, not a spontaneous emanation but a richly earned climax.

I know, I'm sorry. I'll stop.

Imagine my delight to discover, at the bottom of a rabbit hole some years ago, that this maneuver has a name, a pedigree, some disputed etymological elements, a medium-sized Wikipedia entry—all that fly shit that gets the turtledoves hot and bothered. It's called *paraprosdokian*, which breaks down to "against expectation," and it's the same re-parse that happens at the end of *Take my wife,*

Beggin' is bummin', if you nuttin' you cummin' / Takin' orders is sonnin', an ounce of coke is a onion

I got that good dick, girl, you didn't know?

"One More Chance"

73

please or *Outside of a dog, a book is a man's best friend; inside of a dog, it's too dark to read.* It's trickster-deity magic through and through, a device that jumps out of the shadows, spins you around 180 degrees, and sends you back whence you came with a swift kick to the ass. It's intoxicating, and learning its name made me find it more so, not less.

The first device I remember pattern-recognizing in rap was the simile—*I'm coming after you like the letter V*—and ever since I've thrilled to the discovery and identification of countless other verbal tricks, like antanaclasis and zeugma and syllepsis and anaphora and garden-path sentences and bewildering uses of the expletive *it*, which is the 808 cowbell of rap vernacular, I'll explain why some other time. It occurs to me, though, that I almost never hear these terms thrown around by rappers themselves. Even the ones who are outspoken about their craft, who hold forth on their rhetorical strategies in Genius interviews or in Paul Edwards's *How to Rap* series, don't appear to have much interest in the terminological and taxonomic metadata. "I'm kind of into the real technical part of it," Eminem tells Ice-T in the documentary *Something from Nothing: The Art of Rap* after a full minute haltingly describing his approach to rhyming, during which time the most specialized term he uses is *sandwich*.

• •

"Great rap," Jay-Z writes in *Decoded*, "should have all kinds of unresolved layers that you don't necessarily figure out the first time you listen to it. Instead it plants dissonance in your head. You can enjoy a song that knocks in the club or has witty punch lines the first time you hear it. But great rap retains mystery. It leaves shit rattling around in your head that won't make sense until the fifth or sixth time through. It challenges you."

The poem, Wallace Stevens once wrote, in a poem,

I'm not a businessman, I'm a business, man

Jay-Z, in Kanye West, "Diamonds from Sierra Leone (Remix)" (2005)

must resist the intelligence
Almost successfully.

Of course, there's intelligence and there's intelligence. There's the IQ kind and the CIA kind, the debate club kind and the unmanned aerial kind. Same root, *very* different attitudes about problem-solving. There's mastery and there's mastery, solutions and *solutions*. Again, these partially tainted words are everywhere when you start looking.

My intelligence, such as it is, is the kind that likes synthesizing, concatenating, solving puzzles. It likes facts that don't serve an immediate purpose, if only so it can cross-reference them with other facts. It appreciates what Nabokov, the acquirer of languages and the hunter and classifier of butterflies, calls the tactile delights of precise delineation. It enjoys having a name for *paraprosdokian*, a drawer in which to file forevermore this funny little twist-ending effect, and it feels—I feel—that these drawers make for a craftier, more resourceful and rewarding way of looking at the world. I feel, as William Empson puts it, that "unexplained beauty arouses an irritation in me, a sense that this would be a good place to scratch."

You see where this is going. Suppose signifying, playful as it is, is a kind of misdirection in the interest of survival. Survival, says Audre Lorde, is not an academic skill. (Anadiplosis is when you start a sentence with the last word of the previous sentence.) When the unexplained beauty is unexplained by design, when it's the collateral efflorescence of a whole meaning-making system meant to exclude unwelcome attention, what do my excitement and curiosity have to offer? Is the pleasure of discovery inherently acquisitive, colonial? Is cultural knowledge zero-sum? Does the butterfly have to die to satisfy the lepidopterist?

"I can't depend on the world to name me kindly," writes Lorde, "because it never will."

Particularly in a country that has historically treated young people of color as challenges to be neutralized rather than collaborators and equals, I have to wonder what my intent interest has in common with the kind of scrutiny that perpetuates, maybe even characterizes, oppression. I have to wonder whether there's something in this practice of naming and annotating and cross-referencing—in this vigorous, competitive *understanding*—that violates a covenant, that overcomes the poem's resistance by force. I have to wonder if I'm finding puzzles where there are none, if I'm asking the wrong questions, and if so what that says about me. I have to wonder, where Du Bois framed *The Souls of Black Folk* around the question of how it feels to be a problem, what it means to be driven by the desire to solve them.

Or maybe I couldn't solve them if I tried: maybe that's precisely where the beauty lies. There's resistance and resistance, too; maybe this one is less a bitter political struggle and more the resistance of a bicycle in high gear, something that makes you work harder without ever fully ceding to your efforts. Something that cannot be comprehended, to paraphrase Nikki Giovanni, except by its own permission. Something that *plants dissonance in your head* and knows the value of keeping it growing.

Slick Rick:

The girls say "Wow, Rick, you're so unique
"Please tell us how you organize the words you speak"
But my will says chill and I go upon my way
'Cause class will be taught some other day   *"Teacher, Teacher" (1988)*

"The reasons that make a line of verse likely to give pleasure, I believe, are like the reasons for anything else," Empson goes on: "one can reason about them; and while it may be true that the roots of beauty ought not to violate them, it seems to me very arrogant of the appreciative critic to think that he could do this, if he chose, by a little scratching."

76

POWER PLAY

I'm on point like a elbow
Hands red like Elmo
My mama said, "Have you had enough?"
I looked and I said, "No ma'am"

Nasir, in Y.N.RichKids, "Hot Cheetos & Takis" (2012)

• •

"Hot Cheetos & Takis" is a baroque party-rap song, recorded in 2012 by a gaggle of pre-teen moppets in Minneapolis, that would be a clever ode to the dawning of youthful independence and a wry reflection on snack-food dependency if it weren't so busy absolutely fucking *slaying*. Go listen to it, or better yet watch the video: if it doesn't brighten your day, either you're evil or you're in the Arctic Circle in July. Either way, go watch it. I'll wait.

• •

Oh hey. So what Nasir does above, that stagy trick rhyme where instead of the gleeful *Hell no* you're expecting you get a politeness-oozing **No ma'am**: I've seen it filed in a whole bunch of drawers. *Mind rhyme, teasing rhyme, veiled rhyme.* Adam Bradley calls it a *ghost rhyme*, which I love because it suggests ghost riding the

Pull up, hop out, all in one motion /
Dancin' on the hood while the car's
still rollin'

Mistah F.A.B., "Ghost Ride It" (2006)

We ghost ride like Swayze, man

"Ghost Ride It"

whip, that inexplicably jubilant Vallejo, CA move where you dance around and atop your own car while it's rolling along with no driver, which in a way is exactly what **No ma'am** is doing to your brain here, skipping around on the roof of your train of thought as it chugs along down the wrong track. I've heard the device in patty cake—*Miss Suzie went to heaven, the steamboat went to Hello operator*—and read it, via *The Great Gatsby*, in the waggish foxtrot "Ain't We Got Fun"—

One thing's sure and nothing's surer
The rich get richer and the poor get—children

—and dawdled over it in rap too, of course. There's one refrain that's been lodged in my inner ear for more than a decade:

A little bit of this is all I need
Can't wait to get home and smoke... some salmon

Spit so many verses sometimes my
jaw twitches / One thing this party
could use is more [ahem] booze

MF DOOM, in Madvillain,
"Great Day" (2004)

—which I could swear is from a song by these boom-bap bon mot–dispensers from Kentucky called Cunninlynguists, a name that makes so much sense it's obscene, but I can't source it anywhere, meaning this particular rhyme has now ghosted on me twice non-consecutively. Well played, mystery tricksters.

And so here it is again in "Hot Cheetos & Takis," masterfully folding rhyme into a cheeky pantomime of disobedience, making the unexpected sound of it signify. It's a breezy joke with roots in something deeper, in the fantasy of saying *cunnilingus* at the dinner table and convincing your parents you said *prawn linguini* and sending *them* and *their* filthy minds to *their* room without dessert. It's playing with the listener, not not antagonistically. It's a rhetorical whac-a-mole, a homespun science of script-flipping, used here with the purity and good fun embodied by a rapper who could still plausibly get in trouble with his mom for saying *Hell no.*

• •

Here's the signifying monkey legend in a nutshell: one day in the jungle, bored, fed up with all the roaring and preening and bullying, the monkey decides to tell off the lion. *Your daddy's a fairy*, he says, *your mother's a whore*. He lays his aspersions out in some detail, has his fun embellishing them. Why not? When the lion inevitably gets mad, the monkey says he's only relaying the scandalous gossip the *elephant's* been spreading around. Incensed now, the lion prowls off and confronts the elephant, who, resentful of the accusation, beats the cat snot out of him. How the story ends varies by telling: in some, the lion realizes he's been duped and visits a brutal comeuppance on the monkey; in others, he takes the L and the monkey's fun prevails, unpunished, everlasting.

In Schoolly D's 1988 rendition, it's the latter. "Signifying Rapper" doesn't sound all that much like hip-hop, then or now; it's more like a toast or a round of the dozens, funky semi-poetic jive talk that just happens in this case to be extemporized on top of a towering Led Zeppelin loop. But it tells a story about a rapper, who plays the monkey in this scenario, and a pimp, who is the lion, and a "big bad faggot" from around the way as the elephant. Fed up with the pimp's nightly abuse, the rapper takes a stand:

> *But the rapper got wise, started using his wit*
> *And said "Man, I'm tired of this kick-ass shit"*
> *So early, early early in the morning the very next day*
> *The rapper said, "Mr. Pimp, Mr. Pimp, I got something to say"*

Several bars' worth of colorful insult follow, ostensibly second-hand, focused on the pimp's father and mother, his grandma and brother, his sister who is, the rapper reports, *so low she sucked the dick of a little maggot.* Duly wound up, the pimp gets in his Cadillac and races off to find his would-be slanderer. When he does, they fight *all that night, and all the next day / That faggot kick[s] that pimp's ass in a hell of a way.* When the pimp comes back to the projects to lick his wounds, the rapper, *standing up on one of those tall-ass project buildings,* tells him *I shoulda kicked your ass my motherfuckin' self.*

This wasn't the story's first appearance in the proto-rap universe; Schoolly's track is a truncated (and, incredibly enough, less profane) transposition of a Rudy Ray Moore number from the early seventies, in which things don't end quite as happily for the monkey, though he gets in some even better jabs at the lion. Henry Louis Gates, Jr., took the baton in the eighties, tracing the legend's roots and branches and positing it as an interpretive skeleton key to black vernacular culture. By the time Schoolly released "Signifying Rapper," the same year Gates published his critical landmark *The Signifying Monkey,* it was implicitly clear that the trope belonged in conversation with rap and its codes of misdirection and tricksterism.

At base, of course, it's an allegory about power: about those fleeting times when it's possible to renegotiate the balance, when intelligence and irony *are* an even match for authority and might. In the West African context of the legend's emergence it's easy enough to focus on the monkey's quick-witted japery, the pleasure of spirited obscenity—to read the play as play. But in a white-dominated Western culture, one with a long and eerily jocular history of justifying oppression by framing black bodies as simian, literally subhuman, even the levity belies a terrible seriousness. Even the play of doubles is double-edged. The story's moral—that the powerful, be they police or prosecutors or parents, can be fooled and deflated with savvy talk; that they can then laugh it off, or seek punishment all out of reasonable proportion—is ingrained in rap's sometimes adversarial spirit of fun, its calculus of complicity and consequence. But it also models and valorizes, soberly, a kind of resistance, easy as child's play, that makes do with the means at hand, even if it's just keeping your cool while the bully loses his.

WORD AS BOND

Speech is my hammer bang the world into shape and let it fall

Mos Def, "Hip Hop" (1999)

• •

MY MATERNAL GRANDFATHER, who would have hated rap in just about all of its guises, was an ardent proponent of gematria, a Judaic numerological practice that assigns numerical values to Hebrew letters and words, which in turn combine to form more or less auspicious unities. Multiples of eighteen are lucky, for instance, because that's the sum of the two letters in the word *chai*, for life. I won't go deeper into it, because that's about the extent of my erudition, but I will say that the faith it implies in a cosmic order hovering over language's happy accidents has been part of my worldview for as long as I can remember. (While we're crediting David Levin for qualities of mine, I'll note that he also enjoyed puzzles and euthanizing jokes by explaining them at length.)

I recognize a similar attitude in hip-hop culture, this idea that an enlightened handling of words affords access to a vein of meaning that transcends their expressive value, a crunchy sort of oneness with the infinite. In most of the rap I listen to, though, this

81

faith is vanishingly rarely framed as an affirmative personal belief in the power of language. Instead, it's often mediated by an affirmative personal belief in the tenets of the Nation of Gods and Earths, more casually known as the Five Percent Nation, a tradition officially established in the sixties by a Nation of Islam dissident from Virginia who called himself Clarence 13X. Perhaps the best-known Five Percenter catechism, familiar to anyone who's logged any serious time listening to nineties New York rap, is *Word is bond*: three-syllable shorthand for the notion that talk is not just what cements a community socially, but actually what holds together the universe. Conversation is often referred to as *building*, implying that exchanging wisdom and perspective is how you create and catalyze change. Talking *is* doing, essentially. This is the loophole, as I read it, that allows a lot of street rappers to reconcile their professed occupations—as players, as hustlers, as gangbangers—with the fact that mostly, at the end of the day, they talk for a living.

Nation mythology teaches that 85 percent of men and women on Earth are sheeple, unwittingly oppressed by the devilish 10 percent who are manipulative evildoers. The remaining Five Percent are human incarnations of divinity, a spacey talented twentieth made up of poor righteous teachers whose duty is to awaken, enlighten, and civilize the 85, roust them from their complacency and shepherd them into deeper universal consciousness. This is, by the way, what you'll find if you follow the paper trail back from the epithet *conscious rap*—a great many socially aware backpack rappers being either committed Five Percenters or casual affiliates, including a likably trebly group from New Jersey called Poor Righteous Teachers—and the now mainstream albeit increasingly contentious honorific *woke*. Jay Electronica, one of the most outspoken Five Percenter rappers this side of the millennium, recounts his awakening and redemption by the Nation in "Exhibit C":

I ain't believe it then: nigga, I was homeless
Fightin', shootin' dice, smokin' weed on the corners
Tryna find the meaning of life in a Corona
Til the Five Percenters rolled up on a nigga and informed him
That you either build or destroy. "Where you come from?"
"The Magnolia projects in the 3rd Ward slum." "Hum—
It's quite amazing that you rhyme how you do
And that you shine like you grew up in a shrine in Peru"

(2009)

Jay is from New Orleans, but this anecdote is set in New York, birthplace and epicenter of the Nation, not coincidentally coinciding with the golden-age luminaries of East Coast rap: Rakim, Big Daddy Kane, Wu-Tang, Mobb Deep, Nas, AZ, Guru, and probably anyone else you hear saying *Word is bond*, using *building* intransitively, or calling a man *god* or a woman *earth*. (Mos Def, who now goes by Yasiin Bey, is a Sunni Muslim, not a Five Percenter, but there's a ton of overlap between his cosmology of music and meaning and the Nation's.) Rakim is venerated as "the God MC" not just because he's one of the primary architects of lyrical rap as we know it today, but also because, by laying down the mold in which we make and hear hip-hop, he forged something elemental about the world that contains it.

The twin cornerstones of Five Percenter philosophy are the Supreme Mathematics and the Supreme Alphabet, both of which resemble gematria not only in that they assign values to numbers and letters—A is *Allah*, B is *born*, 1 is knowledge, 2 is wisdom; 0 is cipher, also hip-hop slang for a circle of rhymers passing verbal energy around—but also in that they somehow manage to be simultaneously systematic and wildly arbitrary, rigorously methodical and conducive to enormous interpretive leeway. With skill enough, essentially, reality is yours to build. Whatever your truth—say, that the Brand Nubian song "Pass the Gat" doesn't *actually* glorify violence

I'm tryna get this money, god, you know the hard times, kid / Shit, cold be starving make you wanna do crimes, kid

Nas, "One Time 4 Your Mind" (1994)

Say peace to cats who rock MAC-Knowledge Knowledges

Raekwon, in Ghostface Killah, "Daytona 500" (1996)

Three fourths of water makes seven seas / A third of land, 360 degrees

(Eric B. &) Rakim, "No Competition" (1994)

because *gat* also stands for "God Allah's Truth"—it gives you the rhetorical tools to justify it, perform it, *show and prove* it. You invent your evidence not out of whole cloth, exactly, but out of a system of existential perception that's every bit as supple and open-source as language. *Knowledge*, in Nation vernacular, is literally a verb.

Rap's inheritance of all this, as you might imagine, can scan as a little contorted, a little corny, the province of people who eagerly embrace conspiracy theories but wholeheartedly buy into backronyms and the rhyme-as-reason bias. ("In the 5% you have your hypocrites," says Wise Intelligent of Poor Righteous Teachers: "You have your brothers who are not 5%ers, but jive pretenders.") I see my grandfather's cabalist eye-gleam when Guru says **I Self Lord And Master shall bring disaster to evil factions**, when Jay-Z says **Arm, Leg, Leg, Arm, Head: this is God body / Knowledge, wisdom, freedom, understanding, we just want our equality.** (That's 1-2-3-4, if you're up on your Supreme Mathematics.) *God* stands for "gaining one's definition," according to Cee-Lo of Goodie Mob, which itself stands for "The Good Die Mostly Over Bullshit." KRS-One stands for Knowledge Reigns Supreme Over Nearly Everyone. Big Daddy Kane sometimes calls himself King Asiatic Nobody's Equal, dispensing refreshingly with the wiggle words. I'll let you put together *witty unpredictable talent and natural game* for yourself. 2Pac wasn't a Five Percenter, but I don't know where else you get a credo like *The Hate U Give Little Infants Fucks Everyone*. Ditto for Blood-identified rappers like Cardi B and YG, who go out of their way to replace hard Cs with Bs ("Bodak Yellow," "Bicken Back Being Bool") out of a basically ecclesial contempt for the Crips.

And when you're sufficiently steeped in a discourse that plays fast and loose with the standard empirical models of truth, the showmanship in your showing and proving becomes at least as important as the proof. *Take the first letter out of each word in this joint*, raps CL Smooth in a song called "They Reminisce Over You," dedicated to a friend named T. Roy: *Listen close as I prove my point:*

Library broken down is lies buried / To force their beliefs the pilgrims all hurry / Television, tell-a-lie vision / A schism, negative realism

(Pete Rock &) CL Smooth, "Anger in the Nation" (1992)

in Gang Starr, "Above the Clouds" (1998)

"Heaven" (2013)

I guess I'm like the Verbalizer for the fact I'm working backwards / This Asiatic black man is a dog spelled backwards

Grand Puba, in Brand Nubian, "Wake Up (Reprise in the Sunshine)" (1990)

(1992)

T to the R to the O-Y. It's a bright and colorful house of cards, a system of evidentiary hermeneutics cobbled together out of deep arcana, but what religion doesn't have one of those? What subgroup of human civilization doesn't eventually build its own code of existential equivocation? This one at least makes it easy to look past earthly divisions, in its inconsistent way practically even insists on it: even if Clarence 13X and David Levin would have agreed on nothing else, even if in spite of my best intentions I'm a devilish ten percenter, this way of beholding the cosmos promises a dimension in which we can meet, one where the molecular connections that make up reality are fundamentally rhetorical, where the linguistic parts of the world are recombinant and generative, where wordplay is more than just play.

ANTI-SIMILE

I'm the motherfucking king like Oedipus

Qwel, in Typical Cats, "Take a Number" (2001)

• •

"POCKET FULL OF STONES," one of the first singles by the indispensable Texas duo UGK, is about selling crack to an overly willing clientele. *I got a pocket full of stones / and they won't leave my ass alone.* The stones are crack rocks; *they* are the fiends. Libertine listener that I am, however, when this refrain runs through my head—and it does, from time to time, the same way *Mon concept vient d'ailleurs* and a thousand other snippets of language do—both the stones and the *they* represent, well, snippets of language. Lyrics that compel me to rewind, that needle and nag and won't leave me alone until I find something to do with them beyond just rewinding. *I got a pocket full of stones* is itself a stone that I carry around with me, not because it's so incisive or bewitchingly wrought but because it describes with great fidelity a part of my day-to-day experience, one of those things I didn't know I was looking for a name for until I found it. What's that? Yeah, no, I know this is vastly more boring than what the lyrics are actually about. Such is the texture of my libertinism.

(1992)

86

Qwel's one-liner above is the first stone I can recall picking up from a rap song and putting in my pocket. (Like *I'm coming after you like the letter V*, it's so thoroughly a one-liner that it doesn't even seem worth noting its contingent rhyme, but for those keeping score it's *Fuck the fame, say no better, hectic mic fetishes.*) I remember being astonished, the first time I heard it, by its arch simplicity—how had I not found this pun before? How had nobody *told* me? And there it was from then on, unshakeable. I memorized it, sure, quoted it to other people, tried writing it down with quotation marks and without. Nothing exorcized or exhausted it.

Others, needless to say, followed. *The Source* used to reprint entire verses under its "Hip-Hop Quotable" rubric, but for me the slenderer the quip, the more economical, the more portable and urgently communicable. There are even some that time has pared down to the pith: whereas I used to quote this entire stanza, now I keep just the third line in my pocket:

Yeah we be gettin' stupid in your area
Causing all kinds of hysteria
Ad-Rock, in Beastie Boys,   *My beats is sick like malaria*
"Three MCs and One DJ"
(1998)   *Don't worry, I'll take care of ya*

I said earlier that I was first drawn to rap's similes, and sure enough, both *My beats is sick like malaria* and *I'm the motherfucking king like Oedipus* capture something of that initial attraction: not just their quotability but their self-sufficiency, the insularity of their strange paralogical propositions. (Other fine specimens from Qwel include *I won like three thirds* and *You're too weak like fortnights.*) Because that's what they are, molecularly speaking: similes. Comparative equations using *like* or *as*. Metaphors with training wheels.

in Typical Cats, "Qweloquialisms" (2000)

in Typical Cats, "Reinventing the Wheel" (2000)

But at the same time they're not similes, not really. They used to be, but they've since been tampered with, sabotaged, signified on. A simile, after all, is supposed to reconcile. When you say *The*

I'm on point like a elbow

engine purrs like a kitten, you're observing that engines and kittens share the quality of producing a satisfying vibratory thrum, and this one commonality brings them closer together than they began.

"Ain't No Holding Back" (2015)

in T-Wayne, "Listen to Me" (2017)

When Juicy J boasts about having *money long like train smoke* (or T-Pain about having *money long like a tube sock*), he's not saying his money is *long* any more than cheddar is *sharp* or colors *loud*; he's using *long* to telegraph the essence of what he's telling us about his spending power, namely that it's above average in size—*like* a calf-high sock or a lingering plume of locomotive exhaust. When Ad-Rock of the Beastie Boys says *Your rhymes are fake like a Canal Street watch*, he's not saying that poseurs and bootleg merchandise

"Hey Fuck You" (2004)

are exact equivalents, just that both are the opposite of *real* and *authentic*. It's close enough to convey a straightforward idea and an idiosyncratic style at once.

I'm the motherfucking king like Oedipus behaves differently. The appearance of *like Oedipus* bifurcates *motherfucking king* into parallel but unreconciled ideas: the garden-variety boast, intensified by a colloquial filler word you probably haven't taken at face value for years, and its totally literal counterpart. There's the track you thought the train was on, and the one where you actually wind up. *I looked and I said, "No, ma'am."* Qwel isn't emphatically and non-

Hold up: nah, muffuckers, y'all muffuckers / Better run to the post office and get a job, muffuckers / Or starve, muffuckers, 'cause Jay's been the only one eating thus far, subpar muffuckers

Jay-Z, "Hola Hovito" (2001)

specifically saying he's the best; he's *extremely* specifically likening himself to the king of Greek legend who unwittingly beds his mom and then gouges his damn eyes out. Ad-Rock's beats aren't *sick* in the Californian sense, not awesome or cool or excellent; they're shivering with fever. Being held up at gunpoint won't make

I sneezed on the beat and the beat got sicker

Beyoncé, "Partition" (2013)

you resemble Keith Sweat, but it might make you *sweat like Keith*. Instead of reinforcing similarity, the closer look actively undermines it, sours it, perverts it, like when Action Bronson boasts that he's *Hung like a curtain*. The meaning of the first term is diverted along its path to the second, and the culprit is *the path itself*. *I be in the cut*

"The Stick Up" (2011)

Young Butta (& DJ Drizzle), "Money Dance" (2015)

Paul Wall, "Sittin' Sidewayz" (2016)

like Neosporin. The pivoting word doesn't even have to remain the same part of speech: *Trunk bump[s] like chicken pox* is the rattling of a car with a tricked-out stereo (verb), then a spread of itchy varicella blisters (noun). The equation breaks itself down midstream. This is now that, but it is no longer this.

Curiously enough, the thing causing all this mischief is that officiously scorned yet grammatically versatile little word *like*. At face value, *like* signifies simple resemblance; in these strange equations, though, it establishes concord only to destroy it almost immediately, *almost successfully*, leaving behind a sense of similarity that's almost trustworthy. When Dreezy says **I might call your number like bingo**, it's not even clear to me what reading of *call your number* she's pointing to—is it a threat? a flirtation?—but it *is* clear that it has nothing of substance to do with actual bingo. We lean on *like* at our own risk. This and that are superficially the same, says the anti-simile, already receding into the distance, but beneath that affinity lies a bristling and vital world of difference.

"Spazz" (2016)

89

=, ≠

I ain't Q-Tip but I'll make your breathin' stop

Rhymefest, in Go-Getters, "On 10 in a Benz" (ca. 2000)

• •

AND *LIKE* ISN'T even the only semantic banana peel available to the rapper out to confuse you for sport. There's *as if* and *more than* and so *much that* and y*ou would think* and the beguilingly oblique *word to*. There are calculated hyperboles that wouldn't sound out of place, structurally speaking, in a Borscht Belt stand-up routine, like when Jay-Z says *I got more black chicks between my sheets than* Essence (pages, bed linens), or when T.I. says *Brain so good could've swore you went to college* (intellection, fellatio), or when Dr. Dre says *I get plenty of ass so call me an astronaut* (a reach, admittedly). There are sneaky double-negative process-of-elimination plays that tell you how not to parse them—the way enterprising vendors during the Prohibition sold grape juice packaged with anti-instructions to make sure customers didn't carelessly let it ferment into wine—like when Cam'ron says *Not toes or MC when I say "hammer time,"* or when Biggie says *Not from Houston, but I rap a lot.* (Rap-A-Lot Records is a label based in Houston, though the statement would be trivially true regardless, albeit a little cryptic,

Word to Skype, how I see it is how I call it, dude
Young M.A, "EAT" (2016)

"Ain't No Nigga" (1996)
"Whatever You Like" (2008)
"Keep Their Heads Ringin'" (1995)

"Killa Cam" (2004)
in Craig Mack, "Flava in Ya Ear (Remix)" (1994)

90

like when Sha Rock says *I'm not Barbara Walters of NBC, but I'ma rock your mind viciously.*) *in Jazzy 4 MC's, "MC Rock" (1979)*

Or take the line above, in which the Chicago underground perennial Rhymefest threatens to kill you, but also doesn't, while not referencing, but also referencing, Q-Tip's hit 1999 single "Breathe and Stop." Now, Q-Tip, quoted here (but also not) from his first solo album after A Tribe Called Quest began its two-decade hiatus, has never been the type to talk about murdering anyone, in veiled terms or straightforward ones, so it's not that Rhymefest might just leave you lifeless even though he's not Q-Tip: it's rather that Q-Tip's slant idiom *breathe and stop*, coined over a superbly herky-jerky J Dilla beat, happens to sound like *breathin' stop*—an admirably serene way to evoke death, when you think about it—and, lest the aural similarity confuse you, Rhymefest is reminding you that getting down in the club with controlled abandon is the thing he doesn't mean. It's another one of those punchlines that takes exponentially more effort to explain or reverse-engineer than it does to appreciate, which is why at the end of the next verse of "On 10 in a Benz" Kanye West stops rapping altogether to repeat the joke verbatim and complain that he can't come up with anything good enough to follow it.

Each of these push-pulls is another way to revoke and transcend connotation by seeming to conflate two things, only to immediately split them apart: into literal and figurative, into first-degree and second, into face value and allusion hiding in plain sight. And the links between them, the connective tissues of comparison and contrast, function with the simple elegance of mathematical symbols—only it's trickster arithmetic, Schrödinger equalities where it turns out that = somehow means the same thing as ≠.

Sleek and concise as the hinges are, the propositions themselves aren't always: they can be belabored, can miss the memo on efficiency—*Try to play me out like as if my name was Sega*, says Everlast—or get lost for good along the garden path: *in House of Pain, "Jump Around" (1992)*

Some hoes are the Lebron James of playing mind games
And switch their home team up every single time their mind change

Big Sean,
"Deserve It" (2015)

Overwhelmingly, though, from MC Lyte's **He had a head like that of**
a clam to Nicki Minaj's **Gimme that brain like NYU,** they've tended
toward streamlining, so much so that all it takes now to convey
"listen again: here's what I didn't mean" is a simple *no*. Kanye: **I**
got whips, no slave. Fetty Wap: **Wax you, no candle.** Bleek Blaze: **I'm**
tryna get them plaques, nigga, no toothpicks. (This particular device is
the parent of *no homo*, a heavily codified variant of *that's what she*
said that usually works in the opposite way, simultaneously drawing attention to and disavowing the potentially lascivious reading
under the surface. Lil Wayne: **I just shot a video with R. Kelly, but no**
homo though. Jay-Z uses the less offensive *pause* to the same end,
all but asking you outright to press rewind.) It's a thrilling display
of economy not just descriptively but kinetically, a whiplash paraprosdokian effect conjured by no more than a monosyllabic flick
of the wrist. How much more swiftly can a lyric switch your train
of thought to another track? What could reject a single-entendre
world more effortlessly than the word *no*?

"Feeling Myself" (2015)

in Yo Gotti, "Castro" (2016)
"No Days Off" (2015)
in Fetty Wap, "Make You Smile"
(2016)

Thought I came by myself? No
masturbation

CurT@!n$, "36 Chambers of
Death" (2010)
"Dipset" (2007)

No Scantron, don't test me

Key! (& Kenny Beats),
"Demolition 1 + 2" (2018)

92

#

I got bars   sentencing

Nicki Minaj, "Roman's Revenge" (2010)

• •

TRICK QUESTION. The only thing more concise than the word *no* is no words.

• •

"Anyone tuned into slang or youth culture will not be surprised by the large number of sex-related terms," writes Isaac Mozeson in the introduction to *A 2 Z: The Book of Rap & Hip-Hop Slang*, "and those who follow the social problems of the inner city will expect the extensive crime-and-punishment words for categories like theft, guns, rioting, police, arrest and incarceration." Languages accumulate words for the things that matter most to their speakers, modeling their world in ever finer resolution—the old half-truth about Eskimos and snow. In rap vernacular, the realities of the penal system crop up independently, where you'd expect, but also encroach on words that conventionally have nothing to do with it. *Pen* is writing utensil and penitentiary; *box* is radio or vagina or jail cell; to *serve* is to outdo a rival rapper or sell drugs or do hard time. A

Cost me more to be free than a life in the pen / Makin' money off of cuss words, writin' again / Learned how to think ahead, so I fight with my pen

2Pac, in Makaveli, "To Live and Die in LA" (1996)

joint, *the joint* is a depressingly plausible four-word story, at least if its protagonist is nonwhite. **The judge'll say life**, says Malice of Clipse, **like it ain't someone's life.**

When you say *I got bars*, as Nicki Minaj does entirely accurately, you're not talking about thresholds or drinking holes or Confederate stripes or tabs of Xanax, but about musical time, measures on the mic, what happens between line breaks. You're claiming the wherewithal to create space with your words and fill it, all day, with invention and charisma and play. Here, though, after a tiny pregnant pause, Nicki appends *sentencing*, and just like that *bars* means the bars of a jail cell and it's no longer a metaphor but a sobering dramatization, no longer "I'm sick at rapping" but "I've been condemned to prison time"—all of which she manages to do in a statement that is technically, sublimely, *not a sentence*.

What it is, relative to a sentence—on Humpty's indulgence—is decidedly less and also somehow more. It's a juxtaposition, a free association, a fork in the track where you don't have to choose a tine; it's an anti-simile that replaces *like* with a moment of silence, establishing a relationship of proximity between two things and then shutting the door on the specifics. So it's *I got bars, no sentencing* and also *I got bars, yes sentencing* and also *I got bars, and also sentencing*. It helps, I find, to visualize it as a free-floating set of parentheses, or a stagy em-dash, or the # symbol as used on social media to signal categorization or commentary or branded lifestyle mishmosh. As it happens, figurations such as Nicki's here are sometimes referred to as *hashtag rap*. (To be precise, that phrase describes less the device itself than the whole category of rap—clubby, unwriterly—in which a song might be prone to use it.) It's a bit reductive, dismissive, the way *ringtone rap* was thrown around for a time by people who had aged out of rap's target market and begun growing lawns to yell at kids to stay off, without being altogether incorrect. Nicki is very much a hashtag rapper, though she actually has a quiver full of more this-is-no-longer-this strategies than almost any other artist I can think of, from *Tell them bitches blow me #Lance Stephenson* to *I just come through with the six like my name was Blossom*, which is testament to the simultaneously classical and hypermodern gifts behind her bars. Lance Stephenson, for the record, was a shooting guard on the Indianapolis Pacers once filmed coquettishly blowing into Lebron James's ear; Six was Blossom's best friend on the TV show *Blossom*, because focus-grouped nineties youth culture was a hell of a drug.

"Only" (2014)

"The Boys" (2012)

Drake, speaking of nineties television, has also done a lot to normalize hashtagging. He and Nicki both picked it up—this is my historical interpretation, anyway—from their mentor Lil Wayne, who's done it for a couple of decades but who circa 2010 started doing it often enough, and ostentatiously enough, to elevate it from stonery expository shortcut to disruptive rhetorical technology. I mean, it's also deeply lazy, and a too-cavalier usage bumps it back down to tedious word-association exercise: *I'm the best, nigga, period. Kotex.* (There is, however, a great hashtag-avant-la-lettre dialogue-rap by pasty underground stalwarts 7L & Esoteric called "Word Association," formatted as a psych evaluation.) Drake's *About to set it off in this bitch #Jada Pinkett* in the Grammy-nominated 2010 single "Over" isn't exactly worth overthinking; Jada Pinkett just co-starred in the movie *Set It Off*, is all, which is pretty dull as far as cognitive leapfroggings go but still cool because of how it's delivered. To be fair, had Drake said *about to set it off in this bitch like Jada Pinkett* he would at least have avoided one of the other pitfalls of hashtag rap, namely that when your pause is too short the space just sounds like a space, which is why it sounds here like he's calling Jada Pinkett *this bitch*. His hashtag riff in the next verse does not, I fear, fare much better.

Nonetheless, it *is* an exciting rhetorical technology, and done well, with the right measure of empty space and the right footpath

Swimming in the money, come and find me: Nemo / If I was at the club you know I balled: chemo

Drake (& Kanye West, Lil Wayne, & Eminem), "Forever" (2009)

Y'all can't see me—Ray Charles

Lil Wayne, in J.R. Writer, "Bird Call" (2005)

Ace Hood, in Reek da Villain, "Go Off" (2014)

Letterman: great host / Moltar: Space Ghost / Applebee's: tastes gross / Lap dance: pesos

(7L &) Esoteric, "Word Association" (2002)

But I really can't complain, everything is kosher / Two thumbs up Ebert and Roeper

"Over"

between implicit steppingstones, a hashtag punchline can be breath-taking in its economy. When Pusha T says

Two-door preference
Roof gone, George Jefferson

in Kanye West, "Mercy" (2012)

he's invoking the social mobility sung of in the theme from *The Jeffersons*, with its refrain about *movin' on up*, and at the same time letting the air out of that homage by picturing himself riding around in a convertible coupe—did I mention he does this in a Kanye West song?—all in just four words. Four words! Why bother with *Roof gone but I'm not George Jefferson*? Why waste precious breath saying *Come and find me like my name was Nemo*? (Sure, *Come and find me, no Nemo* has a fetchingly Edo ring to it, but you see what I mean.) The point of the exercise is not to forge connections that are impervious or even particularly rewarding to logical scrutiny; the point is to model effortlessness as sound, or rather as the lack thereof. Enough said.

ECONOMY AND TIME

Woke up, last night was all a blur
Four Seasons, three words: do not disturb

Swae Lee, in Rae Sremmurd, "Unlock the Swag" (2015)

● ●

BUT WAIT. What's so special about verbal economy? What makes
breath precious? Talk is cheap, words are free. So why are we—why
am I—so excited by the extreme parsimony of a six-word story like
the one classically if probably wrongly attributed to Hemingway
(*For sale: baby shoes. Never worn*)? Whence the undertone of
approbation with which Alison B. Davis calls the hook to Cardi
B's "Bodak Yellow"—*I don't dance now, I make money moves*—"a   *(2017)*
bildungsroman in two lines"? What's being saved in cases like
these? Just what is economized?

I don't have an argument, really. But these compact narrative
arcs thrill and delight me all the same: their efficiency feels both
spring-loaded, the way *Coke like a caterpillar* does, and inevitable in
an almost geological sense, as though they've been packed down
over millennia to sediment and strata. They make great stones, I
suppose, and the more compact they are the more of them I can fit
in my pocket.

Pusha T, "Lunch Money" (2014)

Willie the Kid (& DJ Drama), "Makin' Money Smokin'" (2007)

Jalil, in Whodini, "I'm a Ho" (1986)

Kevin Gates, "Just Ride" (2013)

Some favorites: the callous opulence of *Lost my bitch, bought a chef*; the gritty urban stoicism of *Mad obituaries printed up at Kinko's*; the gleeful monosyllabic cuckold-baiting of *How's your wife and my kids?*; the old-slaves-to-new historicizing of *This whip can parallel park itself.* I love these for their silence, for the magnitude of what they don't say—how much iceberg they leave concealed under the water, to borrow an analogy accurately attributed to Hemingway. Their mystery, their suggestion. But there's something else I notice seeing them lined up like this: each little gem also dilates or telescopes time in its own way, makes it elastic, moves between past and future with unsettling ease and clarity.

Baby shoes is a three-act structure of anticipation and disaster and regret.

Next thing you know I'm in this bitch's crib, chilling / Told her my story and like this I had her legs in the ceiling / Cooking me fries, fish sticks, hot side of them biscuits / While she doing this the bitch still sliding on lipstick

Ghostface Killah, "Yolanda's House" (2007)

"99 Problems" (2003)

Money moves covers a whole journey from stripping to megawatt stardom without ever leaving the present tense.

Jay-Z's *Foes that wanna make sure my casket's closed* does the same for the future, hypothetically.

Mad obituaries is all aftermath, subtracting the circumstances and motives and players from a murder story, leaving just a vignette of life ending and life continuing—and yet I can visualize it down to the font on the memorial flyer.

How's your wife and my kids directs your attention to the present tense while slyly locating its outrageous insult in the past.

Biz Markie, "Just a Friend" (1989)

You got what I need / But you say he's just a friend dispatches in twelve syllables what the entire history of European cinema is still working out how to say.

This whip collapses the four hundred years between endpoints of one word into a single snoozy materialist flex.

"Warning" (1994)

Biggie's folksily chilling *There's gonna be a lot of slow singin' and flower bringin' if my burgalah alarm starts ringin'* is a death threat so confident that it brackets out everything—the who, the how, the when—but the outcome of the outcome.

Ditto El-P's *As far as I'm concerned I got your ashes in a urn,* which I took at first to be barely cogent trash-talk—this may be because I heard *ashes* as *asses* until like a year ago—but which is actually pristine, scuffless in its adversarial certitude: instead of deigning to describe your defeat, it's moved on to a future where you're history.

in Company Flow, "8 Steps to Perfection" (1996)

This is that unsettling ease again, telescoping and retracting time, making the immediate abstract and the distant present. It's a lot like the way the signifying monkey throws his voice, if you like, except through time instead of space. Candidates for the lion in this scenario aren't hard to come by: it's the angry husband, the police investigator, the nosy paparazzo, the sorry sucker about to turn up on a missing-person report and then a commemorative T-shirt. It's you, immobile at the center of the vortex, left to do the math.

Peep the convo, the address of my condo / And how I changed a nigga name to John Doe

Genius/GZA, "Gold" (1995)

Disrespect my clique, my shit's imperial / Fucked around and made her milk box material

The Notorious B.I.G., in Junior M.A.F.I.A., "Get Money" (1995)

Sometimes this is in good fun; sometimes it's a matter of necessity, sharing with the in-group what you dare not let on to the out-, hiding it in plain sight, making something look like nothing. For people under a lifetime of peremptory surveillance and preemptive suspicion, I imagine, evasion by omission maybe feels like escape, like a way to bracket out the progress and strife and mess of the in-between and jump-cut to the future. A way to wrest control from what Henry Louis Gates, Jr., calls "the tyranny of the narrative present" by turning it into a discrete part of a story whose ending, whether it holds riches or wedding bells or the autopsy of your enemies, you get to write yourself. I imagine it feels like rising above, like getting over—but, again, in time rather than space. Like remembering that now is a time you will one day remember, from elsewhere.

I'm trying to give you sixty seconds of affection / I'm trying to give you cab fare and directions

Jay-Z, in Missy Elliott, "One Minute Man (Remix)" (2001)

I been living life / Like I'll live twice

Slim Jxmmi, in Rae Sremmurd, "No Type" (2015)

SIGNIFYING CHAINS

I take seven MCs, put 'em in a line

(Eric B. &) Rakim, "My Melody" (1986)

• •

"SPEAK THESE NINE words to a true listener and see what happens," writes Jelani Cobb in *To the Break of Dawn*. The response, he promises, will come "like an involuntary reflex or part of a religious catechism":

Add seven more brothers who think they can rhyme
Well, it'll take seven more before I go for mine
Now that's twenty-one MCs ate up at the same time

Some lyrics are indelibly etched in our collective memory, is his point, and Rakim, the God MC, the architect and engineer who upgraded rap from a bottom-heavy 4/4 thump to a Supreme Mathematics of dexterous complexity, did a lot of the etching. *Paid in Full*, Rakim's 1987 debut with the producer Eric B., sits at the magnetic north of my personal rap canon, just past history's border with prehistory: it didn't play a big role in my own upbringing as a listener, but almost all the rap that did points directly back to it.

100

Rakim's influence is obvious, audible both in hip-hop for the two decades that followed and in the homage fully and piously paid him by those rappers and scholars whose work has meant most to mine. But even as I recognize his presence in so much that I hold dear about rap, even though I admire and appreciate him, I do so belatedly—from downstream, sentimentally speaking, of his genius. Around a bend, just out of intelligible earshot. So when *I* hear those nine words, my retrieval reflex comes back with this, from Jay Electronica:

Daddy ain't around, probably committing felonies / My favorite rapper used to sing "Check, check out my melody"

50 Cent, in The Game, "Hate It or Love It" (2005)

(2007)

Bring seven MCs, put 'em in a line
Go get seven other cornballs who think they can rhyme
It'll take seven more before I go for mine
That's twelve sucka niggas with a gash in they perm
Plus nine other motherfuckers drastically burned
It's a horrible lesson indeed, but has to be learned

That's from a song called "Uzi Weighs a Ton," which is a Public Enemy reference but which you may recall from the beginning of this book in "Exhibit C," where Jay says *My Uzi still weigh a ton.* Flashback humor. "As we habitually draw our notions of time from movement in space," writes Howard Nemerov—*downstream*, for instance—"there remains in hiding the idea that whatever is in time is traveling simultaneously in two directions at once, into the future and into the past, and at exactly the same rate." At some point, that is, history ceases to be linear.

I show you my gun, my Uzi weighs a ton / Because I'm public enemy number one

Chuck D, in Public Enemy, "Public Enemy No. 1" (1987)

Pete Rock, "#1 Soul Brother" (1998)

I take seven ill drums, put 'em in a line
And add seven more snares to make it combine
It'll take seven horns before I start my rhyme
Now it's twenty-one beats made up at the same time

When did I discover that the twenty-one star-crossed MCs were a trope, a motif, a meme from back when *meme* meant something else? When did they *become* a meme? For a while I took it for a stock phrase, a commonplace, like *If it don't make dollars it don't make sense* or *The roof is on fire*. I was dimly aware of an echo—it *is* a pretty a specific roll call—and then at some point recognized it as a theme without knowing what to make of it, or without caring enough to find out. Eventually, finally, the persistent inkling of pattern piqued my curiosity. Who were these MCs? Where had they come from? What did it mean for them to think they could rhyme, and what did it *mean* to line them up and eat them? Only much later did I find out that there are twenty-one MCs because Rakim's government name, William Michael Griffin, is three times seven letters, which is both some out-to-lunch Five Percenter shit and a truly wonderful thing to learn.

Take twenty-seven MCs, put 'em in a line and they out of alignment
My assignment since he said retirement, hiding behind 8 Mile *and* The Chronic
Get rich but dies rhyming, this is high science [...]
Now that's fifty porch monkeys ate up at the same time

Nas, "Queens Get the Money"
(2008)

And but *who* were these MCs, I mean in real life? Surely the referent, if there was one, changed as the image was repeated from song to song. Right? That's Nas above, but from when? Why is he firing shots at Dr. Dre (whose first album is called *The Chronic*) and 50 Cent (whose first album is called *Get Rich or Die Tryin'*) and Eminem (who starred in a veiled biopic called *8 Mile*)? Why are there suddenly twenty-seven rappers, then **twenty-three more, from Queens to B-more**, making it an even fifty? Does each repetition of the theme refer directly to Rakim's original iteration, or do some knock into others on their way back upstream? When Jay Electronica signified on Rakim, was he signifying on Pete Rock too? On the *way* Pete Rock signifies on Rakim? What does it mean that

Jay Electronica happened to produce the track over which Nas is rapping this dark fifty-MC fantasy? Is the signifying chain a spoke-hub thing, or is it more of a Jacob's ladder?

Eminem, "I'm Back" (2000)

I take seven kids from Columbine, stand 'em all in line
Add an AK-47, a revolver, a nine
A MAC-11 and it ought to solve the problem of mine
And that's a whole school of bullies shot up all at one time

That's Eminem, but from before or after Nas made that crack about *8 Mile*? What did he think, either way, when he heard Nas's riff, and what did Nas think when he heard this? When did Eminem first hear "My Melody"? When did he first hear the Labi Siffre song "I Got The," from which Dr. Dre took the sample that would power Eminem's breakout single, "My Name Is," but only after Eminem agreed to change some of the lyrics? Did he notice that "I Got The" gave a bass line to Wu-Tang Clan's "Can It Be All So Simple" and a string part to Jay-Z's "Streets Is Watching"? Was Kanye West consciously referencing the Notorious B.I.G. when he rhymed *birthday* with *thirstay* twenty years later? When you sing the *me so horny* line in "Baby Got Back" at karaoke, are you quoting Sir Mix-A-Lot, or 2 Live Crew, or *Full Metal Jacket*?

Walked in the strip club, had my jacket zipped up / Flashed the bartender then stuck my dick in the tip cup / Extraterrestrial, killin' pedestrians, rapin' lesbians / While they're screaming "Let's just be friends!"

Eminem, "My Name Is (original version)" (1998)

LL Cool J, "Pink Cookies in a Plastic Bag Getting Crushed by Buildings" (1993)

I'll take thirty electric chairs and put 'em in a classroom
Thirty MCs and set 'em free from their doom

Paid in Full's title track opens with Rakim, broke, brooding on his immediate future, wondering *how could I get some dead presidents*. He rewinds his life as a stickup kid, thinking *of all the devious things I did*, but those solutions are out: he's on the straight and narrow now. *I learned to earn 'cause I'm righteous.* So he hits the studio, and the rest is—well, the rest is the present. But the way he collapses all that past into the scene he's narrating here, and in turn the song

Thinkin' of a master plan / 'Cause ain't nothing but sweat inside my hand

"Paid in Full" (1987)

I'm listening to and writing about thirty-five years later—the way he tells his story walking, to borrow a phrase from either Jonathan Lethem or Cappadonna—is the same way some lyrics carry *their own catechism* around with them. Whether or not the broadcaster wants it there, whether or not we want to hear it, whether or not either of us knows where it comes from.

I'll take seven MCs, put 'em in a line

Shoot 'em and sell they clothes to get my wisdom teeth pulled

Slug, in Deep Puddle Dynamics, "Rainmen" (1999)

This specific species of confusion—not knowing what refers to what, which dots to connect to which—can be liberating; like most liberating things, it can be disturbing too. An overabundance of pure and unrelated presents in time is how Fredric Jameson describes schizophrenia; Jacques Lacan calls it a breakdown of the signifying chain. Gates reports that the signifying chain dates all the way back to a 1772 slave memoir called *The Narrative of the Most Remarkable Particulars in the Life of James Albert Ukawsaw Gronniosaw*, in which it is *a literal gold chain*. The stream forks toward multiple norths. Memory travels backward and forward simultaneously, in all other directions too. Rap just lets us hear what that sounds like.

RECYCLING

Flow retarded, I'm on some Special Ed shit
The magnificent, twisted like a dread, bitch
And I can get up in a car and drive
And if the record is a smash I can still survive

Lil Wayne, "President" (2007)

• •

"PRESIDENT" LIVES ON a mixtape that came out in 2007, but its beat comes from Jay-Z's 1996 song "Dead Presidents," including the vocal sample it lifts from Nas's 1994 song "The World Is Yours," whose own beat, just barely audible in "President," revolves around a snatch of an Ahmad Jamal song from 1970. The whole track is a loop you can burrow into, a cocoon made of disparate presents, and that's before Wayne—or his sometime protégé Curren$y, a car and weed enthusiast who has an endearing tendency to rap with the petulance of a very articulate nine-year-old—even says a word.

A couple minutes further in, another present joins the fray: Special Ed's "I'm the Magnificent," a refreshing breeze of a song that came out in 1989 and which also contains the confounding threat *You can bet your life that I'ma play you like hooky / on a Friday.*

I'm so sorry if I don't look happy to be here / In your label office but they said I can't smoke weed here

Curren$y, "The Day" (2010)

I'm the magnificent, with the sensational style / And I could go on and on for like a mile a minute / 'Cause I get in it like a car and drive / And if the record is a smash I could still survive

105

In a sense this addition is obvious; indeed, Wayne goes so far as to cite it by title and artist name before his stream of consciousness moves on. And yet I managed to miss the reference for years, so fluently is it woven into his thought-to-thought leapfrogging: he's just used *retarded* in that uncomfortable way that scans as complimentary, then made what appears to be a nod to special education, so it's not necessarily apparent that he *also* means Special Ed the rapper, whose name is of course itself a nod to special education. (The rapper's name really is Edward.) I don't remember when I actually heard "I'm the Magnificent" for the first time, whether it was before or after I first heard "President"; deep in my brain I probably knew **get up in a car and drive** was *from* somewhere, the way *I'm Chiquita Banana and I'm here to say* is from somewhere. But amid all the other sources drifting through "President," it didn't occur to me to triangulate this one.

Elsewhere, Wayne describes this phenomenon as recycling:

But hey, kid, plural, I graduated
'Cause you can get through anything if Magic made it
And that was called recycling, or re-reciting something
'Cause you just like it, so you say it just like it
Some say it's biting, but I say it's enlightening
Besides, Dr. Kanye West is one of the brightest

"Dr. Carter" (2008)

"What separates 'biting' and 'enlightening' is the difference between mere repetition and repetition with a difference," Adam Bradley writes in *Book of Rhymes*, reading the same Wayne quote, whose first couplet draws closely—with two small exceptions, the second line is literally *just like it*—from something Kanye said the year before. (Magic Johnson, diagnosed with HIV in 1991, is still alive three decades later.) I like Wayne's idea of framing this gesture as *recycling*, even as upcycling: not just reusing a similar sequence of words for a similar purpose at a later date, but adding new dimension and implication as well, all while preserving, more or less obliquely, the sequence's origins. Citing, reciting, *re-reciting*.

I don't think Wayne reads much black literary theory, but what he's calling recycling also fits squarely within the common definition of signifying as repetition with a difference. To signify on a text is to repeat it not just for the sake of hearing it again, not just because you don't have anything original to say, but in order to revise or reframe or inhabit it, to poke holes in it or put your own spin on it *'cause you just like it*. That's what's happening when Wayne reaches back from 2008 to borrow a moment from 2007, or reaches back from 2007 to borrow moments from 1989 and 1994 and 1996. It's what's happening when Kendrick Lamar quotes DJ DMD quoting 8Ball & MJG, or when Kanye taps the legacy of horror and protest in "Strange Fruit" to lick his groupie-jilted wounds. It's Lin-Manuel Miranda reaching back from 2015 to borrow a Mobb Deep quote from 1995 and put it in the mouth of Alexander Hamilton circa 1775; it's the Beastie Boys making "Fight for Your Right to Party" in 1987 and Public Enemy making "Party for the Right to Fight" in 1988 and Atmosphere making "Party for the Fight to Write" in 2000. (Nobody has named a song "Write for the Party to Fight" yet, but Three 6 Mafia's "Tear Da Club Up" is basically that song already.) It's the preservation of tradition through reuse and adaptation and commentary; it's "making a future," as Russell Potter puts it in his excellent *Spectacular Vernaculars*, "out of fragments from the archive of the past."

This happens plenty in other media as well, with fluctuating degrees of collateral homage and profanation, which Octavio Paz says are the twin teats of literature. Ask Anne Carson, ask Jack White, ask Quentin Tarantino. But there's something electrifying, I think, about how hip-hop's insularity and irreverence and ancestor worship turn it into a revolutionary practice—in both the radical and full-circle senses of the word—lyrically, lexically, aurally. I

I got twenty-five lighters on the dresser, yessir

I'm only nineteen but my mind is older / When the things get for real my warm heart turns cold

Prodigy, in "Shook Ones Part II" (1995)

Only nineteen but my mind is older / These New York City streets get colder, I shoulder / Every burden, every disadvantage I have learned to manage / I don't have a gun to brandish, I walk these streets famished

Lin-Manuel Miranda, "My Shot" (2015)

wonder what chain of events led Special Ed to use *smash* to mean a commercial flop when the opposite sense has been in the ascendant for almost a century; David Caplan marvels, in *Rhyme's Challenge*, at a Lupe Fiasco rhyme encompassing words that entered the English language more than a millennium apart. Listen to a Pro Era mixtape from 2016 and an Afrika Bambaataa album from 1986 and tell me the former doesn't sound like the past, the latter like the future. Signifying forges a continuum that moves laterally, word to word or line to line, accommodating without flattening as many bygone times as it takes to feel at home.

"It is not so much that hip-hop *tells* history; it's that it is history," Potter writes. "Drop the needle anywhere and you will find lyrical vectors to every other site on the hip-hop map." The map is tirelessly charted, hyperlinked, by rappers and producers acting as archivists, telling their story walking, repeating and revising the whole lineage of hip-hop and its predecessors one borrowing at a time. They know time to move in oblique and unpredictable ways; like Borges's Pierre Menard—the twentieth-century author whose *Don Quixote* is hailed as "almost infinitely richer" than Cervantes's original despite being a word-for-word replica—they trust the same sound to contain different meanings, different effects, depending on how and when it's heard. In this their assumption, their faith, is the same as mine each time I rewind to replay a moment again: that what I experience the next time I hear it won't be the same as the last.

ELECTIVE CHRONOLOGY

Once upon a time in the projects, yo
I damn near had to wreck a ho
I knocked on the door (–Who is it?)
It's Ice Cube, come to pay a little visit to ya

Ice Cube, "Once upon a Time in the Projects" (1990)

• •

I HAVE AN uncommonly vivid memory of the first time I heard
these lines. It was an overcast afternoon and I was riding an unfamiliar bus route, on the way to visit—

Stop, rewind. That's already not quite right. It *wasn't* the first
time I heard those lines, not exactly—that's what made the moment
memorable. Their familiarity but also their difference, their sudden
drift from what I was expecting. I was listening to Ice Cube's words
from 1990 but hearing them as an echo of an Atmosphere song that
didn't come out, as it happens, until ten years later:

Slug, in Atmosphere,
"God Loves Ugly" (2000)

Once upon a time in Minneapolis, yo
I damn near had to steal the show
I stepped on the stage—who is it?
My name is Slug, I've come to kill a couple minutes

This is not, of course, how echoes work. In the chronological sense, it is objectively the case that Slug is quoting and signifying on Ice Cube, not the other way around—that I was responding to a response, not a call. A leapfrogging, a Jacob's ladder, the past signifying on the future. In my own personal echo chamber, though, Slug got there first, and I can't hear the conversation between these two rhymes as anything but Ice Cube quoting and signifying on him. (Let's pause for a moment to appreciate that "Ice Cube quoting Slug" is a contextually legitimate thought that would make no sense if words could mean only what the dictionary told us they did.)

This phenomenon—that weightless moment where you discover that this or that thing comes from an unsuspected source, or that it comes from a source at all—fascinates the hell out of me. Consider this: right now, someone is starting to listen to rap, to learn about its codes and history and arcana, and, assuming she's not a total dweeb, starting not with the very first recording from 1979, but somewhere more or less adjacent to the present, with whoever's hottest and most inescapable in the month and year you're reading this. Her archive, her bank of quotations and allusions, starts at the same moment she does, so how is she supposed to know a Mobb Deep line when she hears it in *Hamilton*, or an 8Ball & MJG-via-DJ DMD line when she hears it interpolated by Kendrick Lamar or ZZ Top? (That... also happened.) How is she supposed to know where the twenty-one MCs come from? We'll also assume she's got better things to do than trawl Genius or WhoSampled while she goes about discovering rap, so how is she supposed to know what's new and what's not, what's a portal to one or multiple simultaneous pasts, without just *knowing*?

This sprawling, swirling mass of words and phrases and memes and ideas, the novel mixed in with the deathlessly traditional: this is rap. This is a *canon*. And what an insane joy it is to be a novice in front of a canon, to begin putting it in order bit by bit, thing after wonderful thing to learn, on your own terms. I saw the *Simpsons* parody "The Shinning" before Kubrick's *The Shining*; I didn't hear Gershwin's "Rhapsody in Blue" as Gershwin's "Rhapsody in Blue" until I already knew it as the United Airlines jingle. I'm still not sure whether "Deep Throat" was the name of a porn movie or an anonymous Watergate informant first. I was in my late twenties by the time I realized that **I'm the epitome of Public Enemy** was a lyric from a Public Enemy song, not just a one-off riff in Weezer's "El Scorcho." (Public Enemy's output, right up there with *Paid in Full*, is another source as densely populated with canonical origins as a Shakespeare play; to listen to, say, *It Takes a Nation of Millions to Hold Us Back* after years spent absorbing mid-nineties hip-hop is to be bombarded with the sensation of *Oh **that's** where that's from.*) It's wild and vertiginous, because so is learning. With each revelation the continuum becomes a little easier to navigate, and a little more doubt creeps in as to why we default to linear chronology when we're trying to make sense of the world.

Chuck D, in Public Enemy, "Don't Believe the Hype" (1988)

It's clear, for instance, that a lot about Atmosphere's *once upon a time* anecdote doesn't come into full flower until you recognize the preexisting framework around it: that's why Slug says **Who is it?**, not to fill a few fractions of a second but because in Cube's original a female voice says it in response to a knock on the door. That's why he swaps out **the projects** of South Central LA for **Minneapolis**, because that's where he's from. It's also an example of his characteristic self-deprecating wit—Slug is white, though his self-deprecation is generally rooted either in his representing for the uncosmopolitan Midwest or in his just being sort of a dirtbag—which is also why in his own story, which takes place in his own hometown, he still needs to introduce himself on stage. That's why, in spite of nobody knowing who he is, he boasts that he can **steal the show**: because Slug would never **wreck a ho**, he'd just prey on her father issues to get into her pants and then ghost her the next day. Only once I learned what he *wasn't* saying, in short, did I register the cleverness of his swerve away from the original.

Who is it?

111

I'd argue, though, that Ice Cube's story is also enriched by the echo. If the original gives Slug's nonce-story dimension and context, the later, recycled version, having conditioned me to expect a humdrum anecdote about the heartland club circuit, primes the original for a sharper punch. In the chaotic universe of Cube's solo debut, *AmeriKKKa's Most Wanted*, a phrase like **wreck a ho** barely registers; upon hearing it in the spot where Slug had already posited **steal the show**, it was all I could do to stifle a little gasp on the bus that gray afternoon.

To date, at least, this sort of thing doesn't go away with experience. I've been wandering around this canon for more than half my life and I still discover masks laid over what I thought was face value. I still connect the dots by following directional cues based on affinity or fantasy or simple ignorance, still assemble my own local signifying chain in leisurely parallel to the objective historical record. (Was Ice Cube clapping back at Slug when he released a song called "Steal the Show" in 2006? There's Ice Cube's answer and there's what David Levin would say.) A song, writes Steve Erickson,

never leaves a trace except with whatever listener can or will attest to it. The listener becomes not just a collaborator with the singer, he becomes the keeper of the song, seizing possession of it from the singer; the listener knows hearing the song more than the singer can claim singing it. If light is a ghost picture that will disappear, time is a child's game of telephone, humming at the beginning of the line a melody transformed by a series of listeners to an altogether other melody at the end—and then who's to say it wasn't that final melody all along?

Believe me or don't, I read this on the one page of a used copy of *These Dreams of You* that had already been dog-eared.

To even presume to want to enter a canon on your own terms, to respect chronology as a playmate rather than an authority, is necessarily to occupy a position of privilege. "History is a burden to be borne," writes Potter; "those who can afford to have already dispensed with theirs." And yet history opens up somehow when it lives in music, becomes almost palpably *present*. It extends to any listener the luxury of assembling and indulging in what Tricia Rose calls "a self-constructed affirmative and resistive history." The power in hip-hop's version of this luxury is how reflexively it affirms the presence and weight of history while at the same time challenging it, undermining the assumption of linearity on which the very notion of a canon depends. Unless, that is, you take the word in its musical sense: that of a song sung in rounds, each voice starting at a different time from the same place, a song perpetually midstream and perpetually starting anew, one with no definitive beginning or end.

Shh, my foot's sleeping on the gas /
No brake pads, no such thing as last

(Drake, Kanye West, Eminem, &) Lil
Wayne, "Forever" (2009)

ANCESTOR WORSHIP

We're not ballin' or shot callin'
We take it back to the days of yes y'allin'
We're holdin' on to what's golden

Jurassic 5, "What's Golden" (2002)

• •

THERE'S A PART in the second verse of Eric B. & Rakim's "My Melody"—a song that, by the way, is almost militantly amelodic—that goes:

They shouldn't have told me you said you control me
So now a contest is what you owe me
Pull out your money, pull out your cut
Pull up a chair and I'ma tear shit up

(1986)

But I first knew it as part of a Jurassic 5 song, released twelve years later, called "Concrete Schoolyard," where it comes just before a kazoo breakdown:

You shouldn't have told me the pyramids could hold me
So now a contest is what you owe me
Pull out your beats, pull out your cuts
(1998)   *Give us a mic (what up?) and we gon' tear shit up*

It's hard to think of a better symbolic distillation than "Concrete Schoolyard" of the supremely approachable blend of street smarts and come-as-you-are edification plied by Jurassic 5. Many of the rap acts I first listened to at length slung ancestor worship as a matter of course—Typical Cats, the Hyde Park trio that put Qwel on the map, have a song called "Reinventing the Wheel," of which almost an entire verse is just a mosaic of Tribe Called Quest song titles—but none did it quite so openly and infectiously as J5. Their six members—yes—made no secret of being didactic, of the degree to which scholarship and language arts were core values of their operation. More than one of their music videos features the group riding around in a repurposed ice cream truck, handing out 45RPM records to kids; in the one for "Quality Control," whose lyrics I committed to memory without ever consciously meaning to, Akil raps a whole verse in front of a city library, the camera cutting at one point to a poster that says *You are about to enter a learning zone!*

What made Jurassic 5 so welcoming, such a positive early point of contact with hip-hop culture for me and a lot of other white rap fans I know—we tended to outnumber attendees of color at their concerts, even more than we usually do—isn't only that their music is impeccably deft and clever and imaginative, but also that their learning zone presents virtually no barriers to entry, no forbidding amorality or gore. They'd swear from time to time, but that was about the edgiest it got. Their songs sound like dispatches from a brighter world, one in which hip-hop has always been rootsy and communitarian and free of any violence that can't be defused by framing it as another kind of language art. (In retrospect, I used to have an awful lot of patience both rhetorically and narratively for

Sucka niggas got me telling 8 million stories help me find my way / Marauding through the midnight, phony rappers need to get a hold

Denizen Kane, in "Reinventing the Wheel" (2001)

I love the power of words, nouns and verbs / The pen and the sword, linguistic Art of War / No folklores or myths in my penmanship / The path of scholar-warriors is what I present

Akil, in "Quality Control" (2001)

Playground tactics, no rabbit-in-a-hat tricks / Just that classic rap shit from Jurassic

"Concrete Schoolyard"

pat conceits like *verbal warfare*, and that's basically all you need to know about why I listened to Atmosphere before I listened to Ice Cube.) *Concrete* is a synecdoche for the streets, but streets aren't necessarily bad if the people there show respect for one another and the community—as they used to, is the implication. The group's name nods to this too, a fourth-wall break and a throwback to rap's primeval crews who had names like the Furious Five and the Fearless Four (also six members) and the Treacherous Three. Implicit throughout their ethos was the notion that the past, old-school values and the listening habits that reinforced them, could always be looked to as a palliative to present ills and excesses. Pusha T shouts out George Jefferson to brag about an expensive convertible; J5 have a song that ends with Sherman Hemsley giving *them* props over the *Jeffersons* theme song.

There are limits to such didacticism, especially for a novice listener. The schoolyard is a great place to learn and be protected, maybe even to be protected *by* learning—again, it's a utopian vision—but it also cloisters you away from meaner, realer streets, the ones where the concrete has blood and broken glass on it. I believe Jurassic 5 trained me ideally to hear the rhetorical rituals and verbal play in grittier kinds of rap, to recognize and appreciate the craft beneath their shock value. But I suspect they also helped keep me sheltered initially, made me a bit more reluctant to learn about ballin' and shot callin', to explore the avenues of rap—raw, anti-utopian, unbecomingly *contemporary*—that hip-hop's elders didn't vouch for.

Still, it wasn't just old-school values and rudimentary verbal derring-do I was learning inside their schoolyard, unaware as I was that I was learning anything at all. I was also internalizing a way of living with the snippets of inherited rhyme that fill rap everywhere, its wholesome streets and dark alleys alike. Jurassic 5 albums are Easter-eggy paradises of recycling in the Lil Wayne sense of the word, of quotations—a line here, a couplet there, a scat interlude or a nonverbal audio gesture elsewhere—so woven into the flow of the rhyme that they're barely called out as such. Even that kazoo breakdown from "Concrete Schoolyard" is a micro-cover of Crash Crew's 1980 "High Power Rap." And even now, when I hear a record by Sugarhill Gang or the Furious Five, or by Rakim or EPMD or Public Enemy (the chorus of "What's Golden" is completed by a scratch-in sample from Chuck D, surely the latest and least starry-eyed source ever to infiltrate the schoolyard), not only do I likely recognize a lyric I first heard in a J5 song; I also hear a tradition selectively renewing itself, not through insult or co-optation but through homage and reverence, through a kind of generosity that makes room for curiosity.

This kind of teacherly patience is extraordinary, I think, especially when so many of your students are novices, culturally and historically, newcomers to the tradition for whom forward and backward are equally uncharted directions. At a time with, I cringe to hear myself remind you, no Rap Genius, no Shazam, no internet-hivemind IV drip, it felt like permission to cultivate and create my own canon, to master history by mixing up time sometimes, to fill my pockets with stones and figure out later, probably, where they came from. This is what it means—and it's not just positive, good-timey hip-hop that does this but any rapper, anyone creating within a canonical lineage—to express your vision of a golden era through what you quote, what you choose to hold onto and keep alive and emphatically yes-y'all. This is what it looks like to entrust that vision to a stranger on the faith that your heritage will eventually become theirs too.

So to prove to y'all that we're second to none / We're gonna make five MCs sound like one

Melle Mel, in Grandmaster Flash & The Furious Five, "Superappin'" (1979)

'Cause it's the brothers on the mic occupying the drum / Taking four MCs and make 'em sound like one

Jurassic 5, "Improvise" (2000)

On a stage I rage and I'm rollin'

Chuck D, in Public Enemy, "Prophets of Rage" (1988)

WRITING/BITING

If you having girl problems I feel bad for you, son
I got ninety-nine problems and a bitch ain't one

Ice-T, *"99 Problems" (1993)*

• •

MY GUESS IS that if there's a voice saying these lines in your head it belongs to Jay-Z, excitable and hoarse, cruising over that rip-roaring Rick Rubin beat. His towering "99 Problems" came out in 2003 and was so ubiquitous for the remainder of the decade that I don't think it will ruffle any feathers to call it its own face-value commonplace, its own apparent endpoint of rap's rhetorical continuum. One of those catechisms, and deservedly so. But none of this changes the fact—and I'm not ruling out the possibility that you're aware of said fact, even if the voice in your head still belongs to Jay-Z—that Ice-T said the same words, in the same order, arguably more dopely, ten years earlier.

Now once upon a time not too long ago / A nigga like myself had to strong-arm a ho / Now this was not a ho in the sense of having a pussy / But a pussy having no goddamn sense, tryin' to push me

Bun B, in UGK, *"Touched" (1996)*

Upon closer inspection—I didn't know this for a long time—Jay's "99 Problems" is a bit of a patchwork. In addition to borrowing the chorus from Ice-T—Chris Rock's idea, according to Rubin—Jay lifts the beginning of the third verse verbatim, give or take a word or two, from UGK's "Touched," and his writeoff just after that of an effete dude—*You know the type, loud as a motorbike, but wouldn't bust a grape in a fruit fight*—a little more subtly from LL Cool J's tacit MC Hammer dis in 1990's "To Da Break of Dawn": *Shootin' the gift but you just don't shoot it right / You couldn't bust a grape in a fruit fight.* All of this is uncredited, even in *Decoded*, whose annotations for "99 Problems" cover only the second verse.

Now, to quote Slick Rick in "La Di Da Di," a song itself arguably eclipsed by Snoop Doggy Dogg's wholesale cover version and liberally sampled elsewhere, *This type of shit it happens every day.* "One can make the argument that rap—like China—is a space where plagiarism simply doesn't exist," writes Ariel Schneller at Genius. Repetition, as we've seen, is in the nature of signifying, perhaps in its purpose too. Sure, it's preferable to hold on to the *with a difference* part, but who's to say changing a couple of conjunctions doesn't constitute difference in a post–Pierre Menard universe?

Nonetheless: this is kind of a lot. Jay-Z, it turns out, does this almost-identical rhyme-cadging thing often enough to blur that already faint line between biting and enlightening. *How much of Biggie's rhymes is gonna come out your fat lips?* asked Nas, back when he and Jay were feuding. Cam'ron, who's also logged his share of time beefing with Jay—he once savaged him for wearing jeans with open-toed sandals, then likened his appearance to that of Joe Camel, Fraggle Rock, and Alf—tallies many of Jay's interpolations of rhymes from Biggie and Slick Rick and Snoop Dogg and Nas and Big L on a circa-2006 track called "Swagger Jacker." Between each audio exhibit of evidence—Jay's rhyme, then the conspicuously similar original—you hear a scribble of tape-rewind, a reverb-drenched sound effect of someone chomping into an apple, and then Jay saying *I'm not a writer, I'm a biter*, a doctored version of this line—

(1985)

"Ether" (2001)

Hold up I gotta rewind I gotta rewind

> *I'm not a biter, I'm a writer, for myself and others*
> *I say a Big verse I'm only biggin' up my brother*

(2003) —from a song called, ironically enough, "What More Can I Say."

The second half of that couplet is in line with the way Jay generally explains his various borrowings from Biggie, who was a close friend of his: "Doing that was my way of always keeping him fresh and keeping his music fresh on everyone's mind." (In a 2010 *New Yorker* "Talk of the Town" vignette Cornel West recalls Jay telling him and Toni Morrison he's "been playing Plato to Biggie's Socrates.") And some of the time this does come across as a perfectly tenable argument: for instance on the 2011 smash "Niggas in Paris," when he says *I'm liable to go Michael, take your pick / Jackson,*

in Puff Daddy, "Victory"

Tyson, Jordan, game six as a riff on Biggie's 1998 *I perform like Mike /*
Any one: Tyson, Jordan, Jackson. Or when he takes Biggie's syllable-

"You're Nobody (Til Somebody Kills You)"

chopping flex from 1997, *My sycamore style, more sicker than yours* and unfurls and dissects it in 2003 as

I was conceived by Gloria Carter and Adnis Reeves
Who made love under the sycamore tree
Which made me a more sicker MC

"December 4th" (2003)

This is repetition with a difference: recognizably related to the prior iteration, unambiguously an echo, but carrying its own narrative, its own distinct context. But then there's the part in "Girls, Girls, Girls, Pt. 2" (whose hook is *also* a micro-cover of Crash Crew's "High Power Rap," for the record) where he reprises Biggie's boast about juggling multiple lovers without getting caught—

Isn't this great, your flight leaves at eight
Her flight lands at nine, my game just rewinds

"One More Chance/Stay With Me (Remix)" (1995)

—by changing it, somewhat confoundingly, to

120

(2001)

> *Isn't this great, my flight leaves at eight*
> *Her flight lands at nine, my game just rewinds*

Or when he picks up a couplet from Slick Rick's "The Ruler's Back":

(1988)

> *Now, in these times—well, at least to me*
> *There's a lot of people out here trying to sound like Ricky D*

and sets it back down in his own "The Ruler's Back":

(2001)

> *Well, in these times—well, at least to me*
> *There's a lot of rappers out there trying to sound like Jay-Z*

Again, Jay's far from the only rapper to appropriate quotations and change a bare minimum of details—*now* to *well*, *and* to *but*, *out here* to *out there*, *hit it!* to *hit me!*—as though scrupulously dodging a YouTube copyright protection algorithm. But if he does it a little too much to ignore, he also never seems to pause to give credit, even when the opportunity overwhelmingly presents itself. In *Decoded* he explains of his 2003 **My homie Sigel's on a tier where no tears should fall** that "the homonym of tiers and tears connects prison tiers with crying—but you can't cry in prison (at least not out in the open)," but neglects to mention that Chuck D used an identical pun in 1988.

So what's this about? Is it pure unabashed mimicry, like Puff Daddy pillaging pop hits from the eighties but without the expensive sample clearances? Or is it possible that the repetition is *itself* the commentary? Notice, if you will, some of the borderline-gaslighting places it happens: when he replaces *Ricky D* with *Jay-Z* in a line that's already about soundalikes and copycats; when he changes Chuck D's first-person prison dispatch

"Moment of Clarity"

I'm on a tier where no tears should ever fall / Cell blocked and locked, I never clock it, y'all

in Public Enemy, "Black Steel in the Hour of Chaos"

121

to a third-person one about his affiliate Beanie Sigel; when he uses *like* to compare himself to any number of famous Michaels. Could it be that **my game just rewinds** is not a brazen admission of petty thievery—*i.e.*, my game is literally nothing but running back other people's tapes—but a boast that he's roping all these echoes into a historically circuitous game of his own magisterial devising?

Nothing gets a certain species of extremely online rap fan exercised like such questions, and I've seen both positions compellingly and stridently defended. (I've also heard a "Swagger Jacker"–style compilation of Cam'ron's own borrowings.) Jay is clearly talented enough that he doesn't *need* to do this, goes one argument, so why would he do it if not in good faith? He's talented enough that he doesn't *need* to do this, goes another, so why does he do it at all? One forum poster expresses annoyance at the negative karma that accrues back to him when he tells his friends that Jay's cleverness isn't really *his*. In that case, wonders someone else, isn't your beef with your friends? "Jay-Z is respecting Biggie by interpolating the narratives," writes Schneller at Genius, "regardless of whether every suburbanite white kid who dances along to 'I Just Wanna Love U' appreciates the reference."

What's *this* about, this compulsion to ensure that suburbanite white kids get the reference, to disabuse your friends of their tragic illusions about the purview of Jay's originality? Why don't the people who do this seem to spend any energy on redressing the wrongs done to the rappers quoted without credit? I'd love to believe that this is something like the extremely online rap fan's version of *doing the knowledge*, that Five Percenter ethos of building by sharing out loud, showing and proving what you know. But I don't believe that's what it is, not really. I think it's more likely suburbanite white kids all the way down, competitively policing the historical record on behalf of imagined novices

When the Remy's in my system, ain't no tellin' / Will I fuck 'em, will I dis 'em? That's what they be yellin' / I'm a pimp by blood, not relation / Y'all be chasin', I replace 'em, unhh!

(2000); also The Notorious B.I.G., "The World Is Filled..." (1997)

because that's somehow less daunting than admitting we've still got gaps in our understanding too.

This, I think—more because of the internet economy and its pernicious sales levers of controversy and gamification than out of any direct philosophical intent—is why Genius inevitably matured from a collaborative educational resource into yet another playing field for performative erudition, with IQ points and leaderboards and whatnot. Communal knowledge work on the internet usually winds up looking less like Jurassic 5's concrete schoolyard and more like LL Cool J's classroom with thirty electric chairs anyway. In a discursive space where veteranship and cred are the supreme capital, you're only ever a couple of degrees away from someone overtly arguing that there's such a thing as too much interpretive liberty.

But that implication is ultimately extrinsic to hip-hop itself, which like any signifying tradition creates in-groups and out-groups through destabilization and insinuation and if-you-know-you-know swagger. If I never hear Jurassic 5 fans grousing about uncredited borrowings or fretting about other people missing references—if J5's song pages on Genius are ghost towns compared to Jay-Z's—maybe that's because those fans haven't yet accumulated enough of that capital to worry about protecting it. Or maybe it's testament to the old-school values J5 worked so openly to keep alive, where it's about liberty and inclusivity rather than material or intellectual wealth, where you can join the in-group without knowing its codes in advance. Maybe those boil down to the same thing. Signifying, remember, is at base about punching up, not down.

• •

Though Jay doesn't mention in *Decoded* that he took the hook of his "99 Problems" from Ice-T's, he does explain that he'd been criticized for his use of the b-word elsewhere, so included *but a bitch ain't one* as "a joke, bait for lazy critics. At no point am I talking about a girl." His rationale, that if you follow the narrative through the song's three verses the word refers to critics, female dogs, and effeminate men respectively, is convincing if you squint hard enough. (In Ice-T's "99 Problems," the word refers to women relentlessly, unabashedly, pornographically.)

"I think that being a player, a real live player, there's nothing you like better than to give props to other people," Ice-T shrugged when asked to comment about the uncredited use of his refrain in the Jay-Z hit. "That's just what you should do. But... you know. That's just how I get down." Not long after this he released a new version of his own "99 Problems" with Body Count, his metal band. "A lot of journalists thought that was Jay-Z's record, and I was like, *Aha, gotcha!*" he later told an interviewer. "It was just something I threw on there as a booby trap for journalists that think they know a lot, so they can just, like, as we say—you can edit this—step in some shit they can't get off their shoe." Booby trap for journalists, bait for lazy critics. Game rewinding.

AGGRAVATED QUOTATION

Beat biter, dope style taker
Tell you to your face you ain't nothin' but a faker

MC Lyte, "10% Dis" (1988)

• •

AT THE END of 1994, a month after 2Pac was shot five times in the lobby of a Manhattan recording studio, Biggie released a track called "Who Shot Ya?" He later claimed to have written it long before the shooting, but it was hard not to hear, between its timing and its overall chest-thumping effrontery, as a boast of involvement. Which is just what Pac did, publicly accusing Biggie, Puff Daddy, and other members of the Bad Boy Records retinue of orchestrating the attack. Then he made an answer song called "Hit 'Em Up," in which he and his protégés, the Outlaw Immortalz, take turns unloading seething bile and rancorous murder talk at all of them. The chorus:

It's on, nigga, fuck all that bickering beef / I can hear sweat trickling down your cheek / Your heartbeat sound like Sasquatch feet / Thundering, shaking the concrete

(1996)

        Grab your Glocks when you see 2Pac
        Call the cops when you see 2Pac
        Who shot me? But you punks didn't finish
        Now you 'bout to feel the wrath of a menace

"Hit 'Em Up" is a chillingly believable display of rage; at one point Pac is silent for about a bar and a half, then comes back frothing with renewed intensity—*Fuck you, die slow, motherfucker! My .44 make sure all y'all kids don't grow!*—as though he had taken a breather to calm himself down but oxygen only made him angrier. (It's actually because he'd taken shots at Jay-Z, Lil' Kim, and Lil' Cease, who his entourage later convinced him were sufficiently neutral in the incident to spare the indignity of being instructed, on record, to die slow.) If "Who Shot Ya?" set a hypermediatized East-West beef on an irrevocable course toward mutual tragedy, "Hit 'Em Up" reads in retrospect as that fiery glint in the eyes, that awful snap of lethal resolve, that extinguishes any lingering hope that it's all still a game.

In this context the song, showcasing as it does the brand of rhetorical violence and no-fucks nihilism that culminated in Pac's murder three months later and Biggie's six months after that, is harrowing, heartbreaking. Unfortunately, there's an alternate context, which in spite of my most solemn efforts is the first one that registers when I hear "Hit 'Em Up": a low-res overdub video by a designer named Ryan Steinhardt that syncs the song's first two minutes to a montage of clips from *Barney & Friends*. To 2Pac and the Outlawz' fiery declarations of contempt, Barney the Dinosaur and four dimpled tweens and a small menagerie of plush puppets sing about dental hygiene and not letting the tap water run irresponsibly. The first time Pac says *Grab your Glocks*, Barney picks up a gigantic toothbrush. It is not so easy, even years later, to dissociate "Hit 'Em Up" from the sight of a purple T-rex gleefully rubbing his boxy fleece hands together alongside darts like *You claim to be a player but I fucked your wife*.

At first it was mostly Barney's situationally inappropriate good cheer that sold the juxtaposition for me, but that was before I heard Junior M.A.F.I.A.'s "Player's Anthem," a song that is not only already the picture of good cheer but also the undeniable source of a certain familiar refrain:

(1995)

> *(Niggas!) Grab your dicks if you love hip-hop*
> *(Bitches!) Rub your titties if you love Big Poppa*

I knew perfectly well that Junior M.A.F.I.A.—the Outlawz to Biggie's Pac—were among the targets of the song's rage. (So were Mobb Deep, for the record, and if you ask me the place where Pac really crosses the line is his making fun of Prodigy's sickle-cell anemia.) But it was a revelation to discover that they were implicated in *this* way, that 2Pac had engineered their party jam against itself, right down to the recurrent murmur of *take money* in the track's lining: a flip of *get money* from the Junior M.A.F.I.A. song of the same name. I'm sure it was meant to be crass and cruel, and I'm sure it was heard that way at the time by the relevant parties, but—the inspired artistry of this cruelty! The thoughtfulness, the attention to detail, even amid such fervent, indiscriminate rage! This was, impious as it feels to say, another wonderful thing to learn.

The clues are always there, in retrospect: a blip in the song's matrix, a bubble in its wallpaper. A cadence that doesn't fit, a sing-song passage that comes out of nowhere. An incongruous moment of silence, a thing the beat doesn't usually do, the sound of someone whooping irreverently in the background. A phrase that never seemed, at first glance, to say anything besides what it said. *You claim to be a player.* Oh, sure.

• •

There remains one wallpaper-bubble that I just can't smooth out. A few verses into "Hit 'Em Up," after Pac has decided that continuing to rag on *you bitchmade-ass Bad Boy bitches* is beneath his station, he hands off the mic to the Outlawz. Following verses by Hussein Fatal and Yaki Kadafi—the Outlawz were named after despots, that was their thing—E.D.I. Mean steps up to the mic with this rhyme:

You's a beat biter, a Pac style taker
I'll tell you to your face, you ain't shit but a faker

It's weirdly melodic and at a different tempo from the rest of his verse, which turns out to be because, besides changing *dope* to *Pac* and adding some ancillary profanity, E.D.I. Mean is quoting verbatim from MC Lyte's "10% Dis," in which she calls out a Bronx rapper named Antoinette for stealing a beat from Lyte's Brooklyn labelmates Audio Two. (Lyte says the track contains only a tenth of the insults she could have leveled, hence the name; she also said later that it was "strictly a war on wax—even then, it was understood completely that it was just business.") Antoinette, it bears mentioning, went on to reuse Lyte's dis against *her*, crowing in the exact same singsong deadpan:

Lyte's out, now the party's over
Homegirl reminds me of my dead dog Rover

Antoinette, "Lights Out, Party's Over" (1989)

E.D.I. Mean isn't nearly as inventive with his turn, to be sure, but I can't help but marvel at his audacity, the sheer pretzel logic of what he does with the borrowing. Within two bars on "Hit 'Em Up" he (*a*) fans the flames of the song's hypermasculine anti-New York bluster by quoting from an amicable rivalry between two New York women playacting total cattiness; (*b*) claims that quoting one person's insult of someone else constitutes telling Biggie to his face; and, most importantly, (*c*) reuses that one person's (Lyte's) words against a second (Antoinette) in order to insult a third person (Biggie) on behalf of a fourth (Pac), and this on the grounds that the third person is biting the fourth *when he himself is biting the first*. I find this almost majestically insane.

Thirty days a month your mood is rude / We know the cause of your bloody attitude
"10% Dis"

So now, even with an eight-year head start, "10% Dis" is haunted for me by "Hit 'Em Up," much the way "Hit 'Em Up" is haunted by that song and dance about dental hygiene and water conservation from *Barney & Friends*. When Lyte says, right after the *beat biter* jab,

> Hit me why don't ya, hit me why don't ya [...]
> You wanna get hurt? Well this is what you do
> You put your left foot up and your right foot next
> Follow instructions, don't lose the context

"10% Dis"

even *Hit me why don't ya* sounds ominous. Like Steinhardt's Barney video, E.D.I. Mean does precisely what Lyte instructed him not to: lose the context. He uproots it, unmoors it, transplants it into something scarier or sillier, something more or less liable to end in disaster. Which is also what the signifying monkey does in the legend about him: he invents a context, weaponizes it, starts shit with the lion not by telling him to his face that he's a bum and a bastard but by *reporting* that the elephant's been saying so. He's signifying the elephant into the fight, the way E.D.I. Mean drags MC Lyte's interborough squabble into his bicoastal beef, the way one might get jumped into a street gang if it were possible to join a gang passively.

It happens. Once you put your words into the world, you can't know that only good and respectful things will be done with them. You can't be sure they won't be distant accessories to verbal homicide, at least to an incompletely informed or chronologically libertine observer. You can't be sure a purple foam dinosaur won't be seen and memorized capering and jiggling to your words, that Jay-Z won't quote you at unseemly length, that a greasy right-wing politician won't gladhand and hatemonger while your song plays over a PA somewhere. It's in the nature of talk to get misdirected; even talk that is itself misdirection isn't immune.

HYPERLINKS

Wikipedia that, if you didn't know

Kool A.D., in Das Racist, "Rooftop" (2010)

• •

(1994)

FOR ITS FIRST year or two, starting back when its name was still Rap Exegesis, Rap Genius's motto was the refrain from Biggie's "Juicy": *If you don't know, now you know.* It sums up the site's aims and ethos with ideal simplicity and exemplary time-compression and insuperable cool, such as I defined it earlier: show up wondering, leave illuminated. Seventeen years later, the Das Racist line above—though surely a lyric about Wikipedia would have been a poor choice of slogan for Rap Genius—is no less on the nose. It's the same principle as Biggie's credo, just updated for an age of shallow knowledge saturation.

It also turns out to be a great description of what it's like to listen to Das Racist, which I enjoy doing sometimes because of and sometimes despite the regularity with which their songs eject me from the song and send me out into the information cosmos to track down a reference to The Diplomats or Captain Beefheart or Gayatri Spivak or whatever. Their songs are an order of magnitude

Jakaya Kikwete, machete machete / Ek Shaneesh, Cheech, Eddie Said speaks / Sheesh—yeah, that's what Ed said

Kool A.D., in "Ek Shaneesh" (2010)

more reference-besotted than Jurassic 5's, but they don't come across as patient teachers so much as obnoxiously, maybe pathologically brilliant students, innately tapped into this rhizomatic network of ceaselessly proliferating meaning that is, as Howard Nemerov once put it, somewhat more like a mind than a thought. It was Das Racist who called out Rap Genius as *white devil sophistry*, but it's also Das Racist whose catalog constitutes the best imaginable use case for Rap Genius, a waveringly legible world after a couple of extra screw-turns. If Jay-Z was complex *like Che Guevara with bling on*, Kool A.D. is

"Public Service Announcement" *(2003)*

"Amazing" (2010)

Eddie Murphy in Shrek, I'm complex
I'm Kanye in whiteface on the cover of Complex

If you prefer, where Jay-Z songs are about Jay-Z and Jurassic 5 songs are about rap itself, Das Racist songs are about aboutness.

For those who doubt it, Typical Cats is 'bout it like Cliffs Notes

Qwel, in Typical Cats, *"Reinventing the Wheel" (2001)*

The group's two MCs met at Wesleyan and ascended to minor but enduring internet celebrity in 2008 with "Combination Pizza Hut and Taco Bell," a stoner novelty that Trojan-horses insurgent critical thought into the hipster karaoke party. They carried on in this unself-serious fashion until they disbanded in 2012, whereupon Kool A.D. and Heems went right on enchanting and confounding in solo rap careers. "Pizza Hut" is about global homogenization and existential cartography, about not knowing where you are in the world, even while it's no less about being drunk and high and not knowing where in the world you actually physically *are*. It's a canny example of the neat balancing act they kept on pulling off, being young and reckless and funny and erudite, and brown, without letting the world get away with writing off the combination as contradictory.

Right here at the Pizza Hut on Jamaica Avenue! Jamaica Avenue!

(2003)

Instead of ignoring the spheres of indirect oppression and direct microaggression they shared with sophists and degree-seeking demons, they put it front and center, aimed it in your face, problematized it in an inconveniently but irresistibly droll way. When Kool A.D. puffs them up as **the smartest dumb guys in the room** a few bars after the Wikipedia line, then rhymes it with **mulatto Jeff Koons,** the homophone of a racial slur is anything but accidental. "They made racial irony signify by dismembering it whenever they saw a chance," Robert Christgau wrote, eulogizing the group in late 2012. Hell, their name is *das racist*, the first word pronounced like a bummy *that's*.

Yeah, shorty said I look like a Cro-Mag too, man
She said I'm half Rasta, half pasta, no Ragu, man   *Kool A.D., in "Shorty Said" (2010)*

What's racist? Aha, well. Everything, sure. The monoculture, the rhizome, life in and beyond these United States. At the same time, though, the absent referent of that *that's* sings out sharply. Like the titles of their first two mixtapes, *Shut Up, Dude* and *Sit Down, Man*—their first and only proper album was called *Relax*— the name is a rejoinder to an offense obscured, known but not identified, everywhere present and felt but [*citation needed*] all the same.

And this is what Das Racist captured about meaning too, about the simultaneously dispiriting and leavening suspicion that everything refers to something else, whether or not you recognize it, whether or not the referent even exists yet. For all their savant manipulation of stereotype and expectation, their intransigent attention to the weird matrix of geopolitical drift and hyperlocal culture, what cements their legacy for me is their weirdly linearity-proof model of time and connection. Somewhere between the highbrow namechecks and the smolderingly juvenile dick jokes you come around to the view that the massive interrelatedness of all things is as tidal a force at the hyperlocal scale as it is at the geopolitical, and their contentedness to both comment on it and simply sit and observe it was the rightest I've ever seen the postmodern condition nailed down. Das Racist were, for too short a time, distillation

132

of and poster child for that future shock, that archive fever, that ouroboric philosophical investigation, sustained by the faith that the dope rhyme, the legitimizing connection, the missing citation is out there somewhere, a few more clicks down the rabbit hole. They showed by example how to make art, or maybe truth, by following that faith until the thicket of allusions laid over the song becomes its own surface, until the bubbles are just the wallpaper itself.

ON CLICHÉ

Kickin' the fly clichés
Doing duets with Rae and A
Happens to make my day

Ghostface Killah, in Wu-Tang Clan, "Can It Be All So Simple" (1993)

• •

YOU KNOW THAT refrain about how the roof the roof the roof is on fire? Of course you do. It's one of those catechisms Cobb talks about, for me and perhaps for you too, and maybe you haven't personally chanted it or heard it chanted all around you but I bet you know how it ends: **We don't need no water let the motherfucker burn.** It's been making the rounds for years. It's been sampled and interpolated by Nelly, The Pharcyde, MC Serch of 3rd Bass, Bizzy Bone of Bone-Thugs-n-Harmony, George Clinton, countless club DJs; it's been punk-rasped by Rancid, white-boy deadpanned by Bloodhound Gang, nü-metal belched by Coal Chamber. It's been reimagined as *The earth is on fire* and *Her hair is on fire* and *My blunt is on fire* and *The roach is on the wall*. It's developed the texture of a traditional party chant, a commonplace calcified into popular usage by years of repetition, and so I admit I was startled, the first time I heard the 1984 party-mover "The Roof Is on Fire,"

134

by Rock Master Scott and the Dynamic Three, to learn that this refrain was actually *from* somewhere. That someone had started this putative fire. The song itself is silly and fun in exactly the way a mid-eighties party-mover should be, less angry mob and more apocalypse rave—but before I heard the refrain in its native context it had never occurred to me that it might have once have referred to actual injury, ill intent, damage, death. **Burn, mother-fucker, burn!**

Commonplaces aren't places. They're hazy, vaporous unities floating along above our heads, unprepossessing, freely borrowed, occasionally renewed. Where quotations begin is in a cloud, says Mary Ruefle. This particular cloud is where the rewind boast comes from, and life being a bitch and then you die, and nothing making sense unless it makes dollars. Rakim's seven-MC theory lived in the cloud over my head for a while, until it occurred to me that I could retrace its forking chain of gonzo arithmetic to an actual source. It's great gratifying fun to climb back up the chain until you reach the cloud, but that's not what it's there for. The vitality of these lyrical themes, their staying power, their contagious communicability, depends in part on how hard it is to imagine—or rather how easy to imagine but hard to *prove*—that they started anywhere at all. Who said **Drop it like it's hot** before Snoop Dogg, and before that Lil Wayne, and before that a pimp in a skit on a Jay-Z album? Who was the first person to instruct a crowd of people to throw their hands in the air and wave them around like they just didn't care, and how recently before that had that person been held at gunpoint by a robber or a cop?

Tradition is another word for this cloud, for expressions that are surely quotations in some sense but that you wouldn't be altogether surprised to see on a throw pillow or a shot glass without expecting anyone to be earning royalties. "Auld Lang Syne," *He who smelt it dealt it*, that sort of thing. If these phrases appear

Now throw your hands in the air / And wave 'em like you just don't care / And if you're not a square from Delaware [...] / Somebody say Oh yeah!

"The Roof Is on Fire"

When the pimp's in the crib, ma, drop it like it's haawwt / Drop it like it's haawwt, drop it like it's haawwt

Snoop Dogg, "Drop It Like It's Hot" (2004)

Now after you back it up, then stop / What, what, what? Drop it like it's hot

Lil Wayne, "Drop It Like It's Hot" (1999)

You run up on your bitches, this is what you tell 'em: / Stick they hands in they panties, grab that knot / Stick they arm in that car window, drop it like it's hot

Jay-Z, "Cashmere Thoughts" (1996)

Hands up, we just doing what the cops taught us

to have no earthly origin, it's because at some point more or less long ago—an interval determined locally, by the beholder—they passed into a kind of public domain where their authorship is not just beside the point but practically athwart it. They're "photographs we have hold of without knowing the names of the subjects in the image," to quote Kevin Young, or volcanoes, to quote Gérard Genette, "in that their first eruption can sometimes be dated but never their last; they may be long dormant but perhaps never definitively extinguished." Both Young and Genette were talking about something else, which I'm pretty sure is my point.

Ghostface Killah, who has always struck me as constitutionally incapable of triteness, has a humbler word for them: *clichés*. We tend to speak of cliché in terms of originality renounced, of effort fallen by the wayside, but it can be of genuine use in those cases where it's not worth the effort to be original. (Like *stereotype*, *cliché* comes from letterpress printing, for the readymade plate that allowed typesetters to reproduce sections or images or entire pages without having to reassemble them over and over again.) And if cliché mostly gets a bad rap, rap has a weird way of making cliché good. Of redeeming it via the same kind of inventive resourcefulness that makes sample-based hip-hop production more than the sum of its recycled parts—what Greg Tate, describing Public Enemy soundscapist Hank Shocklee, calls "that rare ability to extract the lyrical from the lost and found." Isn't that what the roof on fire is, what auld acquaintance being forgot is, what life being a bitch is—something that can be perpetually lost and simultaneously found without undue trouble?

Let's define the category Ghostface is establishing here, the *fly cliché*, as one in which the familiarity of a given image or locution or bromide is the beginning of a journey rather than its terminus, more a search for something lost than something found without searching. Nas:

"N.Y. State of Mind" (1994)   **I never sleep, 'cause sleep is the cousin of death**

AZ, later on the same Nas album:

Life's a bitch and then you die
"Life's a Bitch" (1994)   **That's why we puff la, 'cause you never know when you're gonna go**

Nas, one album later:

Life's a bitch but god forbid the bitch divorce me
"Affirmative Action" (1996)   **I be flooded in ice so hellfire won't scorch me**

Lil Wayne on *Tha Carter*:

"We Don't" (2004)   **Life's a bitch and death's her husband**

And on *Tha Carter IV*:

Life's a bitch and death is her sister
"6 Foot 7 Foot" (2010)   **Sleep is the cousin, what a fuckin' family picture**

Aesop Rock on "Daylight":

Life's not a bitch, life is a beautiful woman
(2001)   **You only call her a bitch 'cause she won't let you get that pussy**

And on "Night Light":

Life's not a bitch, life is a biatch!
(2002)   **Who keeps villagers circling the marketplace out searching for the G-spot**

This chain is slang's evolution, the forced and forking inner mutation of words as they cycle through unattended and unlicensed usages, all of it zoomed out to the level of the thought. It's the churn of idioms and banalities, truisms and snowclones and other units of language we use without quite recalling where we learned them, being parsed and deconstructed into their constituent parts and put back together slant. Notions, scenarios, tropes that would be a headache to reset every time a rapper invoked them: the hypocrisy of people who snubbed you before you were successful, your scorn for those who are cash-poor but rich in luxury items, being fond of your gun to a practically matrimonial extent. (That actually might be just Jadakiss.) Similarities between the rap game and the crack game, your watch being worth more than my car or house or significant other, the breaking news bulletin where a dorky-sounding white anchor reports that one or more dangerous rappers are at large, the greatest of which has to be the skit on Royal Flush's *Ghetto Millionaire* where the guy mispronounces "Canada."

The beauty of the fly cliché is that it treats these things not as filler, not as shortcuts, but as new opportunities for finding. It works because the known quantity of what they say frees us to focus on *how* they're being said. In this way, people who disparage rap for endlessly elaborating the same themes aren't wrong, just looking at it shallowly. These recurring commonplaces, iterated throughout the canon with no perceptible first or last usage, are precisely where thoughtfulness and invention are most visible, most invited: the more familiar the territory, the deader the metaphor, the greater the chance to carve out a new micronarrative connotation, something unexpected or subversive or genuinely novel within the confines of something apparently ageless. Paradoxically, even as each such tweak individuates a new version of the quotation, it also restores it to the cloud overhead, smudging away the fingerprints of the people who've touched it until eventually the thought belongs to no one, which is to say everyone.

Got a quarter tank of gas in my new E-Class / But that's alright, 'cause I'm gon' ride / Got everything in my mama name / But I'm hood rich, la da da da da da da

Big Tymers, *"Still Fly"* (2002)

Rap critics that say "He's money, cash, hoes" / I'm from the hood, stupid, what type of facts are those?

Jay-Z, *"99 Problems"* (2003)

250 drum that's spittin', that's a Hot 97 / Bitch I'm fly 'til I die— mm-hmm, 9/11

(Savage &) No Fatigue, *"FGE Cypher Pt. 6"* (2018)

WHO WORE IT BETTER?

There were times when I used to hide my feelings
Now I'm butt naked in a Lamborghini
And motherfuckers can't see me

• •

POP QUIZ! Who said this? Was it:

> *(a)* Rick Ross
> *(b)* Kanye West
> *(c)* Nicki Minaj
> *(d)* 2Pac
> *(e)* Eminem

Let's think it through. Rick Ross loves talking about Lamborghinis and appearing topless in public: strong contender. Kanye West takes evident pleasure in antagonizing his haters through outrageous deeds, but when has he ever hidden his feelings? Nicki Minaj likes luxury goods and titillating levels of undress as much as the next maneater, but would she really say *butt naked*? 2Pac was rhythmically nimble enough to make good on the five-syllable differential between the second and third lines here, plus invisibility was a substantial part of his late-career fantasia—legend has it he was closely monitored by COINTELPRO until he died. (Erik Nielson's essay about surveillance quoted earlier, "Can't C Me," is named for a song Pac made with George Clinton.) Best choice so far, I'd say. Eminem actually seems like a Nevernude to me, but who can really say what goes on in that guy's mind?

The answer is none of the above: it's noted epicurean and tilapia connotation-scrambler Action Bronson, who crows in the following verse about **getting topped off in the front row of the opera**, in case you were wondering about sonority's role in cultivating new slang about oral sex. Apologies for the ruse. The exercise wasn't about the answer anyway; it was about how the same set of words shifts shape and inflection when attributed, even hypothetically, to different voices. It was about the speaker-specific interpretive data that is functionally the same thing as personality, and how much of it is derived directly from the source *especially* in a world where so many rappers draw from the same well of tropes and narratives. When you're one of a hundred street kingpins rhyming about selling crack and stacking paper, the story you're telling matters less than the idiosyncrasies you come up with while telling it, the texture of the pulp, the reflective qualities of the fish scale.

I would even argue, in fact, that it's the minimal variations on those fly clichés that do the most to distinguish rappers from one another. I bet it's possible to predict your allegiance to Biggie or 2Pac to a high level of accuracy based solely on whether you prefer the ornateness of

"Baby Blue" (2015)

·

All-purpose war, got the Rottweilers by the door
And I feed them gunpowder, so they can devour
The criminals tryna drop my decimals

or the chilly simplicity of

I got two Rottweilers by my bed
I feed them lead

(The 2Pac line is the second one, which once again illustrates his intuitive knack for ironing out lines of uneven length, not that that's why I brought it up.)

You can run this experiment indefinitely; I certainly do. Incidentally, when you ask who else might plausibly have said an Action Bronson line, the answer is impressively often nobody, so specific are his vernacular and sense of self, his fetching blend of depravity and dorky opulence. But for my money no one has a tighter lock on this phenomenon than Kanye West, that rare author who is with his every uttered word becoming more purely and irrevocably himself.

A friend asked me not long ago what *If they don't wanna ride I'ma still give 'em raincoats* meant. She thought maybe it was a safe-sex joke, but Genius had other suggestions, the more credible among them including clothing drives, Noah's Ark, and the hoses turned on civil-rights marchers in Alabama. I didn't and still don't know, but there was a moment before I remembered who'd said it—it's Chance the Rapper in his flyly pious verse on Kanye's "Ultralight Beam"—where it could have been practically anyone, and accordingly could have *meant* practically anything. What if it were DMX? What if it were Lauryn Hill? What if it were Ghostface? I can't count the number of times I've heard a Ghostface line and been like, "I don't know what that is but I bet it's dirty as fuck." When Guru says *Lemonade was a popular drink and it still is*, it sounds bafflingly, incuriosity-baitingly pointless. When Kool A.D. says *Shout out to Wesley Willis / He was a popular man and he still is*, it sounds like he's signifying on Guru. When Jay-Z says *You know you made it when the fact that your marriage made it is worth millions / Lemonade is a popular drink and it still is*, right after his wife drops an album called *Lemonade* whose central narrative conceit is his infidelity, it sounds less like signifying on Guru than like an ungainly attempt to cash in on some golden-age rap cred. (As Tom Breihan points out, it's also borderline incoherent that he says *is* twice in the second line.) If De

The Notorious B.I.G., "Warning" (1994)

2Pac, "Picture Me Rollin'" (1996)

You could find me playing tennis with my dentist, Dennis

in Samiyam, "Mr. Wonderful" (2016)

I am a god / So hurry up with my damn massage / In a French-ass restaurant / Hurry up with my damn croissants!

"I Am a God" (2013)

(2016)

Then I asked these young ladies do they buff helmets / They said "Fuck you," took a sniff, and then they didn't tell me

Ghostface Killah, "Big Girl" (2006)

"Special Forces" (2014)

in Fat Joe & Remy Ma, "All the Way Up (Remix)" (2016)

La Soul said it it'd sound deep as hell; if Lil' Kim said it it'd sound like a reference to watersports. Ditto the line about raincoats.

What I mean is that rappers occupy language at different angles and so perforce occupy ambiguity the same way. Imagine these lines, clichés or otherwise, not only as vectors for rappers' individual idiosyncrasies but also as verbal entities of their own. Commonplace clouds drifting across the landscape of language, some pregnant with personality, some light and unique and waiting for someone to pull them down and inhabit them for a spell. Gérard Genette again:

What I said once belongs to me and it can be parted from me only by being given over through a voluntary or involuntary transaction, officially acknowledged by a pair of quotation marks. What I have said twice or more ceases to belong to me; it now characterizes me and may be parted from me by a simple transfer of imitation; by repeating myself, I am already imitating myself, and on that point one can imitate me by repeating me. What I say twice is no longer my truth but a truth about me, which belongs to everyone.

Rap, as you may have heard, is funny about plagiarism. It claims in its lore to abhor biting and faking as mortal sins, but it's no secret that plenty of rappers write other rappers' rhymes—Big Daddy Kane for Biz Markie, Biggie for Lil' Kim, Jay-Z for Foxy Brown, GZA for Ol' Dirty Bastard—and have done so more or less formally ever since Big Bank Hank appeared on "Rapper's Delight" reading lyrics straight out of Grandmaster Caz's notebook. (You may have wondered why he introduces himself as *C-A-S-N-O-V-A F-L-Y.*) Jay-Z's success and influence are undiminished by Cam'ron and some nerds on the internet grousing about how much he borrows from Biggie; Meek Mill tried to character-assassinate Drake in 2016 on the grounds that Drake sometimes outsources his lyrics, and failed because nobody's affinity for Drake is based on the assumption that he writes his every word. (Also because

Drake completely eviscerated Meek with his answer song "Back to Back.") "I think often that the mistake made in rap music is that people feel a vocalist should write their own lyrics," says Chuck D of Public Enemy. "That's been a major, major mistake in hip-hop, because not everyone is equipped to be a lyricist and not everyone is equipped to be a vocalist."

For the most part, that is, rap's legendary contempt for copycats is a red herring. What counts is not so much whether your rhymes belong to you as what you do while they're momentarily in your possession, how you build on or bracket out their existing affiliations, how persuasively you sell them to the present moment. Even the most beaten down cliché can be fly if you make it fly, yours if you make it yours.

This is for y'all that think I don't write enough / They just mad 'cause I got the Midas touch
(2015)

Coke like a caterpillar, I make butter fly

DENIABLE PLAUSIBILITY

Might look light but we heavy though
You think Drake will pull some shit like that? You never know!

Drake, in Rick Ross, "Stay Schemin'" (2012)

• •

I HAVE A pet theory according to which Lil Wayne is the Homer Simpson of rap because, during their peak eras, respectively roughly 2004 to 2009 and 1992 to 1997, it was functionally almost impossible for either of them to be out of character. Nothing was beyond them. Their range was too immense, their individual deeds outlandish in too many different ways: who they were, who they could be, was enveloped in a kind of blurry omniplausibility. Just as Homer could be up on theological arcana or American jurisprudence or the sex appeal of Oliver North in one moment and return to being an inconsiderate boor the next, Wayne could flash a soulful or erudite or kittenish side without breaking his stride as a drug-gobbling alien mobster. He could wander from obscure to lewd to crude to menacing to playful back to obscure in the space of a verse, and it's not that he didn't seem unfocused; it was that his lack of focus was not a distraction from his persona but a fundamental part of it. He was that malleable, a true hybrid of human and cartoon. Like

Ten addresses, and I dresses / Like I thinks I'm the motherfucking best there is / And I'm about to bubble and she catch that fizz / And I'm straight from Claiborne, nigga, just ask Liz

Lil Wayne, "Get High Rule the World" (2007)

peak Homer, peak Wayne is a personification—to borrow Ayodele Ogundipe's description of Esu-Elegbara, the Yoruba trickster deity on whom the signifying monkey is based—of flux and mutability.

If Wayne is Homer, his Canadian protégé Drake is Ross from *Friends*: a little nerdy, a little clingy, sort of tastefully swarthy. He—Drake—is a brooding bon vivant and a dreamy drunk-dialer, buoyant and sentimental and callow and prone to minor cruelties like trawling mall food courts and *telling every girl she the one for me when I ain't even planning to call*. (That's from the same song with the *come and find me #Nemo* line, and honestly a helicopter-parented clownfish toddler feels like a pretty good spirit animal for him.) And part of his massive success, I think, has been this sense of transparency, this notion that what you hear on record is or at least aspires to be a candid reflection of who he really is, how he's been spoiled and deadened and wokened by megastardom. He'll be petty and nostalgic and drop verifiable hints about past dalliances that he's still hung up on. He'll rap about his grandma. He is dependably talented and reliably—even in the plush throes of impossible wealth, even brooding cinematically in an empty mansion—*relatable*.

Somewhere along the way, though, let's say circa 2011's *Take Care*, he also started dabbling in darker, streetier tropes. A bit of thug life here, a bit of mafioso acculturation there. Not so much that his stories themselves got more sinister; more that he began spinning them with more allusions to danger and violence, peppering his boasts and avowals of emotional recklessness with intimations of deadly firepower. His signaling got hazier. *I seen a lot of you die*, he says of rival rappers on "Free Smoke," after establishing an elaborate rhetorical framework for the concept of death. *You gon' hype me up and make me catch a body like that*, he says in "Headlines": *'Cause I live for this, it isn't just a hobby like that*.

To catch a body, you may recall from Dej Loaf, means to kill someone, to rack up a murder as you might rack up parking tickets or divorces. (A gun with bodies on it is one that can be tied to a

"Forever" (2009)

The one that I needed was Courtney from Hooters on Peachtree / I've always been feeling like she was the one to complete me
"From Time" (2013)

Tuck my napkin in my shirt 'cause I'm just mobbin' like that
"Headlines" (2011)

(2017)

And I ain't playin' with nobody / Fuck around and I'ma catch a body

145

homicide.) Like quite a lot of terms for violence in hip-hop vernacular, though—see *bang* and *bump* and *hit* and *wet* and *smash*, see *break you off* and *hit a lick* and *get rubbed*—it can also refer to sex. There's a whole song where Dreezy—I get that it's confusing to bring her up right now given that Drake sometimes calls himself Drizzy, but so it goes—uses *catch a body* as an extended metaphor for lovemaking. **You about to catch a body if you ain't careful,** like her **I might call your number like bingo,** is a remarkably sure-footed highwire walk between flirtation and threat.

In plenty of idiolects, of course, the most elemental themes accumulate the most versatile and context-dependent signifiers—and few people understand this slipperiness as intimately, and exploit it as cunningly, as Drake. So while he's conjuring power and menace when he threatens to **catch a body like that,** he's also sowing enduring doubt through his choice of words and images: is he the kind of jealous guy who's liable to murder someone, or the kind who's liable to have revenge sex with a hostess from the Olive Garden? Is he tucking his napkin into his shirt because that's what mafia guys do, or because his sweater is made from a natural fabric that's a real chore to get alfredo sauce out of? It's practically obnoxious, his knack for crossing wires to keep us guessing, for floating ultimata he can easily walk back in the next line—but he's just too good at it to begrudge. **I got enemies, got a lot of enemies,** he says in "Energy." **Got a lot of people tryna drain me of my energy.** A list, we find out shortly thereafter, that includes **bitches asking me about the code for the wi-fi.**

• •

Drake spent a spell in early 2012 feuding with the veteran Chicago MC Common, allegedly over both rappers' romantic involvement with Serena Williams. In a guest verse on Rick Ross's "Stay Schemin'" Drake takes his shots—in the lyrical sense, not the martial or medical or alcoholic senses—without ever naming his target, calling him one of *the gods* and goading him into response by framing his beef as disillusionment:

"Stay Schemin'"

> **Back when if a nigga reached it was for the weapon**
> **Nowadays niggas reach just to sell they record**

It's brilliant how plausibly this could be a self-own, nostalgia for a bygone era of pistol-packing being even more of a reach for Drake than it was for Common, who by 2011 was basically a sentient perfume commercial. (The next thing Drake says is *spaghetti Bolognese in the Polo Lounge.*) Common makes a similar argument in his answer song, ninety seconds over the "Stay Schemin" beat, telling Drake to give up the charade and cop to being catty rather than dangerous. *Everybody know you sweet, what the problem is?* he says. *You ain't wet nobody, nigga, you Canada Dry.*

You used to call me on my self-owns

Common, "Stay Schemin" (2012)

Now, I don't know Drake. To clarify: I don't know Aubrey Drake Graham of Toronto. But I know Drake the global rap star reasonably well, and when he hits the triumphant third-person checkmate call above—*You think that Drake will pull some shit like that? You never know!*—my immediate and categorical reaction is *Nah, I do, and he won't.* He's not keeping me guessing here. I don't believe he's liable to *pull some shit like that*, at least not in the way he wants me to; I believe the shit he'll pull is to continue shrewdly treading the thin line between genuine vendetta and public beef as competitive celebrity exercise, then go celebrate another platinum single at Hooters. Again, I claim no authority here. The blogger Ernest Baker once spent a few evenings at Drake's Hidden Hills compound and reported that "the guy who walks around politely checking on everyone at his party is the same one who can't wait to let his new Beretta go," and I have no reason not to believe this is true of Aubrey Graham. I'm just saying, wrong or right, I don't think I'll ever listen to a Drake song and think *This is definitely a guy who owns and routinely uses firearms.*

Here's Drake on "No Frauds," a 2017 Nicki Minaj single that also features Lil Wayne:

Niggas see me like, "What up, Killa?"
Man, please stop bringin' up my past
I'd really love to leave that behind

If you know that the first two of these lines are lifted wholesale—recycled, not upcycled—from Wayne's 2008 song "Mr. Carter," you realize Drake is borrowing Wayne's gangster bona fides to imply that his own past is checkered by bodies rather than talky beefs over celebrity love triangles. And we know with a strong degree of certainty that it's not: we know Aubrey Graham had a bar mitzvah and acted in a Canadian teen soap opera and now co-owns a record label and a whiskey brand. We know Drake to be a smart and hard-working and neurotic guy who's capable of sportive mall-jiltings, sure, but *murder*? There are no doubt parts of his past he'd love to leave behind, same as anyone; it's because he's so gifted at his noncommittal rhetorical shapeshifting that he's able to wrap himself in the aura of Wayne's menace without entirely eliminating the possibility that he just wants us to stop talking about his multiple seasons on *Degrassi: The Next Generation*. (This is an inversion of the loophole Jay-Z uses to shirk responsibility for saying *bitch* in "99 Problems" because Ice-T said it first. As in the signifying monkey legend, he's not *saying* your mother's an easy lay—he's just *quoting*.)

So what about Wayne? We also know with a strong degree of certainty that Dwayne Carter has never killed anyone, so why doesn't it land as flat when he enumerates his own sordid deeds and warns us politely, *in the same words as Drake*, not to go sniffing around his past? Flux and mutability. If, as Foucault suggested, identity is the decoder ring that tells us the particular sense to make of an author's words, peak Wayne's is permanently on

Don't listen to the lies / I swear they all lies
"Cameras"

Don't quote me, boy, 'cause I ain't said shit
Eazy-E, "Boyz-n-the-Hood" (1987)

Flip your vehicle, split your windshield / Whack your baby mama but I let the kid live
Lil Wayne, "BM J.R." (2004)

the fritz—and far from being a burden, this is a boon. The illusion of dependability without the promise.

Being a compelling character, in short, isn't the same thing as being a consistent one; Wayne, like Homer, is an object lesson in attaining the former by rejecting the latter. Perhaps Drake was too successful too early on at doing the opposite—at effacing the distinction between person and persona—to enjoy the same mobility. From his gilded VIP section he can only envy the liberties of Wayne; or of Nicki Minaj, who says whatever she wants through *actual* personas with names and accents and everything; or of Kendrick Lamar, who balances direct introspection with an opera's worth of alter-egos on each album; or of Missy Elliott, whose "refusal to discuss her personal life," Rachel Kaadzi Ghansah reports, "has allowed her to deftly deflect any inquiries about her real life toward her surreal life: the one she inhabits with her many costumes and her various personalities." The more Drake tells me I'll never know what he's capable of, the less I believe him. His insistence only shines a light on what he's otherwise so gifted at obscuring, namely that he too does what Nicki and Kendrick and Missy do outright, what Wayne does so thoroughly he never seems to do it at all: play a character.

ON FIRST PERSON

Now get it from the underground poet
I live it, I see it, and I write it because I know it

Eazy-E, in N.W.A, "Niggaz 4 Life" (1991)

• •

AND OF COURSE rappers play characters. It's all but impossible to miss. When Nicki says *I got bars #sentences*, she's not Nicki Minaj but her alter-ego Roman Zolanski; when Eminem joins her later in the song, he's not Eminem but his alter-ego Slim Shady. Ghostface Killah sometimes calls himself by his government name, Dennis Coles, but more often goes either by Ironman, which is also the title of his first solo album, or by Tony Starks, which (give or take the final S) is the real identity of Iron Man in the Marvel Comics universe. Last I checked, the nine core members of the Wu-Tang Clan had a collective seventy documented aliases and heteronyms. MF DOOM, who has released work under names including but not limited to Zev Love X, King Geedorah, Viktor Vaughn, and DOOM tout court, never appears in public without a metal mask on—MF stands for *metal face*—and sometimes hires impostors to take the stage in his place. "I remember a George Clinton interview from when he was younger where he said that characters

150

live on longer than human beings do," says Shock G of Digital Underground, better known for his lapses into a novelty-nosed, Slick Rick–voiced character named Humpty Hump, even though for a time nobody knew Humpty was the same person as Shock G and he had to remind listeners on "The Humpty Dance" that they'd already met him in an earlier song. "They don't burn out as quickly," G explains. "So that was an inspiration."

"There is nothing authentic about a rapper's identity," writes Katja Lee, "for it is designed to be sold."

Still, sometimes we forget to parse the character from the human being. We know performing is performing, sure, but most of us prefer not to think about it unless we have to. There's an essay where Robin D. G. Kelley describes Ice Cube's "A Bird in the Hand" as a song in which "Cube plays a working-class black man just out of high school who can't afford college and is regularly turned down for medium-wage service-sector jobs," and I bring it up because it's the single time I can recall seeing the verb *play* used to describe the way a rapper occupies a song's first person.

Kevin Young:

> We live in a culture where we expect to learn about the "lives" of the famous, to know people from screens as if they are more than just two-dimensional entertainments. In the case of hip-hop, we often have gone beyond the mask of, say, someone who raps as a persona (Ice Cube) with a name his momma did not give him who then "acts" as other characters (some of which once were admittedly close to the Ice Cube persona itself), using that same stage name. This, admittedly, may not prove fundamentally different from any stage name, but surely results in a form a bit more extreme and playful in its refractions of the real and represented. The mask puts on another mask, yet we expect to see a face.

Or maybe a better analogy than acting would be wrestling, which has gone from a spectacle of excess in Roland Barthes's assessment—mask upon mask—to what Jeremy Gordon calls "a

I sang on "Doowutchyalike," and if you missed it / I'm the one who said "Just grab him in the biscuits"

in Digital Underground, "The Humpty Dance" (1990)

151

stage-managed 'reality' in which scripted stories bleed freely into real events, with the blurry line between truth and untruth seeming to heighten, not lessen, the audience's addiction to the melodrama." Rap has heroes and heels, rivalry and redemption, vendetta and amity and bloodlust that all seem pretty realistic even when we have every reason to remember they're elaborately fabricated. Some rappers are even upfront about the influence of pro wrestling on their worldviews, from Kanye and Pusha T to Antwon and the Griselda crew to Quavo of the Migos: *I growed up looking up to wrestling / I found out it was fake and started hustling.*

in The Alchemist, "Jabroni" (2015)

Hustling is, handily enough, another word that straddles the concept of legality, most immediately connoting robbing or pimping or drug-dealing even though it also just means working hard. Our interest in the objective difference is "a lie we tell ourselves, especially when it comes to our entertainment," Hanif Abdurraqib writes in an essay called "Johnny Cash Never Shot a Man in Reno. Or, The Migos: Nice Kids from the Suburbs." "Violence sells, but mostly when it is a myth. Something invented and then expanded on by the person painting the picture."

So, as a rule, our lens when we examine the gap between character and human being is a bit blurry, and deep down that's probably a legit aesthetic preference. Who would want Qwel to rap *I'm not actually the motherfucking king like Oedipus, but imagine if I were?* First person is all the proof of authenticity we need, or rather all we *want*. It's hard not to be swayed by its narrative authority: think of how few great rap songs don't use it. Jean Grae's "Lovesong" and Eminem's "Lose Yourself," whose protagonist is the Eminem-based character Eminem plays in *8 Mile*, start in third person but downshift to first by the end of the song. Even prophetic parables like Grandmaster Flash & the Furious Five's "The Message" and 2Pac's "Brenda's Got a Baby" are framed by ancillary first-person narrators. (MF DOOM dips into third person all the time, but he's basically the Schrödinger's cat of rappers.) The covenant simply falls

I suggest you hand over the formula, doola / A villain in your land, in his land a ruler

MF DOOM, "?" (1999)

down if we can't suspend disbelief, if we have to endlessly evaluate the story's 1:1 relationship to the teller's lived experience. The whole thing about the American dream is that you can make your own identity, propagate your own myth, commit as deeply as you wish to the mask or masks you've chosen to wear. This isn't what people mean by *let a player play*, but imagine if it were.

I wish I got paid by rappin' to the nation, Ice Cube raps as the recent high school grad in "A Bird in the Hand." Circa 1991, factually speaking, this was exactly how Cube, who has an architectural drafting degree, got paid.

"It gives you something else to do, you know?" Cube's N.W.A bandmate Dr. Dre says of rap in the documentary *Rhyme & Reason*. "Everybody's not fortunate enough to be a doctor or a lawyer."

• •

One of the Miami rap impresario DJ Khaled's likably strident credos—and after his exemplary work as a casting director for John Woo movies in rap-album form, he's basically all strident credos—is *Don't ever play yourself*. Khaled, who when you think about it embodies the word *doge* in both the sixteenth- and twenty-first-century senses, in that he is both an influential figure in a port city and frequently enthusiastic bordering on inarticulacy, is using *play yourself* in the sense Jia Tolentino defines as "working against your conscious intentions": "It's what you do when you *think* you're serving your own interests but are actually betraying them—often through significant effort, often in a spectacularly public way." Meek Mill played himself when he tried to start a rap war with Drake and got so breezily destroyed by Drake's response that he didn't even try to have the last word. New York City pols in the seventies played themselves when they invested $20 million in a chemical wash to remove graffiti from subway cars that wound up not only damaging the trains but also causing health problems in transit workers and children who lived nearby. The lion plays himself when he believes the signifying

Rhyme sayer, and I'm here to lay a load / So watch a player when he's playin' in player mode
LL Cool J, "Eat Em Up L Chill" (1990)

Battlin' me is hazardous to health / So put a quarter in your ass, 'cause you played yourself
Big Daddy Kane, in Marley Marl, "The Symphony" (1988)

Niggas writing for you 'cause you know you never did shit
Meek Mill, "Wanna Know" (2015)

monkey's outlandish and baseless claims, then picks a losing fight with the elephant to preserve his wounded pride. Playing yourself is the penalty for not *getting it*. Sometimes you get hurt when you play yourself; sometimes other people do too.

But, again, wrestling. I personally spent the whole heavily covered non-starter of a feud between Drake and Meek Mill interested less in the outcome, such as it was, than in whether Aubrey Drake Graham and Robert Rihmeek Williams had any real animosity toward one another or were just letting their avatars clash for the spectacle of excess. Don't get me wrong, the spectacle was successful, especially as game to be sold. But how do you trust any public actor to act according to genuine, first-degree motivations when you're also pretty sure everything is a carefully orchestrated performance anyway? How do you not assume everyone is a convoluted apparatus of concentric selves, an onion skin of authentic interiority, each layer carefully calculating how the next one out should behave? A logician could spend twenty minutes diagramming the ways Drake occupies the word *I* when he quotes Lil Wayne asking us to stop asking him about his past, or the ways Kendrick Lamar, a platinum rapper playing a teenage version of himself aspiring to rap like a successful rapper, is and is not the *I* who has twenty-five lighters on the dresser. *I* is a nest of quotation and posture and ventriloquism, mask upon mask upon mask stacked as high as the incoming attention goes deep. *I* is like *tilapia*, like *lobsterhead*, like *like*. It means what it means in the moment.

I believe most people get, intellectually and intuitively, that it's possible for an *I* to represent, stand for, *signify* a self without corresponding directly and comprehensively to the person voicing it. On some level I think it's even desirable that the hustler on record *really* be a person who pays taxes and feeds his cat and feels strongly about the merits of certain pentameters, so long as he *seems* plausibly to live a life wholly indifferent to such things. That's how we enjoy the characters peopling the street operas rap stages for us, how we sidestep the squeamishness of possibly endorsing or bankrolling robbers and pimps and drug dealers. It's why we buy Wayne warning us not to pry into his past even though, as Robert Christgau pointed out in 2008, "the Reality Police know that his guns, cocaine, pimping, murdering, etc. are the formal play of a beat jacker who at 24 has spent half his life as a professional musician." It's why Rick Ross's career barely skipped a beat after he was exposed as a former corrections officer and not a lifelong druglord who used to pal around with Manuel Noriega.

It only gets complicated, I think, because of the story rap tells about its contempt for liars and biters and studio gangsters, about the cardinal sin of faking the funk. This too is a story we've agreed to pretend is real. *That's why when you talk that tough talk I don't feel you,* says Jay Electronica in "Exhibit C." *You sound real good and you play the part well / but the energy you giving off is so unfamiliar / I don't feel you.* (*We need something realer!* yells Just Blaze behind him.) That's why a man in a video strongly implying that he lives in a dank cellar and subsists on bugs and slime is allowed to spit *I heard your album and I don't believe a word of it.* That's why the climactic scene of *8 Mile* finds Eminem's character delivering the coup de grâce to his freestyle-battle nemesis by outing him as a kid who plays thug but went to a posh private school. *He ain't a gangster, his real name's Clarence!* says Jimmy, played by Eminem, whose real name is Marshall Mathers, which is another one of Eminem's alter-egos. We buy into the spectacle of excess's insistence on its own epistemological parsimony because what else are we supposed to do if we don't want to suck out all the fun? And that's when we get tempted, maybe, to take shortcuts, to stop keeping track of the aliases and heteronyms and overlapping fabulist identities, to buy into the fiction that it actually strains credibility to inhabit the role of a stone-cold lothario or a psychopathic murderer without on some deeper level actually being one. It gets complicated when we stop thinking of playing a character as the opposite of being yourself, and instead start thinking that *being* a character is the opposite of playing yourself.

(2009)

Nine, "Lyin' King" (1996)

Eminem, "8 Mile: B-Rabbit vs. Papa Doc" (2002)

TRUTH AND CONSEQUENCE

Calling her a crab is just a figure of speech
'Cause she's a apple, a pear, a plum and a peach

Kangol, in UTFO, "Roxanne, Roxanne" (1984)

• •

I SUBMIT TO you that there is no finer two-word poem in and about the English language than *answer song*. I mean no disrespect to fans of *Jesus wept*, a darker though equally compelling candidate.

For a minute in the eighties, a flock of answer songs led to the invention and sustenance through collective yes-anding of a young woman named Roxanne. Roxanne is, in the UTFO song that kicked it all off, a girl from around the way who has thus far managed, improbably enough, to resist Kangol's swagger *and* Doctor Ice's book smarts *and* EMD's rap. In 1985, I suspect, the dominant connotation of the word *rap* was still patter, smooth talk, *doing* talk: cajoling talk that gets you into someone's good graces and/or pants, or institutional talk—*bad rap*—laid on you against your will. It was *jive*, basically, with like 20 percent more sex. Legend has it that after UTFO's song made the rounds a fourteen-year-old from Queensbridge called Shanté took a break from doing her mother's laundry to record a rejoinder from the perspective of the

She'll take to my rap 'cause my rap's the best

"Roxanne, Roxanne"

156

impenetrably fly Roxanne, and one take later "Roxanne's Revenge" was ready to pave a path for future generations of catcall-proof lady rappers—

I met this dude with the name of a hat
I didn't even walk away, I didn't give him no rap

—and making a regional celebrity out of someone who did not, technically, exist.

In counter-response, UTFO hired a vocalist named Elease Jack to play the *real* Roxanne on a second answer song—both Jack and the song were billed as "The Real Roxanne"—which took its cues, and some of its lines, from Shanté's and UTFO's tracks. Later, due to label issues, Jack was replaced by *another* Real Roxanne. And at some point these rejoinders and bifurcations hit critical mass, giving way to what David Toop calls a "vinyl soap opera" in which the whole village turned into a chorus of observers, reporters, rumormongers: Roxanne's parents, her brothers, her sisters, her doctor, her younger self, the undertaker who declared her dead of too much rap. Word got around that she was in the right, she was in the wrong, she was really a man, she was real fat, she **died of too much rap.** Sting, so far as I know, said nothing.

She said, "How'd you know my name?" I said, "It's getting around / Right now baby you're the talk of the town"

"Roxanne, Roxanne"

I am the father of Roxanne / And rappin' on the mic is what I command

Tony Gigolo (& Lacey Lace) "The Parents of Roxanne" (1985)

Inevitably, there were squabbles and disputes about profanity and copyright and beat-biting—this was still the music industry—but you don't hear any of that when you listen back to the Roxanne Wars, as they've come to be known. I don't, at least. What I hear is the generosity and creative abandon of fiction being treated, in a movingly optimistic way, as a collective labor. There's no sinister edge to it, unlike the perniciously immersive fictions we engineer and then get trapped inside today; there's nothing the fiction *wants* from you. It's pure, big-hearted, fun. It's signifying for sport, a head-fake, a pantomime where you say *No no, I'm just kidding, she's not an actual crab* and then go right on kidding, keeping a straight face

Well let me tell you a story that's definitely true

Jalil, in Whodini, "I'm a Ho" (1986)

the whole time. ***She's a apple, a pear, a plum and a peach.*** It's play that plays with the suppleness of reality, the kind where you're allowed to use your imagination. It was obvious that Roxanne wasn't an actual person—to the point that there were multiple Roxannes and two of them were called the "Real" one—and everyone was cool with that.

But she had to not exist. Everyone had to know she didn't exist—or, to put it in a sunnier way, had to know they got to participate in creating her.

• •

On January 20, 1992, Ice Cube woke up peacefully, had a wholesome family breakfast, played some basketball, got laid, had a meaningful encounter with a blimp. Nobody he knew died. These plot points come from his 1992 song "It Was a Good Day"; the date comes from Donovan Strain, who in 2012 spent fifteen minutes—he was also watching *Space Jam* at the time—cross-referencing evidentiary factors on his iPhone (a day with no smog, a Lakers victory over the Supersonics) before arriving at the conclusion that see beginning of paragraph. He ruled out November 30, 1988, which checks all boxes except the availability of beepers for consumer purchase; I don't know the back story, but the uncredited use of Strain's deductive legwork in Rick Famuwiya's 2015 film *Dope*, when its protagonist is asked to defend the academic merits of his essay "November 30, 1988: A Research Thesis to Discover Ice Cube's Good Day," strikes me as a very Jay-Z kind of appropriation.

No barking from the dog, no smog / And Mama cooked a breakfast with no hog / I got my grub on, but didn't pig out / Finally got a call from a girl I wanna dig out

And everything is all right / I got a beep from Kim, and she can fuck all night

"It Was a Good Day"

"It doesn't make any sense at all," said Ice Cube in 2014, asked on a late-night show to comment on Strain's findings, "but it's cool."

• •

Outside of perennial intra-rapper squabbling, much of the confusion and trumped-up finger-pointing around rap's relationship to objective truth can be sourced to the deathless phrase *keeping it real*, which I don't recall hearing in an actual rap song since the turn of the century. Keeping it real means representing your own personal truth over and above the dictates of politeness and lawful conduct and adherence to mainstream values; extrapolated to an ethos, it suggests that rap is duty-bound to deliver unembellished and unflinching eyewitness accounts of underclass struggle and urban decay because it's less a form of art than a tentacle of black resistance to social pressures.

This isn't untrue, just distracting. *Keeping it real* is ambiguous as much because of the way it's been heard and internalized by ideological dogcatchers and dogged literalists alike as because of rap's innate technologies of polysemy. As becomes intuitive after you've listened to rap for more than a few minutes, *realness* has a hereditary bond but not a complete overlap with *reality*. Keeping it real doesn't mean being exhaustively autobiographically truthful; it means being good and noble and original and genuine and down for your people. It means being true not the way a fact is true but the way a friend or a lover is, even or maybe especially if that means lying on your behalf. It means being true the way a novel or a poem can be true, can *feel* real without *being* real. It means being rooted in and inspired by lived experience, your own or someone else's, but tightening or loosening or otherwise embellishing the details without sacrificing what made the experience resonant in the first place. It's a real-life dramatization that resembles what Kevin Young calls *the counterfeit*, a practice among black writers of "telling lies to get at a larger freedom—and truth." It embraces the Whitmanian ethic of contradiction in that, if the story isn't fully consistent with the objective historical record, very well. Reality is vast. Reality contains irreconcilable multitudes.

Take Eminem, whose fantasias of unabashed hatred and libidinous violence have made him a millionaire many times over. "The multiple and contradictory selfhoods he performs do not 'denature' a profound reality," Katja Lee writes, "because no profound reality

Dress it up and make it real for me / [mirthless chuckle] Whatever that fuckin' means

Future, "March Madness" (2015)

But even still you support me like a superstar / I sport my wedding band in honor of how real you are

Count Bass D, "Seven Years" (2002)

is present in the music." "My mom had a shotgun in the closet and I pretended it was mine in the rap," Eminem told Steve Stoute of his teenage fantasy of intervening after seeing a neighbor beating his girlfriend, which would eventually inform the domestic-abuse dramatization "Love the Way You Lie." "In the story," he explains, "I ended up shooting the dude to protect the girl and saved the day."

You hear qualifiers like "in the story" time and again when rappers break down the way they've taken a real experience and colored it in for dramatic effect. Schoolly D, on "Saturday Night" (*Forgot my key and had to ring the bell / My mama came down, she said, "Who the hell?" / "Wait, mama, wait, it's me, your little son!" / Before I* (1986) *knew it, my mom pulled a gun*):

My mom didn't have a gun, but it *felt* like she had a gun. She did catch me plenty of fuckin' times trying to sneak somebody in the crib, and she fucked up my room and kicked some ass. It's truth, just a bit exaggerated.

Slick Rick, on "Children's Story" (*He was only seventeen, in a madman's* (1988) *dream / The cops shot the kid, I still hear him scream*):

I saw that scene in real life, so I just put it on paper and added a little fiction to make it more interesting. I didn't see the people get shot, but I saw the people go to jail and ruin their whole lives.

Snoop Dogg, on his breakout single, "Deep Cover" (*"Hmm, let me think about it" / Turned my back and grabbed my gat / And guess what I told him* (1992) *before I shot it*):

I made it about me getting caught selling drugs to a undercover officer [...] but I put a little fiction on it.

Accounts like these use *fiction* like an ingredient, as though objective truth were a flavorless protein and narrative embellishment a spice,

160

seasoning for that majority of palates to which shooting an under-cover cop is dramatically tastier than being arrested by one. The argument that adding too much fiction profoundly alters the story is relevant only if the story is advertised as pure non-fiction; to paraphrase Lee, a pinch of paprika, even a cup of it, doesn't *denature* an omelet if nobody's claiming the omelet is scrupulously non-paprika.

If all of this sounds self-evident—and I certainly feel a little pedantic going on about it here—consider another term that took on outsize influence on rap around the same time as *keeping it real*. *Reality rap* was a crafty marketing hook dreamed up to accompany gangster rap's rise to national prominence and commercial gold, and it was preemptively defensive to an almost legalistic degree: the rappers most prone to violent storytelling were merely products of their environment, it said, ergo they couldn't be blamed for the rough material in their songs, which merely reflected their everyday lives. "We call ourselves underground street reporters," Ice Cube said while he was still in N.W.A: "We just tell it how we see it, nothing more, nothing less." This, like Humpty Dumpty's claim about selective word meaning (or for that matter like Humpty Hump's claims to personhood), isn't quite true: it's both more and less. N.W.A's *Straight Outta Compton* is neither straight reportage nor straight fabrication; it's a recognizable portrait of Los Angeles amidst the violence and racial tension of the late eighties, seasoned liberally with fiction. It's reality dressed up and made *real*.

The short-term victory of *reality rap* was that it provided a robust framework in which rap could be read as non-fiction and *keeping it real* as literal; the Faustian twist was that it worked so exceptionally well. If a single moment made *rap* indistinguishable from *gangster rap* in popular usage, it was this one. "The more that mainstream America got to know about rap through its pop hits," writes Toop, "the more convenient the genre became for shouldering the burden of urban collapse." ("The genre" means gangster rap, but I'm skeptical that the dogcatchers were all that

I like big butts and I cannot lie
Sir Mix-a-Lot, "Baby Got Back" (1992)

I live it, I see it, and I write it because I know it
Eazy-E, in N.W.A, "Niggaz 4 Life" (1991)

161

interested in distinguishing between N.W.A and Rakim.) Take the Body Count song "Cop Killer," a song written and narrated in fictive first-person by Ice-T, but that musically speaking contains no hip-hop content whatsoever: it was called "vile and dangerous" by Tipper Gore and boycotted by politicians and police unions, precipitating a furor over an "offensive rap record" the likes of which never happened to Bob Marley for claiming to have shot the sheriff, much less to Slayer or Pantera for their violent—and musically very similar—wet dreams. My point isn't that this hurt rap's market value in the long term, quite the opposite; my point is that Chuck D's oft-quoted remark describing rap as black America's CNN means two very different things depending on whether your lens is *reality* or *realness*.

The hysteria simmered down as the social unrest of the Rodney King riots faded into the flannel patchwork of the early nineties, but street rap's veneer of true-crime reportage didn't go away. The artistic and commercial imperatives hadn't changed. Reality rap remained in demand well into the next century, way more so than actual reality did. "If black ghetto street life were really being represented," writes Tricia Rose,

we'd hear far more rhymes about homelessness and the terrible intergenerational effect of drug addiction. There would be much more urban contemporary radio play of songs about fear and loss, and *real* talk about incarceration. [...] Where are the stories about women who work two and three jobs to keep their children fed while hundreds of thousands of black fathers languish in American prisons? Where are the outrage about white racism and the anger and frustration about police brutality, economic isolation, and unemployment that define too much of black ghetto life? Is this not keeping it real?

But just as getting locked up for selling drugs to a plainclothes cop is a less zesty narrative than murdering one, being disenfranchised by the ongoing wages of systemic racism is a less zesty narrative than terrorizing the streets with your posse of heartless and heavily armed thugs. So street rap kept conveying the kind of gritty storytelling that made N.W.A's underground poets into Calabasas millionaires, kept stoking what Stephen Lester Thompson calls "a fundamental confusion about whether hip-hop lyrics mean communicatively or narratively, whether they aim at genuine truth or merely as-if truth." And the ambiguity kept paying dividends. Rap got to have it both ways, to be both marketed as authentic and, as Imani Perry puts it, "sold for its gore like an action flick." (There's that *like* again.)

"If we understand rap simply as fact—as it would seem many Americans do—then it's no wonder that so many are scandalized by it," writes Adam Bradley.

> But if we treat it as fantasy, as entertainment, then its offensiveness becomes indistinguishable from that of other explicit material that those very same Americans who criticize rap seem to have a voracious appetite for consuming when it comes in the form of movies or television, books or graphic novels. Rap's difference from these other forms is not one of substance but of rhetoric, not of content but of packaging. That packaging is both the product of corporate media and the stuff of the artists themselves.

In this climate, absent any incentive on rap's part to change its strategies of presentation, how was the obscurely freaked-out literalist to distinguish N.W.A from Rakim when even Rakim was saying things like *How do I plead to homicide? Lyrics of fury!* and releasing songs with names like "Musical Massacre"? The Roxanne Wars were a sustained bait-and-switch game with objective reality; this was just plain baiting. "To provoke someone in power enough that they call for your music to be banned was rap's greatest trick, especially in the late eighties and early to mid-nineties, when the government was easiest to provoke into such responses," writes Hanif Abdurraqib. "It didn't take rappers long to realize that their

"Lyrics of Fury" (1988)

Bitch, I had a rose gold kit in '06 / Really it was '04 but '06 went with the flow
Payroll Giovanni, "Came Up Off Work" (2016)

particular brand of storytelling wasn't the type that could gain sympathy or understanding from white people in power, so why not play into the inevitable fear? When people in power who enforce and back violent policies pretend that the 'rawness' of rap makes its creators less human, there is no use in imagining much of a bridge."

That is, if there were going to be consumers and lawmakers no matter what who came to rap in search of violence and danger and anger and black hate—what Russell Potter calls "a titillating gift-box that ticks but does not explode"—then why not sell that image back to them at a profit rather than correct or apologize for it? Why not commit even further to the blurry line between murder as metaphor for rap and vice versa? *I use my rhymes like a Glock automatic*, says Guru. *My mind's my 9, my pen's my Mack-10*, says Biggie: *My target? All you wack niggas who started rappin'.* 2Pac, a few months before he died: *This ain't no freestyle battle, all you niggas gettin' killed.* It all looks pretty grim in retrospect, but I have to imagine it was more fun, while it lasted, than *I'm here to show and prove / Our favorite pastime is not robbing you.* I have to imagine there's something thrilling and cathartic in performing the power to sow fear and terror, even when you have no intention of using it. What else would make gifted young black men band together and call themselves gangs and mobs and clans?

As seductive as it is, though, like Roxanne, the threat has to not exist. Everyone has to know where to draw the line between realness and reality. "Pass it off as harmless fun and you miss its self-conscious use of form," Kevin Young writes about "An Ante-Bellum Sermon," a quietly subversive dialect poem by Paul Laurence Dunbar: "if you believe it is entirely truthful, or uncoded, you are by definition excluded from it: you are, in fact, the literalism the poem protests against."

"Rap is really funny, man," says Ice-T, "but if you don't see that it's funny, it will scare the shit out of you."

in Gang Starr, "Who's Gonna Take the Weight?" (1991)

in Junior M.A.F.I.A., "Player's Anthem" (1995)

"Hit 'Em Up" (1996)

Cut Master D.C., "Brooklyn's in the House" (1986)

If it's 'bout beef, I'll take your whole team to Arby's / Figuratively

A-Wax, "It's Nuthin'" (2015)

Even today, decades after the boycotts and FBI raids and mandatory parental advisory labels, to ask Ice-T or Ice Cube to tell stories from the point of view of a father rather than an oversexed urban superpredator, to ask Lil Wayne or Future to rhyme as professional musicians rather than extraterrestrial gangster pimps, is to ask them to choose reality over realness in a landscape where reality doesn't sell. Well, that's not quite it: rather, in a landscape where what sells *because* it's marketed as reality—this is as true now as it was in the nineties—has nothing of substance to do with what Lee calls "profound reality." Reality television has replaced reality rap, and twenty-first-century politics has underscored the degree to which instead of picketing or prosecuting reality TV stars we allow them to build empires on whatever toxic bullshit they have to shill. Meanwhile rappers go on telling it slant, narrating into existence a world as complex and malleable and messy as actual truth; meanwhile the will to litigate it, to pursue a clean binary between reality and fiction, lives on among the literalists and dogcatchers. I wish I could say the latter are only playing themselves in this, but the real story, so to speak, is somewhat darker.

CRIMINAL SLANG

*Key for Key, Pound for pound I'm the biggest Dope Dealer and I
serve all over town.*
*Rock 4 Rock Self 4 Self. Give me a key let me go to work more
Dollars than your average bussiness man.*

Derek Foster, *from* U.S. v. Foster, *939 F.2d 445 (1991)*

• •

THE WORDS ABOVE were written in a notebook found on Derek
Foster, along with a kilo of cocaine and ten gallons of liquid PCP,
when he was arrested at a train station in Chicago in 1989. The
ensuing trial, which ended in Foster's conviction for possession of
illegal drugs with intent to sell, was one of the first U.S. criminal
cases to admit rap lyrics as evidence. It wasn't the last. The practice
has only gained currency in the decades since; as scholars like Erik
Nielson and Charis Kubrin document, it's not uncommon now for
prosecutors to use raps written by defendants, or even more inci-
dental cues—such as selling rap CDs or appearing in rap videos—to
lobby for a "gang enhancement" to add time to felony prison sentences or demonstrate motive and lack of moral character.

The judge'll say life like it ain't someone's life

Now, sound unheard, I can see plenty of reasons to pass judgment on Foster based on his *Key for Key* rap, which is awkward

166

and trite, rhythmically stilted and prosodically misbegotten—but none of the reasons that come to mind is his *actually being a dope dealer*. These lines read to me more like the sauced freestyle mutterings of a junior i-banker on the Metro North home to Cos Cob than the confessional scribblings of an overzealous drug kingpin. Indeed, the lyrics weren't the smoking gun in Foster's conviction—the coke and PCP were plenty—but in the court's opinion they proved sufficient knowledge of the practice of narcotics trafficking to discredit his claim that he had been unaware he was transporting illegal drugs.

So far, tough but fair. Most courts are careful not to admit rap lyrics as evidence unless they're more probative than prejudicial—that is, if they lend support to arguments about motive or intent or knowledge with a "strong nexus" to the specific crime being charged. In the high-profile case of Acquille Pollard, rap name Bobby Shmurda, who was imprisoned in 2014 for murder and drug trafficking, his lyrics only corroborated information already obtained by wiretap. Still, *prejudicial* lies at the bottom of an awfully slippery slope. Sam Lefebvre, in a stomach-turning 2015 report for the *East Bay Express*, follows testimony from the trial of the Bay Area rapper Deandre Mitchell, rap name Laz Tha Boy, finding it "fraught with ahistorical statements masquerading as objective truth." Surveying the records of that case and rap's run-ins with the criminal justice system more broadly, Lefebvre turns up numerous instances of lyrics mistranscribed, quotations not recognized as such, and police officers, testifying as experts, supplying misguided or prejudicially skewed interpretations. ("Hooded sweatshirts are fairly common to wear if you're gonna commit a shooting," one officer testifies.) In over 150 pages of "expert testimony" in Mitchell's case, Lefebvre explains,

Mitch caught a body 'bout a week ago

I'm tryna stack cheese probably taller than the Eiffel / That's why I stay posted on the block like a light pole
Laz Tha Boy, "What U Do It Fo" (2010)

And feds buy mixtapes, yeah, I'm aware of that

there is no acknowledgment of the figurative language or poetic devices that Laz Tha Boy employs—which include neologism, hyperbole, parody, portmanteau, and allusion—presumably because the prosecution wished to avoid signaling to jurors that Mitchell deals in creative invention. Likewise, the inadequacy of semantically analyzing a lyrical form in which content and meaning hinges upon delivery and vocal style wasn't brought up, nor were Mitchell's array of past personas. Put simply, [prosecutor Satish] Jallepalli and [detective John] Lopez ignored the distinction between author and narrator that's extended to other genres and forms of expression.

In a paper called "Poetic (In)Justice?" law professor Andrea Dennis identifies three assumptions underpinning the admission of rap lyrics as evidence in criminal trials:

(1) interpreting and understanding rap music lyrics is not a subject requiring specialized knowledge;
(2) rap music lyrics should be literally understood; and
(3) rap music lyricists depict accurate, truthful, and self-referential narratives.

I've listened to enough rap to say with confidence that the second and third assumptions are false: that boasting about being the biggest dope dealer in town is pretty much meaningless, that nobody raps about being a low-level street hopper (at least not in the first person or the present tense), that spouting platitudes about living a certain kind of life does not a liver of that life make. I'm not bragging; this seems to me like common sense, albeit in a postmodern type of way. What I mean is that I don't believe literacy in rap's codes of misdirection and exaggeration should count as specialized knowledge. I don't believe understanding that Laz wasn't *actually* piling up wedges of gouda, or that Rakim didn't *actually* eat twenty-one people at once, should make me some kind of industry expert. I don't believe Foster's lyrics could have been admitted as prejudicial *or* probative without some consensus that a *dope dealer* was someone who sold drugs rather than art or used cars, though who's to say how things would have gone if he'd scribbled instead about selling tilapia all over town.

• •

In 2003, a Detroit sanitation worker named D'Angelo Bailey filed a defamation lawsuit against his former classmate Marshall Mathers over the song "Brain Damage," in which Mathers, as Eminem, recounts being bullied by Bailey and exacting his revenge with a makeshift weapon. Judge Deborah Servitto awarded in favor of Eminem, delivering her verdict in a sporting (if also prosodically misbegotten) rap:

> *The lyrics are stories no one would take as fact*
> *They're an exaggeration of a childish act*
> *Any reasonable person could clearly see*
> *That the lyrics could only be hyperbole*
> *It is therefore this Court's ultimate position*
> *That Eminem is entitled to summary disposition.*

Servitto is recognizing here that a *reasonable person* should be able to tell that a story in which Eminem is beaten by his mom until his brain falls out of his skull is probably not an unvarnished account of events as they actually transpired. A reasonable person could most likely be expected to assimilate the fact that Foster and Pollard and Mitchell had all written about the illegalities for which they were on trial and not rush to draconian conclusions about their real-life deeds. But signifying isn't about reasonableness. Popular culture, I would argue, is not about reasonableness. To expect and demand that rap not require the "specialized knowledge" of being able to distinguish hyperbole from confession, that its objective truth value be visible at all times, is to have either suspect motivations or impaired critical faculties. "If you think rap music is real," Jack Hamilton writes in *Slate*, "you shouldn't be listening to it, nor

He looked at me and said, "You gonna die, honky!" / The principal walked in and started helping him stomp me
(1999)

Everybody say they got bread / Racks stuffed inside the mattress / But you'd be the dumbest motherfucker ever born / If you sittin' around believin' that shit
Bun B, in Kodak Black, "Candy Paint" (2017)

should you be driving, voting, reading *Slate*, or doing much else besides enjoying the remainder of your time in elementary school."

Lefebvre notes rightly that this double standard afflicts rap disproportionately, even when you correct for the extent to which rap songs are disproportionately about breaking the law. Jay-Z—whose debut album is called *Reasonable Doubt*—dilates on this theme in *Decoded*:

Rappers, as a class, are not engaged in anything criminal. They're musicians. Some rappers and friends of rappers commit crimes. Some bus drivers commit crimes. Some accountants commit crimes. But there aren't task forces devoted to bus drivers or accountants. Bus drivers don't have to work under the preemptive suspicion of law enforcement. The difference is obvious, of course: Rappers are young black men telling stories that the police, among others, don't want to hear. Rappers tend to come from places where police are accustomed to treating everybody like a suspect. The general style of rappers is offensive to a lot of people. But being offensive is not a crime, at least not one that's on the books. The fact that law enforcement treats rap like organized crime tells you a lot about just how deeply rap offends some people—they'd love for rap *itself* to be a crime, but until they get that law passed, they come after us however they can.

Murder fanatic, killer fantastic / Swerving semi-conscious with half a blunt and an automatic / Bought it to snort it, just in case I meet with static / What I deliver to your address is dead tragic

"Monster" (2003)

Talkin' about you gangsta, drive your mama PT Cruiser / Run up on T-Bizzle, I'ma hit you with my Ruger

T-Bizzle, "PSK da Truth" (2010)

Killer Mike, the veteran Atlanta rapper who is simultaneously a vital voice of reason and no stranger to creative declarations of plausible menace, has spoken out in court testimony and newspaper editorials to a similar effect. "Anyone who is learned in law is capable of separating art and lyrics, whether you agree with them or not, and actual human behavior," he wrote in an amicus brief filed to the Supreme Court in support of Taylor Bell, a Mississippi high school senior suspended in 2010 for recording a rap that invoked violent acts against two coaches accused of sexually harassing students. "I think the courts understand it when it's Johnny Cash. I think they understand it when it's Robert Nesta Marley."

170

What strikes me in Mike's argument is the faith it puts in our Reasonable Person's ability to parse between edgy art and lawless anarchy; what strikes me about it is that it's precisely this benefit of the doubt that isn't extended in the other direction, precisely this trust and decency that go unreciprocated. Imani Perry points out in *Prophets of the Hood* that legal scrutiny of rap is often rationalized on behalf of impressionable listeners and viewers, who we *just can't be sure* won't read hyperbolic or parodic or allusive evocations of shitty behaviors as pure glorification. "Artists should have the right to represent their perception of today's society," radio exec Rick Cummings said in 1993 in response to a flap about the use of the words *bitch*, *ho*, and *nigga*. "However, we cannot be certain that the youngest part of our audience is capable of discerning between artistic interpretation and endorsement."

The outrageous irony, of course, is that it's the legal and commercial powers that be who can't seem to manage this discernment, who remain almost resolutely myopic in their literalism. The disclaimers that have begun preceding rap videos—"any props used in this video that show resemblance to any illegal material are merely props and should not be taken seriously," *e.g.*, or "the prop guns that were used in this film are fictional and do not have any connectivity in real life"— aren't there to edify that "youngest part of our audience." (Can you imagine that even *working*?) They're there to placate Tricia Rose's ideological dogcatchers, whose "ideology" appears to be rooted in what Jay-Z calls "the failure, or unwillingness, to treat rap like art, instead of acting like it's just a bunch of niggas reading out of their diaries."

I get that there are gray areas. I get that there really are impressionable listeners and viewers out there, that we have laws against threat and defamation for sound reasons. I won't deny that it can be hard to stomach the concentrated volatility of a grip of teenagers throwing gang signs at the camera and brandishing assault weapons whether they're props or not. But I don't think you insist on so systematically missing nuances that are factory-standard in so

We'll hang you from the neck just for calling me a name / Same guns from the video'll hit you broad day

Baby Smoove, "Freestyle" (2020)

It oughta be a crime just to feel
this good / Swear it oughta be a
crime just to be this hood

*Young Jeezy, "And Then What"
(2005)*

many other forms of expression unless you intend to criminalize the people who are overwhelmingly drawn to and identified with this one. As Killer Mike suggests, no reasonable person thinks Johnny Cash was confessing to a random pleasure homicide in Reno, nor Bob Marley to shooting Sheriff John Brown; no one takes metal bands to task anymore for piously glorifying gory death unless, in the case of Body Count and "Cop Killer," the lead singer happens to daylight as a rapper. It's hard not to see racism at work in the practice of using rap lyrics to seek a conviction the same way it's hard not to see racism at work in the war on drugs or in felony disenfranchisement and mandatory minimums or in redlining and price discrimination. It's hard not to see racism at work in the choice of what gets embraced as unflinching social commentary and what gets penalized because of its intimate, specialized knowledge of the troubled and troubling conditions of American life.

"There is a difference between hip hop and the nightly news," writes Perry, "and that is that hip hop is written by black men instead of white."

"The more public opinion, political leaders, and policymakers criminalize hip-hop as the cultural example of a criminal way of thinking," writes Rose, "the more imaginary black monsters will surface."

"Every instance of a legal authority using a rapper's creative output as proof of character or crime," writes Briana Younger, "whispers that the power of imagination doesn't belong to disenfranchised black and brown people."

• •

Often left out of retellings of the signifying monkey legend is the ass-beating the lion hands the monkey once he realizes he's been made to play himself. Here's Henry Louis Gates, Jr., again:

The Lion, though slow-witted enough to repeat his misreading through the eternity of discourse, realizes that his status has been deflated, not because of the Elephant's brutal self-defense, but because he fundamentally misunderstood the status of the Monkey's statements. As still another poem represents this moment of clarity:

> Said, "Monkey, I'm not kicking your ass for lyin',
> I'm kicking your hairy ass for *signifyin'*.

Out of all the social inequity and selective enforcement and predatory scrutiny that Kubrin and Nielson and Dennis and others have inventoried, this is the thought that scares me most: that deep down our criminal justice system and the institutions intertwined with it have it out for rappers not for any real wrongdoing, not for any consistent "strong nexus" to verifiable acts of crime, but for making it tricky to tell the difference between one thing and another. Between word and deed, art and reality, criminal slang and criminal activity. That this is white America punishing someone else for our own confusion and fear. A reasonable person might be frightened by lyrical vérité about drugs and murder and the whole gamut of unruly livelihoods native to rap mythology, but fear makes us less reasonable, not more. When it wins, it edges out empathy, and fairness, and the ability to recognize and admit when we're wrong, when we're uncertain, when we're afraid.

The monkey starts his shit with the lion not only because he's annoyed by all the roaring and ass-kicking, but also because he's bored. Signifying originates, David Toop says, in "situations of enforced boredom, whether prison, armed service or streetcorner life." The cycle, that is, begins elsewhere. Where it ends I have no idea. Gates warns that to equate the monkey with black America and the lion with its historical oppressors is to ignore the essential presence of the elephant—the figure who finally restores a dark kind of moral equilibrium to the jungle, who delivers the lion's comeuppance for all his misdirected rage. But I don't know who the elephant is in this version of the story. I don't know whose memory is long enough to fill that role.

SELLING WORK

The dope I'm selling you don't smoke you feel

Ice-T, "I'm Your Pusher" (1988)

• •

NOT ALL RAPPERS commit crimes, obviously, but sure, some do. Like Jay-Z says, some bus drivers and accountants commit crimes too. Some librarians are Proud Boys. We still have laws because some percentage of people in the world are at any given moment engaged in breaking them; the thing is that among people in the world the presumption of breaking the law, and the opportunities to get paid by telling stories about it, are very unevenly distributed.

Rap tells vivid stories about and/or gestures obliquely at a whole range of antisocial malfeasances, from tagging walls and driving drunk to pimping and racketeering to carjacking and homicide. There's a whole scene mushrooming up as I write this in which kids from Detroit rap breathlessly and with no particular finesse about elaborate online gift-card scams. Hip-hop is a folk art; folks are wild. But at bottom, and for as long as I've been paying attention, the default rap hustle, the suite of infractions that carries the most weight, pun not really intended, is the drug trade. Slinging dope, serving fiends, making butter fly. Fishscale aquaculture and all that.

When you go hit the bitcoin you can't be petty, bro / Put your money in but can't be nothing under a hundred, though

Teejayx6, "Swipe Lesson 1" (2019)

174

Rappers rap about selling drugs so much at least in part because a lot of them—a lot of the most talented ones, at that—actually did it, or do it, in real life. Biggie dealt, Jay dealt, Pusha, 50, Snoop, most of Wu-Tang. Ice-T dealt for a while, among other things—word is he robbed some banks too—before he decided to start rapping as a kind of existential money-laundering maneuver. "Hustlers and players, they want flashy shit," he writes in his foreword to Shea Serrano's *Rap Year Book*. "That's all a hustler'll think about. He wants girls, he wants jewelry, he wants cars. I did, too. And I was getting it on the street. But when I saw a lane where I could have all that and not go to jail, it was like, 'Aw, yeah, that's what I wanna do.'"

He takes pains to blur the distinction on "I'm Your Pusher," from his 1988 album *Power*, a song partly framed as an exchange between a smooth-talking dealer and a sniveling fiend, both played by Ice-T. There's a whole venerable micro-category of songs where rappers appear as their own uncredited guests—Jay-Z as a patronizing highway patrolman pulling over Jay-Z in "99 Problems," Eminem as a fan scribbling out increasingly obsessive letters to Eminem in "Stan," a nasal-voiced Biggie getting out of jail and going on a robbing spree with a regular-voiced Biggie in "Gimme the Loot"—but "Pusher" sits on a plane of its own, and that's partly because of how authentically Ice-T straddles and complicates the moral divide between rapper and hustler. *You know where I can get a ki?* asks the fiend. *I know where you can get a LP*, the dealer replies coolly. They wheedle each other for a while, in the intro and then between verses, the dealer exhorting the fiend to clean up his life and elevate his mind while still upselling him on his potentest product. The fiend accepts almost everything on offer with panting enthusiasm but turns his nose up at LL Cool J. By the end of the video, he's a swaggering player himself, posted up at the club flanked by babes, draped in gaudy chains. He is, alas, played by a different actor.

I was four, but I have to imagine that this kind of sustained ambiguity was novel at the time. In my imagined version of rap

I do this in my sleep / I sold kilos of coke / I'm guessing I can sell CDs

Jay-Z, in Kanye West, "Diamonds from Sierra Leone (Remix)" (2005)

A ki of coke is a pie

Big L, "Ebonics (Criminal Slang)" (2001)

prior to this period, an MC copping to doing *devious things* was still talking about basically standard mischief, not wholesome but not horrifying either—*We usually take all niggas' garments*—and not hardcore narcotraficante shit. Rap was addictive, sure, but to its practitioners, not its clientele. *I fiend for a microphone like heroin,* said Rakim the same year "Pusher" came out: *Soon as the bass kicks, I need a fix.* The drug dealer wasn't yet a real three-dimensional figure in hiphop's narrative universe, wasn't part of what Tricia Rose calls the "gangster-pimp-ho" trinity; hustlers showed up in stories of life on the streets, but without much in the way of first-person interiority. And then here was this song that "[glamorized] hiphop's outlaw status among the young and criminal-minded," as Greg Tate put it, "pushing 'dope beats and rhymes' *and* 'just say no.'" Here was Ice-T with an allegedly anti-drug anthem whose conceit—that great rap music is the only dope you need—could have made the rap game sound depressingly like the dead-end crack trade but instead made it sound freaking *great* to be a drug dealer. *I'll be the biggest dope dealer in history / 'cause all the fly'll be high off that Ice-T,* he says at one point, a couplet I can't help but think could have taught Derek Foster so much.

Vocational similarities thus posited, the next generation of more or less reformed hustlers with rhyme skills set about making the commonalities into a commonplace. *Sometimes the rap game reminds* *me of the crack game,* says Nas. *If I wasn't in the rap game, I'd probably* *have a ki, knee-deep in the crack game,* says Biggie. (Oddly, "crack game" is defined in the Stavsky–Mozeson *A 2 Z* glossary as "a car insurance fraud.") *I'm serving, my rhymes like nickels and dimes,* says Snoop Dogg. Just in case you needed a finer point put on it, Jay-Z's "Rap Game/Crack Game" is two and a half minutes spent annotating the perils and best practices of both trades, from the value of ground-up promotion to the benefits of a flexible distribution apparatus. It samples that Nas line above, as well as Outkast: *See* *that rap shit is really just like selling smoke.* Let's say, approximatively, that by the turn of the century the comparison was so internalized in street rap and beyond as to be table stakes. Even Kanye, whose narrative interest in drugs is strictly recreational, couldn't resist the chance to belabor the metaphor:

> *Cook it, cut it, measure it, bag it, sell it*
> *The fiends cop it, nowadays they can't tell if*
> *That's that good shit—we ain't sure, man*
> *Put that CD on your tongue, yeah, that's pure, man*

(2005)

(That song, "Crack Music," also features hard-nosed Compton rapper and definite ex-dealer The Game, though inexplicably only on the hook. Let me also pause here to assure those readers who have never used a compact disc that there is ordinarily no licking involved.)

Belabored or not, it's a metaphor that works, tirelessly, from the abstract level down, as granular as you feel like going. Yes, rap is a product to be sold at volume. Yes, it's a controlled substance made by putting one volatile verbal element next to another, a potent synthesis cooked up in the lab. Yes, it's an intoxicating concoction that practically peddles itself to an enraptured public, which if you're uncharitably inclined you can interpret as evidence of profound civic decay. Yes, it's dope, it's crack, it's piff. Like *picking cotton*, the potential meanings resonate on two separate wavelengths that turn out to be less estranged than we might have hoped; like "I'm Your Pusher," it's wholly possible for the two readings to be reconciled and incarnated within a single character. Possible, that is, but still ambiguous. Whether they're really criminals or not, it's in rappers' best interest for us to believe they plausibly *could* be, without knowing for sure either way.

But how and why this is true, so far as I can tell, has shifted seismically. I suspect it was a genuinely useful tactic for hiding in plain sight circa "I'm Your Pusher," that there was substance to the

The studio is the lab
"Ebonics (Criminal Slang)"

White folks say it controls your brain
dead prez, "Hip Hop" (2000)

Patty cake, patty cake, I'm the baker's man / I bake them cakes as fast as I can / And you can tell by how my bread stack up / Then disguise it as work so the Feds back up
Malice, in Clipse, "Grindin'" (2002)

Naw, I'm not a dealer, I'm a poet at large

Black Thought, in the Roots, "Stay Cool" (2004)

in Diplomats, "Dipset Anthem" (2003)

(2015)

(2014)

way it allowed ex- or current hustlers like Ice-T to represent their real lives without the hassle of having that representation read as testimony. I figure there was a good decade or so after that when it was a way for drug aficionados of all stripes, dealers and casual users alike, to tweak the occasional dogcatcher convinced rap was as dangerous as drugs but mostly just have fun signifying on the fly cliché that was the comparison. *This on my wrist is nothing / Yeah, it's just yellow hearts and pink diamonds*, says Cam'ron, the guy who came up with the riddle about coke and the caterpillar. *Where I get the money for this? Don't think rhyming.*

And since then, even as rap lyrics started making their way into legal evidence, this rap-as-metaphor-for-drugs-as-metaphor-for-rap prevarication has become fair game for any frisky indoor kid who can be bothered to rhapsodize about finessing plugs and slinging pies with the calculated vagueness of Drake cooing about catching bodies. (Consider the sublime calling-her-a-crab tricksterism of the shot in the "Trap Queen" video, synced to the moment when Fetty Wap yowls *I be in the kitchen cooking pies with my baby*, where a young woman gingerly takes a literal pie out of the oven.) "I live in Atlanta," shrugs the hip-hop crooner iLoveMakonnen in an interview where he's been asked to break down his song "I Don't Sell Molly No More," revealing a little sheepishly that the line *I got the gas and the coke* refers to actual gasoline and actual Coca-Cola. "We got Dasani water, all that."

Is this... *moral?* Is it better to co-opt the vernacular of a fundamentally wholesome language art as a way to keep hustling without going to jail, or to pretend to have sold drugs simply because that's the done thing? Is it wrong to compare the two, legitimate drug trafficking against unauthorized beverage resale, in terms of authenticity? Where we've arrived, I think, is that aside from some imaginative fabulists and some ambitious prosecutors, no one really cares very much. Audiences clamor for trap houses and triple beams, not thesauruses and breath control, no matter which one more closely resembles their own lived realities. The rap–drugs proxy is so ingrained, so spacious—and hip-hop vernacular so proficient at making any old word sound like oblique underworld slang—that the literal legal truth just no longer seems to hold any sway. Dope *is* dope. Butter *is* fly. Rap—by its own volition or by cultural happenstance, as wicked mastermind or as unsuspecting vehicle—went and made selling drugs cool.

• •

Like any other tradition so deeply invested in the creation and husbandry of cool, rap requires the appearance of effortlessness, of utter sui-generis self-evidence, to truly function. "An audience listens to rap to be entertained, not to be impressed with the formal sophistication at work," writes Adam Bradley. "The purpose of sophisticated poetics is not to call attention to itself, but to absorb itself so fully within the art that it is invisible to the naked eye—or ear." Ease, or the illusion of it, testifies to that magical facility, that extraterrestrial other-other nextness so sought after by artist and consumer alike. *It must not sweat,* Toni Morrison said in 1981, speaking of good writing in terms that could just as well describe a kind of ecstatic intoxication:

Roll the Ls tight, keep the rhymes light / Yo, I just made this motherfucker up last night

Angie Martinez, in Lil' Kim, "Not Tonight (Ladies Night Remix)" (1997)

As you doin' the dance you might hurt your back / Just look at the crowd, say "I meant to do that"

Joeski Love, "Pee-Wee's Dance" (1986)

> The language, only the language. The language must be careful and must appear effortless. It must not sweat. It must suggest and be provocative at the same time. It is the thing that black people love so much—the saying of words, holding them on the tongue, experimenting with them, playing with them. It's a love, a passion. Its function is like a preacher's: to make you stand up out of your seat, make you lose yourself and hear yourself.

I'm still speculating here, but back then I bet cool in rap looked pretty different—looked like Wonder Mike humbly promising to **try to move your feet**, like Run-DMC tempering their hyperbolic braggadocio with comically reasonable flexes like **Nothing too deep**

"Rock Box" (1984)

and nothing too dense / And all our rhymes make a lot of sense. Sugarhill Gang and Run-DMC weren't rapping about selling drugs; they were rapping about rapping, which was still subversive and new enough to be the same thing as rapping about cool. The crack epidemic was still a few years off. Rap wasn't code for drugs, and drugs certainly weren't code for rap; if the word *rap* meant anything besides itself, it meant sex. But it didn't have to mean anything besides itself, is my point. It was novel, next, magical and other-other even to the people making it. Nonchalance—what Kevin Young calls letting the song sing you—was in no danger of being misinterpreted as a lack of mastery. *He gets better 'cause he knows he hasta,* Run-DMC declaimed about their DJ, Jam Master Jay. *Only practice makes a real*

"Jam Master Jay" (1984)

Jam Master.

Facile as it is to map my own listening trajectory onto the whole history of rap, I think a lot about how my own travels, from Jurassic 5's concrete schoolyard inward to Jeezy's brutalist trap house, ended up a little scale model of the genre's own fatal attraction to crime and misdemeanor. First came run-ins with the law for writing graffiti and puffing on blunts, then came stick-up kids wanted for snatching chains and selling coke, then came kingpins dodging federal indictment while ordering hits and architecting illicit empires. I came of age more or less as this alchemy was taking root, as it was becoming a marketable truism not only that the rap game was awfully similar to the crack game but also that, to the listener slavering for realness, there was no *real* difference.

Sharp with the needles, found no IVs for the feeble / Y'all fiending for the sequel and the beat's not even EQ'd

staHHr, in King Geedorah, "Next Levels" (2003)

One consequence of which for street rap, say what else you will about its sociopolitical implications, was the dematerialization of that sense of potency and prowess and mastery, its creeping abstraction into a version of cool whose stakes are purely economic, unsentimental, coldly transacted rather than lovingly cultivated. Game to be sold, not to be told; product dealt but not grown. Even as a mythical pusher, Ice-T admitted that the hustle was work: *I don't play when it comes to my dope,* he says, *I check my lyrics close, like*

with a microscope. But eventually *work* stopped working that way. Cool stopped being effortless effort; cool became a new high, less organic and more efficient, brought in from elsewhere at someone else's expense and peril. Its potency is ruthless, steely, vacant, so committed to not sweating that it's forever draped in icy chains and dirty money. It must be *cold*. And I wish, or feel I should wish, that this made me like it less.

I see she wearing them jeans that show her butt crack / My girls can't wear that / (Why?) That's where my stash at

Lil Wayne, "Fireman" (2005)

ON VALUES

I'm out here making sense 'cause I'm out here making dollars

Project Pat, in Three 6 Mafia, *"Poppin' My Collar (Remix)" (2006)*

• •

CANDIDLY, THIS FLY cliché does nothing for me. I would retire it from rap if I could. Like, we get it: one is perforce making *sense* if one is making dollars, because a dollar is made up of a hundred *cents*. And a door is not a door when it's *ajar*. I know that by my own argument it's only a matter of time before someone renews and redeems this trope, breathes into it the kind of life Jay-Z did when he said, of an ex-friend whose baby mama he's just kidnapped, **About his whereabouts I wasn't convinced: I kept feed-**

"D'Evils" (1996) **ing her money 'til her shit started to make sense.** Nor am I oblivious to the vaguely Five Percenter felicity of the mere fact the homophone works for American English—*If it don't make rubles then it don't make kopeks* doesn't have the same ring—but still, but still. It's played out and tired, a dad joke wrung dry by decades of overuse and underthought. It sounds, no pun, spent.

All the same, it's a fascinating thought when you dissect it morally, especially when it's as stark as Project Pat's causal reductio here: that money is proof of sense, of logic, of credibility. It's a pragmatic cliché, certainly, and also a particularly sad one. Ends, not means. It's a telling example of how rap prizes and scorns money at once, how it valorizes and trivializes it, covets it absolutely but condemns it absolutely too. Money is not to be saved or invested but to be dispersed explosively and with a flair closely resembling contempt: blow a bag, drop some stacks, fuck up some commas, make it rain dead presidents over a strip-club stage floor. It is at once the realest thing in rap's narrative universe—its oxygen—and something suspiciously unreal. It's a compact, a handshake, a promissory note, a story about value agreed upon by some people behind closed doors and sold aggressively to everyone else. It is the master's tools. Fuck-you money; fuck you, money.

I find these revaluations of value, as it were, contagious. Why should it be more honorable, more boastworthy, to be rich from selling drugs than to be rich from writing and recording rhymes, even rhymes *about* selling drugs? What does it mean for an audience to keep faithfully spending money on rhymes about making money by selling drugs? Is selling drugs always wrong just because it's against the law? Should laws be obeyed even when they mostly benefit the people who made them? If you break the law does that make you evil? If you uphold it does that make you good? If you do evil deeds to get rich but then buy your mother a house, what's the moral sum total of your actions? As Clipse ask, **Is dirty money really that bad?** What would clean money even look like? If dirty money is real and clean money is frivolous or devilish or better left undiscussed, what even *is* money anyway? What is its purpose if not to perpetuate itself? What good is a promissory note of worth appreciated over time to someone who's **out here** hustling, whose retirement fund is a gold chain or a shoebox stashed under a floorboard?

I *trust* rap for the unapologetic way it espouses and exposes me to values I find unintuitive and sometimes alien, outlooks on life and liberty that are terrifying and also persuasive, troublingly

Fuck your twenty-eight Grammys, I want twenty-eight grams, nigga
Cuz Lightyear, "Pots N Pans" (2017)

Thank the lord I got blessed with some trap money / But the devil got me working for that rap money
Jeezy, in Kodak Black, "Feeling Like" (2017)

Pusha T, in "Dirty Money" (2006)

All my life I hustle just to get that moolah / And stack my change up and go see the jeweler
Young Greatness, "Moolah" (2016)

As a child, hip-hop made me read books / And hip-hop made me want to be a crook

Slug, in Atmosphere, "Party for the Fight to Write" (2001)

As long as I'm alive I'ma live illegal

Havoc, in Mobb Deep, "Shook Ones Part II" (1995)

I don't tell my homies be safe / I tell 'em stay dangerous

Jay 305, "Stay Dangerous" (2017)

All this blood and I don't feel a thing

Styles P, "Think Lox" (2016)

alluring just inside the bounds of the rhetorical. I like the way it confronts me with propositions whose verbal expression captivates me even as their moral content challenges or contradicts what I've always assumed I believed. What does it mean if I'm suddenly willing to entertain the possibility that saying something awful in a particularly fly way is not only worthy of fascination but also maybe excusable? Yeah, rap regularly makes me think, there's a bigger picture here. There are more sides to the story of value and propriety. Maybe I'd sell drugs too if I had to. Maybe I'd rob banks. I don't understand how someone *could just kill a man*, but maybe I want to. Maybe what rap's critics fear is antisocial imitation is really a kind of abstracted, vicarious, even involuntary empathy.

And then where does abstract empathy tip over into desensitization? I can stomach things now in rap that I couldn't have ten or twenty years ago, and more and more I can stomach them outside of rap too. I can listen without flinching, at least not much, to stories about violence and debasement and hopelessness and exploitation, to an American kind of rage that's not so much hatred as cruelty for lack of any compelling alternatives. Is that growth or regression?

• •

Hell Hath No Fury, the second of two absolutely bulletproof Clipse albums, gets at this with a rare candor. True to the crack-rap genre, it's mostly made up of unabashed encomia to drug trafficking and money laundering with the sporadic side of murder, told in immaculately crafted and magnetically delivered coils of high-level wordplay. (It may also be the coolest-*sounding* album I've ever heard, in the sense of cold, of ruthless and steely and vacant.) But unlike so much of the genre it's washed in this beguiling, riveting darkness, its vanity and pride and shoptalk laced with a palpable sense of how empty life can be when dollars are the primary guarantors of existential sense. It's straight-up depression masquerading as machismo, as Joan Morgan puts it. It gets under my skin not

Cook money clean through Merrill Lynch / Accountant just gasp at the smell of it

Pusha T, in "Keys Open Doors" (2006)

Still I creep low, thinking niggas tryna harm me / Hoping my karma ain't coming back here to haunt me

Pusha T, in "Nightmares" (2006)

184

because it sounds like a cry for help, not because it's any more socio-logically damning than the next crack-rap cri de cœur, but because what if the dizzying nihilism, the sanguinity about so much violence and loveless luxury, is inextricable from the joyous wellspring of descriptive invention? What if the ruthless dollar-mad paper chase is a non-trivial part of *why* it feels so meaningful? What does it mean if language can be used in divine ways for devilish purposes?

I don't have blind faith in many things, but I have blind faith in language. I want to believe it's good. I *do* believe it's good. I believe it connects us to each other and to ourselves, that it makes art and science possible and accessible and is itself an endlessly rewarding species of both. Maybe that keeps me from truly seeing the picture an album like *Hell Hath No Fury* is painting, makes me experience its eloquent tales of sordid industry as invigorating instead of terribly discouraging. If that's true, I can't tell where it leaves me morally. I've heard myself describe the beat from "Ride Around Shining" with fathomless approbation as *evil*. Here is something so good at talking about being bad that I struggle to believe anything about it could actually be *bad*, and that's… not not frightening to me. Because what could misdirect me like this, what could so flatter my analytical faculties and so numb my moral ones, if not language itself?

It's a horrible lesson indeed, as Jay Electronica says, *but has to be learned*. That language, sublime as it can be, is not values, is not righteousness, is not truth. That there are people, not just personas but *people*, who are ignorant and immoral and inhuman and who use language the way I imagine angels would, if angels were inter-esting. That language is pure but we are not, magical because we are not, omnipotent so we don't have to be. A reasonable person may be vulnerable to seduction and sinister persuasion by guile and beauty, but guile and beauty have no morality of their own. Beauty may be truth, but truth can still be ugly. It can still hurt, maybe even for no reason. The how does not cancel the what. Words are holy but do not confer holiness: only sense.

185

ON THE B-WORD

Who you callin' a bitch?

Queen Latifah, "U.N.I.T.Y." (1993)

• •

LIKE PUNK ROCK, street rap retails with an implicit no-tomorrow worldview. "Where the Sex Pistols chanted 'no future,'" writes Kevin Young, "gangsta rap said there wasn't even a present." Is this part of my readiness to forgive rap its lapses into the conceited and grim? Quite possibly. Life *is* a bitch and then you *do* die.

Nonetheless, time makes fools of us all—punks in particular—and it's oddly refreshing to watch entertainers' lived realities peel away from their characters, their youthful edge dulled by maturity and money. *Teenage angst has paid off well*, per Kurt Cobain's first words on Nirvana's last album: *now I'm bored and old.* 50 Cent reportedly made $8 million inadvertently by accepting payment for one of his albums in bitcoin, a report he later denied while filing for bankruptcy. Snoop Dogg kicked his weed habit for two years—imagine anyone else trying to sell his deadpan "it kicked me back" afterwards—then a while later converted to Rastafarianism, changed his name to Snoop Lion, and co-founded a cannabis-oriented VC firm. Jay-Z, net worth in the high nine digits, started rapping about credit and investment. DJ

I bought some artwork for one million / Two years later that shit worth two million / Few years later that shit worth eight million / I can't wait to give this shit to my children

Jay Z, "The Story of O.J." (2017)

186

DMD rerecorded "25 Lighters" as "25 Bibles." Run from Run-DMC became a Pentecostal minister and starred in a reality television show for a time; reality TV's bottomless chum bucket also claimed Flavor Flav, Salt-n-Pepa, 50 Cent, Snoop Dogg, and Ice-T. Ices T and Cube have both played detectives in film and on television. "That's acting," said Cube when the *New York Times* asked whether he thought that was ironic given that he had once made a song called "Fuck the Police." "It would be ironic if I was a real cop."

One fly cliché to emerge from all of this is a cautionary moral about the pressures of parenting when you're still a hellion at heart. **The coolest playas and foulest heartbreakers in the world**, says Nas in a song partially about his daughter's Instagram photo of a box of condoms on her dresser, **God gets us back: he makes us have precious little girls.** Kanye West, who has three kids and a family of sisters-in-law molecularly composed of reality television, wrote a queasy introspection in 2018 about his daughters called "Violent Crimes"—**Curves under your dress, I know it's pervs all on the net**—but anticipated the turn as early as 2005:

I got twenty-five lighters on the dresser, yessir

"Daughters" (2012)

> **Feelin' better than some head on a Sunday afternoon**
> **Better than a chick that say yes too soon**
> **Until you have a daughter, that's what I call karma**
> **And you pray to God she don't grow breasts too soon**

"We Major"

Which oversized limerick is a little marvel of narrative economy, in that it actually ages itself while you listen: as it broods fatalistically about growing up, you see its diction mature, from *head* to *chick* to *daughter* and finally to *breasts*—likely not the word the narrator of three lines earlier would have chosen. There you are enjoying the indolent pleasures of young lust, and ten seconds later you're less concerned with getting off than with showing up at church just to vouchsafe your precious daughter's innocence for a little while longer. *Karma.*

187

I don't have kids, nor have I ever been accused of being a cool player or a foul heartbreaker, but this is not wholly academic to me. I don't deal drugs to get by or for fun, and I don't spend fuck-you money on cars or watches, and I don't have run-ins with the police because of what I look like. But I do have people in my life whom I love and care about and very sincerely want to thrive unmolested by the world's many cruelties, and I don't know how to reconcile that with how much time I spend immersed, happily, in a vernacular tradition that's so reflexively, breezily hostile to them. One where Biggie names a heartfelt tale of romantic devotion and loss "Me and My Bitch"; one where Fetty Wap's partnership anthem "Trap Queen," which Hanif Abdurraqib astutely calls an Ultimate American Love Song, concludes with a tossed-off threat to break into my house and fuck my ho. One where women and queer people are so often present as ornaments at best, faceless scorn-receptacles at worst, stripped of identity and individuality and lumped in with an undifferentiated mass of golddiggers and fairies and skanks. I don't call people those names, but I love a lot of songs that do. I've reproduced parts of some of them in this book. So there's that gap again between the values I think I hold and music that openly, gleefully flouts them. *You know I spell girl with a B*, says Ice Cube.

"I have to wonder if there isn't something inherently unfeminist in supporting a music that repeatedly reduces me to tits and ass and encourages pimping on the regular," writes Joan Morgan in *When Chickenheads Come Home to Roost*. "Perhaps the non-believers were right, maybe what I'd been mistaking for love and commitment for the last twenty years was really nothing but a self-destructive obsession that made a mockery of my feminism."

• •

Here's a broad-strokes summary of women's trajectory through rap. I won't pretend to be able to do the story justice; Morgan's *Chickenheads* is a superb first-person reckoning, and Gwendolyn

We just set a goal, talkin' matching Lambos

(2015)

I asked her her name, she said blah blah blah / She had 9/10 pants and a very big bra

Biz Markie, "Just a Friend" (1989)

in N.W.A, "I Ain't tha 1" (1988)

Pough's *Check It While I Wreck It* and Kathy Iandoli's *God Save the Queens* do valuable work respectively theorizing and historicizing the progress female MCs have made, and the obstacles they've encountered, in the record industry and the broader public discourse. I also love Chinaka Hodge's *Dated Emcees*, which muses on love and devotion under the influence of hip-hop's ingrained male chauvinism, and Ashon T. Crawley's *The Lonely Letters*, a close-reading of sexuality more broadly within black musical culture.

But for the sake of argument, I'll describe the journey inward from the margins for everyone besides straight cis male rappers as a slow process of either overcoming objectification—reduction to appendages, accessories, sexually essentialized vessels of fantasy about dominion or possession or repugnance—or leaning into it hard enough to come out, as it were, the other side. Beginning with Sha Rock—the first lady MC to appear on record, rhyming with her group, the Funky 4+1, on whose songs she sometimes calls herself "the Plus One More"—the struggle's basic object was to be validated as a person, to be recognized as having agency and interiority, desires and joys and pains. We geek out about "Roxanne's Revenge" today not only for the matter-of-fact way it shatters the fourth wall, but also because it showed us a woman responding to men who were talking locker-room shit about a woman as though she didn't exist—because in point of fact she didn't—and standing up to say a real person was listening, had some opinions and a voice and could smoke a microphone too.

After that era the field largely split into sex kittens and Nubian goddesses, to use a distillation proposed by the New Jersey badass Rah Digga, plus some outlying G-funk femmes fatales and shouty militants and girl groups, though vanishingly few. For the most part the industry preferred adjustably raunchy young ladies who would pair off and spar, sometimes bitterly, sometimes as proxies for their male labelmates or bosses, for the same artificially tiny spot in the

Me, the Rox, give up the box? / So you can brag about it for the next six blocks? / Where's the beef? You guys can't deal it / I need a man who can make me feel it

The Real Roxanne, in UTFO, "The Real Roxanne" (1984)

center of attention, as though audiences would only assimilate or stand for one rap diva at a time. Iandoli wraps it up as follows:

Really, though, what is it like to be a female rapper? To be told you're not pretty enough or sexy enough, then too sexy to the point of slutty? If your lyrics are too hard, you're trying to be a man (and maybe you're even gay), which depletes your selling power in a market that wants femininity. If your looks are too light, then you're pandering to the mainstream and out to kill the last pure drops of hip-hop left. Do you band together and love each other, or do you disband and wage a war?

Spoiler: to date, more disbanding than banding. Hence MC Lyte trading barbs with Antoinette, Lil' Kim squabbling with Foxy Brown, Nicki Minaj throwing shade at Cardi B and Cardi throwing a shoe at Nicki. This is the same adversarial energy rappers have always leveraged for attention, except there just weren't many alternative lanes for ladies to take. "Back then that's how you got your foot in the door as a female, challenging somebody," Salt recalls in the documentary *My Mic Sounds Nice*. "Dissing," Pepa adds before Salt finishes her sentence.

If you ain't know then now you know, nigga / I wasn't welcome, I imposed, nigga / I put this dick inside her soul, nigga / Just to get up under niggas' skin / Fucking with the same sex, they say it's a sin / But I'm a dyke and she a femme, it's a synonym

"No Mercy (Intro)" (2019)

No name for people to call small or colonize optimism / No name for inmate registries that they put me in prison

"no name" (2018)

This emphasis on rivalry has subsided as the market has found room for archetypes besides the oversexed maneater and the ethereal enchantress, as the grimacing gangster and the fly shopaholic and the stoner revolutionary and the cosplay nerd have forged niches for themselves; if these don't quite supersede the category of *lady rapper*, they at least help erode its relevance. There aren't many openly queer high-profile rappers as I write this, but between the riveting effrontery of Young M.A and the exacting chops of Cakes da Killa and the wide-angle visions of Kevin Abstract that moment doesn't seem so far off. Where Sha Rock wore "plus one" virtually as a second name, now the supremely thoughtful Chicago MC Fatimah Warner can call herself Noname just on principle. It's a start.

Nonetheless, the vernacular has been slow to purge its toxins. Rappers aspiring to mainstream success can't say *faggot* without repercussions, but they can still say *bitch* with commercial impunity. Kanye says it on the album with "Violent Crimes"; Nas and Jay say it too, as do Eminem and Macklemore and Kendrick Lamar. The message this sends is not just that old rhetorical habits die hard, even when the times call for you to embrace the complex personhood of your fellow MCs or family members—but also that there persists a belief in ways of using the word that are exceptional, situationally appropriate, redeemable. "I don't use it to degrade women or anything," the Harlem rapper Sheck Wes, born in 1998, who scatters the word around his songs like buckshot, not in verses so much as tourettic ad-libs, told the *New York Times*. "Any time you hear me say *bitch*, it's because it means something."

And sure, once more, context. *Bitch* isn't just Cube's *girl with a B*; it is, qua word, a word with a handful of shades that really can approach *le mot juste* even if they're not *redeemable*. It's true that it's inseparable in certain situations from preexisting angers and social pressures, and that it was around long before rap existed. ("Anybody older than me knows they were saying *bitch* before I was born," Snoop Dogg told *Playboy* in 1995. "I didn't make up that shit. If I did, I mean, damn, give me some money!") It's true, in an analytically defensible way, that it's not *just* a slur, not *always* meant to disparage or dehumanize. "I mean worldly, sophisticated, independent, badass bitch, you know—the kind of hoes every man wanna marry," explains Def Jam mogul Russell Simmons in the concert documentary *The Show*. "I know people will be watching this who ain't hip-hop who might not understand when I say *bitch* I mean *bad bitch*."

Still. What good is a lecture about social pressures and polysemy to a person who experiences the word as a slap in the face— "ugly imprints," Morgan writes, "left on cheeks that have turned the other way too many times"? What difference is there between a carefully aimed bullet and stray buckshot to a person who's just been hit? Is there some actionable truth to the distinction between

See, y'all really shocked but I'm really not / You know how many girls I took to the titty shop? / If she get the ass with it, that's a 50 pop / I still bring the bad bitches in the city out

"Yikes" (2018)

Why I say bitch so much? Let me explain it / It's the only word where I could feel and hear all my anger / It ain't got nothing to do with, like, bitches, it's just... / Bitch! BITCH!

"Gmail" (2018)

I need a gangsta bitch: she don't sleep and she don't play / Stickin' up girls from around the fuckin' way / Strapped but lovable, hateful but huggable / Always in trouble and definitely fuckable

Apache, "Gangsta Bitch" (1992)

bitch and *bad bitch*, or is this just making excuses for the morally inexcusable? Is there a middle ground between the fact that rap contains coarse and demeaning words laden with their own deep contextual pockets—words that can be purgative to use or gratifying to hear or intended wholly innocently—and the fact that it has a tendency to afford those words gratuitous exposure and tacit, even explicit, approval?

I don't know, and that's on me. I can enumerate multiple connotations of the word *bitch*, all the more if you add adjectives before it—bad bitch, basic bitch, boss bitch, bottom bitch. I don't personally experience the word as a slap in the face—plus I live for lectures about polysemy—and what's more, when I think about it, I find, alongside my desire for everyone everywhere to enjoy equal respect and self-determination, that I'd be disappointed to live in a world devoid of the sleek multiform impertinence of the Compton slang-slur *ya bish* or the spring-loaded rhetorical action of *no homo*, a world without idle arguments about the orthographical distinction between Too Short's *biatch* and E-40's and Snoop Dogg's. I'd hate to have to disqualify a slick turn of phrase like **My mission's to flip your bitch into missionary position** from analysis or admiration just because one of its parts is a historically shitty word whose greatest redeeming value in context is its vowel sound. I'd hate to believe it's necessary to throw out the baby with the bathwater, murky and stale as it may be. But life's a bitch like that.

You lookin' like a easy come up, ya bish

Kendrick Lamar, "Money Trees" (2012)

Matlock, "God Damnit" (2001)

Yo tell 'em what's the mission

••

Whose baby? Aha, well. The other thing about *bitch*—and *ho* and *thot* and *hoochie* and the rest of that misogynistic menagerie—is that it turns out to be just as polysemous and impertinent on a female tongue as on a male one. Nicki and Cardi and Megan Thee Stallion bandy it around a *lot*; Lil' Kim and Foxy Brown used to even more. Bhad Bhabie, born in 2003, has a song called "Hi Bich" (a thousand times *sic*) that went gold in 2018. In part this proves that ladies can debase and sexualize themselves and others as prolif-ically and ingeniously and grossly as men; see Kash Doll's "Coastal Rota," a fuck-buddy inventory every bit as graphic and dispassion-ate as Ice-T's "99 Problems." But I think it also suggests that the semantic charge of the word is changing, dissipating, becoming less what Michael Eric Dyson, writing about 2Pac's use of *bitch*, calls "a one-word thesaurus for male supremacy" and more like what the French rap critic Pierre Evil, writing about Snoop Dogg's use of *biatch*, calls a semicolon. It underscores the word's shift, perhaps, from a hurtful epithet toward a lexical commonplace that lies dor-mant until it's modified, like when Kash says *No motels, I'm a presi-dential suites bitch* or when Dreezy spends a whole song elaborating what she means by "Bad Bitch," or when Leikeli47 says *I ain't the type of bitch to do a lot of barking / The only thing that I need validated is my parking.*

Investing a slur with meaninglessness can be its own radical act of resistance: a riskier kind of leaning in until you emerge on the other side. Intentionally or not, this is work being done by male and female and nonbinary rappers alike, gradually shifting *bitch* from a word that objectifies people into a word that personifies objects. *Call me what you want, I done heard the worst / And if it's Cris in this bitch, bet I'm poppin' it first*, says Foxy Brown. (That's Cristal, the champagne brand whose relationship to hip-hop is a story for another time.) *Meanwhile I'm turned as fuck*, says Queen Key: *I left my pizza in the oven, that bitch burnt as fuck.*

Maybe this wasn't what Danyel Smith had in mind when she wrote, in 1994, that "it would be thrilling to hear girls go beyond trying to do to boys what boys do to them." But then maybe it was. Even as these usages work to empty *bitch* of meaning, they also play at the opposite, something trickier and more valuable: they make it individuate, invest its object with personality and personhood. That's what I hear Queen Latifah doing in the anti-defamation and anti–domestic abuse anthem "U.N.I.T.Y." While

I got a nigga out west who make me wear a vest / Niggas be shootin' at him, wanna fuck me when he stressed / Got a nigga down south, when I go to his house / Don't even let him fuck, just put this pussy in his mouth

(2019)

"Cheap Shit" (2019)

Yeah I get it but I go hustle like I ain't had shit / If I got paid to piss you bitches off I'd be mad rich / Flexing on the gram but broke in person, that's a catfish / Got her own money and a crib, now that's a bad bitch

(2016)

"Zoom" (2020)

"Baller Bitch" (1999)

"My Way" (2017)

assuring the listener that *You ain't a bitch or a ho*, she's also posing the question openly, open-endedly: ***Who you callin' a bitch?*** That is, who's the bitch you're talking about? Who's the person, or the pizza, you're talking *to*? Can't bitches be queens? Can't queens be bitches? Lil' Kim:

Queen bitch, supreme bitch
Kill a nigga for my nigga by any means bitch
Murder scene bitch
Clean bitch, disease-free bitch

"Queen Bitch" (1996)

Miami rapper Trina, self-proclaimed second name Da Baddest Bitch, professing to be not just any ho but

A little nasty ho, redbone but a classy ho
Young jazzy ho, and don't be scared 'cause if you're curious, just ask me, hoes

"Da Baddest Bitch" (2000)

Latifah herself, five years after "U.N.I.T.Y":

Today I'm not your Queen, your sister, role model, or friend
Today I'm that bitch that'll shoot you a fair one—this don't exclude men

"Name Callin' Part 2" (1998)

And Lizzo in 2019:

I just took a DNA test: turns out I'm 100 percent that bitch

"Truth Hurts"

My pussy teaching ninth-grade English /
My pussy wrote a thesis on colonialism /
In conversation with a marginal system
in love with Jesus / Y'all still thought a
bitch couldn't rap, huh?

Noname, "Self" (2018)

"While it's true that your music holds some of fifteen- to thirty-year-old black men's ugliest thoughts about me," writes Morgan, "it is the only place where I can challenge them." Indeed, this space sounds more and more like the place where an artist can determine whether their *bitch* is the baddest or the hottest, the dirtiest or the nerdiest, the realest or the bitchiest, and inhabit it affirmatively. It's a place that can accommodate multiple voices, multiple contradictory archetypes, and thus one where, answer by willful answer to Queen Latifah's question, it might be possible to take back the privilege, monopolized for too long by too few, of deciding what distinguishes a redeemable usage from a useless one.

Forget the baby boys, it's the biggest mama Mia / Unladylike diva, lyrical maneater

Mia X, in Master P, "Make 'Em Say Uhh!" (1997)

I just come through with a couple bossy bitches / They get money too, they some "don't cross me" bitches / Flossy bitches, Sergio Rossi bitches / And if we at the game then it's floor seat, bitches

Nicki Minaj, in YG, "My Nigga (Remix)" (2014)

ON THE N-WORD

I'm shooting for her heart, got my finger on the trigger
She could be my broad and I could be her —

Slimkid3, in The Pharcyde, "Passin' Me By" (1992)

• •

THE RHYME IS not actually veiled: there are some versions of "Passin' Me By" that don't censor the word *nigga*. Most do, though, clipping it at the reverby inside tip of the *N*. The video, for instance, does this. When the sudden silence drops, as the word's absence hangs in the air, Slimkid3 furrows his brow for just a second before the shot cuts away.

On one hand, polysemy! It doesn't take a particularly careful reading to see that the word as used here is not pejorative, is in fact quite sweet. It's a term of endearment, of steady alliance, of people being *real* to one another. It's like he's saying **I could be her man**, but tuned to the quaintly hammy register of **my broad**. *Her fella*, maybe. It *does* mean a man, mostly, generically, though not always: when Method Man says **You my nigga** to his lady in the velvety devotional "You're All I Need to Get By," Kevin Young glosses it as "you're not just my girlfriend but my friend girl, my homie, my partner, my one—you're down with me, wherever down is."

My nigga Sing he used to sling on the sixteenth floor

The Notorious B.I.G., "Somebody's Gotta Die" (1997)

196

Elsewhere, depending on context, it can mean other things. It can mean *brother* or *rapper* or *sucker*, to name three that are also pretty good two-syllable substitutions. ("There's a certain rhythmic seduction to the word," says Cornel West. "If you speak in a sentence, and you have to say *cat, companion,* or *friend,* as opposed to *nigger,* then the rhythmic presentation is off.") It can mean any old person, irrespective of race—*We usually take all niggas' garments*—or it can *seem* to mean any old person until it turns out to be racially coded after all: *We harass niggas like we was the po-po.* It can mean *me* if you put an *a* in front of it, the way *yours truly* or *ya boy* does, the way it works in *Help a brother out* or *Let a player play. I'ma spit it 'til TRL get it and Hot 97 hit a nigga with a bomb drop,* says Jay Electronica. (*Are you sure you wanna go this route?* says Lil Jon, chivalrously, in a song about busting out of the friend zone: *Let a nigga know before I pull it out.*) It can be a sort of prosodic placeholder with no particular connotation, a throat-clearing dummy-trochee, a hashtag pivoting from setup to punchline: *Might not let a nigga hit but if he get impatient I'll let him lick it,* says Dreezy. *If I gotta make a call we gonna set it off, nigga, Jada Pinkett.* It can signify obscurely, obliquely, impiously, but above all potently. It means hard.

On the other hand, it's not like they weren't going to censor it in the video.

The word *nigger,* you don't need me to tell you, and forgive me for even mentioning it, is gnarled by centuries of oppression and brutality and contempt. It doesn't just bear the scars of those things; by some sinister transubstantiation it has come to *be* those things. It is an index of white privilege and power so entrenched, so towering, that it doesn't even have an equivalent pointing in the opposite direction. No word in English describes *me* that way: not *honky,* not *cracker,* not *kike.* Not even *bitch* dehumanizes so efficiently. It's a word that Damon Young calls "the greatest and most impersonal slur in America's lexicon," that Ta-Nehisi Coates calls "the border, the signpost that reminds us that the old crimes don't

Jurassic 5, "Quality Control" (2000)

"Eternal Sunshine" (2007)

Lil Jon (& The East Side Boyz), "Lovers and Friends" (2004)

"Spazz" (2016)

197

disappear. It tells white people that, for all their guns and all their gold, there will always be places they can never go."

The word *nigga*, its scrappy and selectively rehabilitated cousin, polices that border a bit differently. Kinetically, self-possessedly; playfully, almost. It's the electricity coursing through the fence between old crimes and present day, and it's possible, I think, standing on the latter side, to hear it used skillfully enough for long enough that it starts to sound like a clean, renewable source of approval and respect, of dignity and pride and even love, like an earthbound version of the Five Percenter *god*. It daps across gender, as with Method Man, and even across race— think of the rapacious inclusivity it oozes in *Training Day* when Denzel Washington calls Ethan Hawke *my nigga*. And all of this, it seems to me, tells white people like myself that maybe, precisely because of its radiant semantic versatility, because of its context-dependent endearment and rhythmic seduction, maybe this is a place we *can* go: a place we can visit from time to time, dropping the *R* at the door like an inverted password. A place we can *hang*.

Of course this is a lie. It's not a password, it's a shibboleth, a lure, a test. *Miley, what's good?* We're not supposed to say it; we don't *get* to say it, don't get to participate in its rehabilitation, even innocently, even eruditely. By *we* in this case I don't mean anyone who isn't black—French Montana, who is Moroccan, and DJ Khaled, whose parents are Palestinian, and Big Pun, who was Puerto Rican and whose song "Nigga Shit" is just a litany of archetypical ratchet behaviors, get to use it because they're people of color, because they live closer to the barrel of the gun that is ingrained American bigotry than they do to the trigger. By *we* in this case I mean white people. And this is an uncommon position for us to be in: to have the solidarity and authority and privilege flow *to* us rather than from. "It symbolizes one of the most important and difficult dynamics of hip-hop," writes Jason Tanz in *Other*

In every Jeep and every car, brothers stomp this / I'm Never Ignorant, Getting Goals Accomplished

2Pac, "Violent" (1991)

I'm just with my niggas hangin'

That nigga shit, talkin' loud at the flicks / That nigga shit, fried rice and rib tips / That nigga shit, lookin' fresh with no ends / That nigga shit, beatin' on my sisters' boyfriends

(2000)

People's Property: "it means one thing when black people use it and another thing when white people do." What could be more fascinating and treacherous than a word like that?

"Take the group's full name, which derives its power from its use of an epithet that a huge percentage of its audience is simply not permitted to say," journalist Jonathan Gold wrote about Niggaz Wit Attitudes—N.W.A to many—in 2015. "In early interviews, MC Ren took full advantage of the disparity, goading reporters, including me, into repeating a word many of them simply were incapable of even stammering. If you rose to the bait, you were a racist. If you didn't (I didn't), you were a wuss. There was no middle ground."

"We don't say *nigga* as a racial thing," Ren's bandmate Dr. Dre told *Spin* in 1991. "Anybody can be a muthafuckin' nigga." Moments later in the same interview: "Depends on how you say it. Say it wrong, we fuck you up."

Why do I call myself a nigga, you ask me? / Because my mouth is so motherfuckin' nasty / Bitch this, bitch that, nigga this, nigga that / In the meanwhile my pockets are getting fat

Dr. Dre, in N.W.A, "Niggaz 4 Life" (1991)

• •

It seems like common sense and decency to accept that there's just no way, for a white person, to say it right. And yet. Against all logic, the word remains a reliable cause of white people playing themselves, an endlessly renewable opportunity to get twisted into awkward little pretzels of hypersensitivity and self-righteousness. ("I'm not afraid to use the word at all," says a white survey respondent in Michael P. Jeffries's *Thug Life*, "not that I use the word, but if I did, I wouldn't have any qualms about it.") A white person may say it heedlessly—like the woebegone white roommate in *How High* who ventures an overeager "I love Niggaz With Attitude!" and gets a sucker punch and a lecture from Method Man—or use it excessively gingerly, like Ben Horowitz, a venture capitalist in the habit of using rap lyrics as epigraphs to announcements on his firm's blog, opening a 2015 post called "The Past and Future of Systems Management":

"I said that I'mma ride for my motherf*ckin' n***as
Most likely I'mma die with my finger on the trigger
I've been grindin outside all day with my n***as
And I ain't goin' in unless I'm with my n***as
My n***as, my n***as
My n***as, my n***as (My muthaf*cking n***as!)
My n***as, my n***as (My n***as, my n***as)
My n***as, my n***as"

—YG, "My N***a"

A white person may use it and then invoke colorblindness or post-racialism or the difference between use and mention ("It's the title of the song!" protested Gwyneth Paltrow at the backlash to her tweet calling a live performance by Jay-Z and Kanye West "Ni**as in paris for real"), or performatively not say it—the asterisks, the dropped *R*, *brother* and *rapper* and *sucker* and, ugh, *ninja*—which is perhaps, arguably, worse. Horowitz's blog post is, in its way, an ode to the kind of ride-or-die loyalty that the word conjures when *said right*; at one point he recalls looking at a colleague knuckling down for a daunting technical challenge and thinking to himself, "My guy." But then why choose this song over any number of less fraught allegiance pledges in the rap canon—there's even a radio edit of the YG song, called "My Hitta"—if not to borrow its badass edge, its unpredictable bite, if not also to make a show of muzzling it?

I'm not trying to sound sanctimonious here; I too have fucked up and let the word escape my lips while reciting this or that rap catechism, usually in no one's presence, though once while trying tipsily to keep up with Lil Wayne at a karaoke bar. I've chosen to reproduce it plainly when I quote or mention it in this book; I also, when I was ten, took a marker and blacked out every instance of it in the liner notes to the *Natural Born Killers* soundtrack (which shortly afterward I tearfully handed over to my mom, who had forbidden albums with parental advisory stickers in the house; I don't think she was mad so much as bewildered). My point is there's no elegant solution, just unbecoming compromises all the way down. Here is a word that flies in the face of what I said earlier about words being free and unregulatable, a word not even my birthright as a native speaker of the most promiscuously acquisitive language on the planet entitles me to claim as mine. Here is a word that white people have always treated as a window but that reveals itself, over and over, to be a trick mirror in which we just gaze endlessly at our own ability to make everything about ourselves. Here is something I *can* understand, intricately and thrillingly, and still cannot repeat with dignity intact.

And here is rap, a field and a vocabulary that joyously traffics in it, that blurs use and mention for sport, that seduces me with rhythm and invites me to talk about it, to talk in time with it, to amble and fuss through this terrain strewn with landmines, booby traps, bait for lazy would-be rappers-along. That there's no good look for me to take that bait is itself a kind of justice, a karmic balance restored—not exactly that of the elephant trouncing the lion for believing the monkey, but not so far off either. "*Nigga*, in its loud articulation, has presented a large space of social discomfort, a line in the sand which the artists continually ask their listeners to cross, enticing and challenging," writes Imani Perry. "It marks a provocative irreverence with potentially large but unknowable consequences. It is tricksterism par excellence."

What this particular tricksterism sells is the fantasy that words can shed their historical scars, like tigers their stripes, by sheer force of solidarity and understanding and good intentions. But *nigga* still comes from *nigger*, still wouldn't exist without it, still hyperlinks back to it sooner or later. "As we're already in the practice of comparing words to plants," writes Lauren Michele Jackson in *White Negroes*, "it makes much more sense to think of them as trees with roots and branches where each branch is another possibility for meaning that exists in relation to other meanings. And if one of

Kings of New York with these underground killers (nigga, fuck them niggas, nigga) / Kings of New York with these underground killers (nigga, fuck them niggas, nigga) / Kings of New York with these underground killers (nigga, fuck them niggas) / Kings of New York with these underground killers (nigga, fuck them niggas, nigga)

A$AP Mob, "Underground Killa$" (2012)

those branches once provided so many switches with which to strip humanity from generations of people, we can't assume that branch has rotted off and died simply because another, unexpected branch has grown up and out from the same mother tree. 'Nigger,' like so many other racial, gendered, and sexual slurs, hasn't lost any branches yet."

ON WHITE PEOPLE

Please listen to my album
Even if you're white like talcum

Del the Funky Homosapien, "Catch a Bad One" (1993)

• •

I'M TALKING ABOUT how, like, white people can't even go outside into the sunlight without contracting a disease, like skin cancer, drawls Heems in the introductory patter to Das Racist's "All Tan Everything." *(2010)* (Heems is of Punjabi Indian extraction; a few bars in, he refers to himself as "Young Melanin.") If I'm being candid, I've caught myself more than once hearing this remark and chuckling along, thinking *lol, yeah, stupid white people.* It's deflating to remember that I'm a white person myself, but it doesn't altogether erase the feeling of assent.

Whiteness has a long history of regarding itself as colorless, as default, as a pure essence instead of an obvious metaphorical whitewashing of pinkish beige. Like Russell Potter says about history, those who could afford to dispensed with their skin color long ago. "The central trope of 'white' is, I think, the luxury not to think doubly," he writes, recasting Du Bois's double consciousness in *The Souls of Black Folk*, "to see the world through the one-eyed vistas of privilege, rather than having to account for one's own identity within and against a fundamentally multiple culture." White culture is high culture, white English is standard English. Whiteness is single consciousness, with an army and a navy and a shitload of banks.

More and more of late, though, just as there's long been this thing called black people—and brown people, and poor people, and immigrants, and criminals, and so on—there's been this emergent cultural bloc called *white people*, and imagine our surprise to find out that belonging to so massive and undifferentiated a demographic category based on something as vague as skin color actually sucks. Who knew? *White people* are brittle, fussy, eminently clownable. ("I just don't understand white people," Mike D of the Beastie Boys, America's premier white rap group, told an interviewer in 1994. "White people like stuff that is so overtly wack: Soul Asylum, Rush, *Sports Illustrated*.") We're both a wholly invented cultural signifier and a direly real social force, architects and beneficiaries of the starkly unequal institutional privilege that serves as backdrop and prologue to most American rap songs ever recorded. We're the man, the wind chill in the cold world, the gravity against which one has to keep one's head up. We're the reason it doesn't make sense unless it makes dollars, and we're *super humorless* about all of it. Somehow it seems like whenever we play ourselves someone else ends up getting punished. *Monkey, I'm not kicking your ass for lyin', / I'm kicking your hairy ass for **signifyin'**.*

Prior to the widespread reckonings of the last few years, borne by the Black Lives Matter movement and the civic unrest to which it attends, rap did more than anything else to broaden and deepen my perspective on the complicated realities of race in America. Through argumentation, through allusion, through out-to-lunch conspiracy theories and sampled snippets of venerated Black Panthers and Five Percenters waxing militant about power. But at the same time rap is awfully hospitable to the kind of recreational, palliative escapism that is the forgetting of self—that evasion of justified shame that's often mistaken, confusedly if not entirely incorrectly, for consuming or coveting blackness. White people are present in rap as prologue, as its implicit consumers and tastemakers and financiers and critics and dogcatchers, but as characters we manifest only in certain very circumscribed roles—as white cops or white prison wardens or white bosses or white landlords or shady white label execs or white floozies fed up with being sexually unsatisfied by their lame white husbands. Which, because I don't identify with any of those roles at a more intuitive or granular level than our common pigmentation, allows me to keep on picturing myself as an unimplicated observer. "Whiteness is not who you are," writes Eula Biss. "Which is why it is entirely possible to despise whiteness without disliking yourself." Pay the man, whitey.

Some hypotheses: it's possible that rap has grown to make structural allowances for what Robin D'Angelo calls white fragility—the way our lifelong insulation from racially coded stress and recrimination, from thinking about ourselves as even having a race, much less as perpetuating that stress in others, leaves us unable to engage rationally with criticism or confrontation. (See the music video for Kanye West's "All Falls Down," in which the words *white man* are censored while multiple instances of the word *nigga* remain audible. "We didn't want to offend anyone," an MTV executive allegedly said.) Maybe, conversely, white people just don't *belong* in rap's narrative universe, have no place in its ethos of insularity and open-secrecy. Maybe we're always just listening in. "I do records for black kids," Ice Cube told bell hooks once, "and white kids are basically eavesdropping on my records." Maybe our presence is tolerated, as Del suggests when he invites us to listen to his album in spite of our whiteness, because of the cultural or material capital we bring to the table. Or maybe rap is, rappers are, simply better at letting people be people, at accepting that *brothers* and *MCs* and *suckers* can comprise constituents of all colors without their having to be racially inventoried. Maybe the discourse around rap is

If I wasn't rappin', baby / I would still be ridin' Mercedes / Comin' down and sippin' daily / No record 'til whitey pay me

Pimp C, in Jay-Z & UGK, "Big Pimpin'" (1999)

Drug dealer buy Jordans, crackhead buy crack / And the get paid off of all that

(2004)

Y'all act like you never seen a white person before

Eminem, "The Real Slim Shady" (2000)

I can't blame no one for this, I'm aight with that / Can't be racist 'cause I sell too much white for that / So I decided I'ma milk these crackers for all they milk and crackers / Until I'm rich and these mills don't matter

Juelz Santana, in Diplomats, "The First" (2003)

preoccupied with these questions in a way that rap itself just isn't. Race, Ta-Nehisi Coates says, is the child of racism, not the father.

I suspect all of the above are true in fluctuating measure. But I also suspect that if there are so few characters within rap's narrative universe who look like me, it's less because rappers don't want to contend imaginatively with white people and more because white people don't want to. This, I think, is why white fans in particular can be so jealously protective of their own relationship to hip-hop, so quick to dismiss as parvenus listeners who haven't been attentive as long or committed as deeply: we don't want to see more of ourselves crowding out the view. This is supposed to be *our* elsewhere. Our secret language, our flag of enlightenment planted in wild foreign soil.

There is a well-meant fantasy in white patronage of black culture, one that's no less racist for its good intentions: that our attentiveness and commitment will earn us a unique kind of credibility that functions alternately as absolution and protection. ("I entertained fantasies of a gaggle of armed black men wearing army fatigues and shimmering 1970s-era Afros," writes Tanz of purchasing his first Public Enemy album, "storming our neighborhood with their fists in the air, only to retreat, impressed, when I held up a copy of my new CD.") That our connection to this music, if it's sufficiently wide-ranging and open-eared and solemn, might blossom into a conduit of repentance and remediation and, at last, mutual acceptance. "If I was a white guy," Carvell Wallace writes,

I would probably like this aspect of hip-hop the most. The idea that I can become an honorary member of blackness just by listening. Hip-hop makes that easy. The songs are readily available. The hood is explained to the uninitiated. No longer would I have to feel that the Blackness of Black People represents mystery or the unexplained. And if I was the kind of white guy who thought about the fact that Black people have experienced a sustained and relentless brutality in the name of protecting people like me, then I would seek reassurance from every black face I saw, every black voice that I heard, that we were cool. I would look to hip-hop to absolve me.

This is an obvious pipe dream, but maybe there's potential in it. Maybe, if it can't make amends for four centuries of cruelty on the unsolicited behalf of people like me, it can at least hack away at the same species of racial binary that props up the fantasy in the first place. The one where all you want is to be recognized not just as a white person, not just one of the good ones or one of the bad, but as an individual who transcends skin color and simple demographic categorization. Maybe it can foreground, in its way, the plea I as a white person am so unaccustomed to having to make: please see me as myself.

ON SECOND PERSON

If that's your chick then why she textin' me?
Why she keep calling my phone speakin' sexually?
Every time I'm out, why she stressin' me?
You call her Stephanie? I call her Headphanie

Young M.A, "OOOUUU" (2016)

• •

"THERE'S A LOT of women in the world named Stephanie so it goes," says Young M.A in a Genius annotation from her breakout single, "OOOUUU." "A lot of people named Stephanie will be like, 'Why did she have to come at me like that!?' That's the new Becky now."

Becky, you may recall, has come to mean "basic white girl" thanks to the intro to Sir Mix-a-Lot's "Baby Got Back," the way *Stan* has been shorthand for "obsessive fan" since Eminem's song of the same name or the way *Chad* and *Karen* have become all-purpose lame-white-person archetypes. (Beyoncé drove home the equivalency with her archly dismissive **He better call Becky with the good hair**.) M.A's claim about *Stephanie*'s market penetration may be a little bit exaggerated; I don't recall seeing the name used that way, or for that matter any way, since "OOOUUU" came out. And this might be because the joke is... not that good? Just putting that

"Sorry" (2016)

208

out there. I adore Young M.A and am usually in ecstatic alignment with her rhetorical energies—just look at the slurry slant rhyme morphing through the quatrain above, the simultaneously flippant and weirdly prim swagger of her your-chick-chose-me chest-puff—but I confess I don't really get what's funny about *Headphanie*. I feel like I'm either too dumb to get it or not dumb enough. Like, *Headphanie* because she's into oral sex? Or is it like *heifer*, like a cow? "Not Headphanie, Heffanie," writes a Genius commenter, "key word being 'heffa' meaning she's being a 'bitch.'"

"It's a metaphor," M.A explains with a shrug on the red carpet at a BET award show, speaking to an interviewer whose name is actually Stephanie. "It's not necessarily a person's name." *This* is true: but for the very loose chain rhyme starting with **textin' me**, Stephanie might have forever remained *your chick*, or *your girl*, or *your bitch*, *your ho, blah blah blah.*

Now she reppin' my clique 'cause it's better for her, says Future, in an alienated song about having sex with groupies. **She a ho and a slut and a metaphor.**

"Because Future don't LIKE her AS like a simile," reads a Genius annotation of that line that had been, at the time of this writing, marked for review on the grounds that it is "a stretch."

• •

Why is everyone being so chill about all of this? How can we sit idly by when our chicks are out swanning around town, ignoring our calls and purring seductive nothings into Young M.A's ear? Easy: we either accept being baited and wound up as part and parcel of rap's innate adversarial attitude, its inheritance from the hand-to-hand sparring of toasting and the dozens, or we don't listen to rap. M.A takes infectious delight in stealing your girl if *you* are a man, but her sexuality doesn't have much to do with why she goes there or how she does it so well. Really, everyone across the demographic spectrum gets to take their disrespectful jabs, to

"I'll Take Your Man" (1986)

throw some rhetorical cuckold-crowns around and sound great doing it. *I'll take your man*, warn Salt-n-Pepa. *Call me what you like*,

"If That's Your Boyfriend (He Wasn't Last Night)" (1993)

says Me'shell Ndegeocello, *while I boot-slam your boyfriend tonight.*

Munchin' on my Takis like I just don't care, chirps Dame Jones of the Y.N.RichKids in "Hot Cheetos & Takis," *then I walked up to your*

(2013)

girl, and she askin' me to share.

I've been insulted on this specific grounds in a thousand variations—my bitch flipped, my slut buttered, my honey teabagged, a song called "I Left It Wet for You"—and I almost always think it's terrific. How can I not love this Fabolous burn—

You looking for your girl? She just left
Her and my dick just became BFFs
Then I threw her out like Jazzy J-E-F-F

"I'm Raw" (2010)

Her and my dick just became BFFs

—when it so brazenly corrupts "best friends forever" into an obliquely gross euphemism for sex, when it rankles my inner grammar scold with its ungainly object pronoun, when it immediately contradicts itself since if he force-ghosts her after sex it's more like she and his dick became best friends extremely temporarily? (The beat also does this great little flute-flutter when he spells out *Jeff*, like you're watching Jazz get tossed out of the Banks' Bel Air mansion in slow motion.) I've heard tact defined as the ability to tell a man to go to hell and have him happy to be on his way. What do you call the ability to tell a man you've loved up and ditched his significant other and have him enumerate the ways he's delighted by the news?

The way it never occurs to me that *my* girl has recently concluded a short-term dalliance with Fabolous or blown through our family data plan sending nudes to M.A is not so different, I don't think, from the way I can hear white people clowned on in the aggregate and not feel personally implicated. It's cultural, but also grammatical. (Six-word distillation of entire book alert.) In both

210

cases the people involved are ideas, abstractions, thought experiments. My girl is Roxanne, basically: whether or not she really exists, it is necessary to invent her over and over again.

And the same goes for me. I am no less a rhetorical chess piece, no more actually me, except it's the song itself that invents me over and over again. Whether or not I have a girl to steal or a glock to grab or a whip to ghost ride, the song expands me into a vessel of whatever shape and size it requires for the narrator to establish dominion, to prove he or she can make the nearest bystander rewind, jump around, put their hands up, **shake it like a Polaroid picture.** In the past week alone I have been saluted by a rap song, embraced by a rap song, cajoled, clapped amicably on the back, hit on, romanced, robbed, scammed, threatened, offered drugs, incited to violence and singalongs and dance routines, called *bitch*, called *nigga*, called *my nigga*, called *player* and *pimpin'*, called *fool* and *mark* and *son* and *girl*. Occasionally I can tell it's not me—in a very public rap beef, for instance, or in the kabuki conflict of a freestyle battle—but most of the time it might as well be, and this simply because the figment of imagination at hand happens to go by the same name I answer to: *you.* Rap's first person is structurally complex, but the second is an almost literal hall of mirrors.

How you take this at a broader level is up to you. Reading Jay-Z's exemplary dis track "Imaginary Player," all fluent and flamboyant disdain for an unnamed second-person chump, Questlove sees demographic alienation disguised as good talk: "Within the first ten words of the song, Jay Z ensures that no one in his audience can identify with the experience that he's rapping about. He would never want to be in a club that would have you as a member. But this doesn't offend his audiences. They love it. They want to be just like him so they can exclude people just like them." But what if it's just good talk? What if we read Jay's dis, at least parts of which are allegedly directed at

You mad cause my style you're admiring / Don't be mad, UPS is hiring

The Notorious B.I.G., in Craig Mack, "Flava in Ya Ear (Remix)" (1994)

Andre 3000, in Outkast, "Hey Ya!" (2003)

I got blood money, straight up thug money / That brown paper bag under your mattress drug money / You got show dough, little to no dough / Sell a bunch of records and you still owe dough

(1997)

Yeah, thanks to all the hustlers / And most importantly you, the customer

Jay-Z, "Roc Boys (And the Winner Is...)" (2007)

211

Is there beef between us? We can settle it / With the chrome and metal shit: I make it hot, like a kettle get / You're delicate, you better git—who sent ya? / You still pedal shit, I got more rides than Great Adventure

Ma$e, or Biggie's endlessly quotable 1997 "Kick in the Door," which is probably about Nas, or DMX's little jewel of haterade in "Party Up (Up in Here)," as no more and no less than exemplary signifying tricksterism?

You wack, you twisted, your girl's a ho
You broke, kid ain't yours, and everybody know
Your old man think you stupid, you be like, "So?
"I love my baby mama, I never let her go"

(1999)

What would I be without youuuuu /
I only think about youuuu

Ja Rule, "Put It on Me" (2000)

What would rap even be without this ritualized art of self-glorification via pulling someone else down, and isn't the joke on us especially if we miss that the disser also depends on our presence for the narrative to go anywhere?

"Imaginary Player" takes its core sample from a silky 1981 René & Angela song called "Imaginary Playmates," and here's why that's a wonderful thing to learn: for the four minutes Jay spends dunking on me for being broker and stupider and less successful than him, I become the loser he requires, someone getting a well-deserved verbal lashing for faking the funk and putting on playerly airs. But I also become a playmate—a partner in the fun, a participant in a sparring match taking place entirely within our temporarily shared imagination. I'm not every audience member, I don't and can't hear myself in every *you*-shaped gap, but I'm in the conversation. And so long as it doesn't spiral out of the rhetorical realm—*Who shot ya?*—it's not a bad kind of crossfire to be caught in. "It was just, like, the perfect word," Young M.A says on the BET red carpet, putting her hand on the interviewer's shoulder. "I'm sorry, Stephanie."

212

IS RAP POETRY?

I wouldn't've came and said my name and run the same weak shit
Puttin' blurs and slurs and words that don't fit in a rhyme
Why waste time on the microphone
I take this more serious than just a poem

Rakim, "My Melody" (1987)

• •

THIS IS RAKIM, canonically held to be god and/or father of *lyrical rap*. Which meant, in his day, to mark a break with first-generation hip-hop's carefree, rudimentary approach to assembly, its lockstep end-stopped patter. This rap is lyrical in its care, its complexity, its attention to detail. In the pitch and density of internal rhymes. In the way the word *rhyme* doesn't appear to rhyme with anything until the rhyme, which is *time*, pops up where you weren't expecting it. In the manicured indifference to the difference between *more serious* and *more seriously*.

It's not that *lyrical* doesn't still mean all this; it's just that now it more often means to mark a break preemptively, nostalgically, with an *n*th-generation crop of so-called post-language rappers who are more interested in mood and sonority than they are in wordplay or prosody, and for whom *lyrical* is like *conscious*, or

Basketball has always been my thing /
I like Magic, Bird, and Bernard King /
And number 33, my man Kareem / Is
the center on my starting team
Kurtis Blow, "Basketball" (1984)

I wouldn't've came and said my name
and run the same weak shit / Puttin'
blurs and slurs and words that don't fit
in a rhyme

213

woke, namely something to be wary and not altogether proud of. Something basically good, taken to an extreme. *I ain't no backpack rapper, I ain't no lyricist / And if we ain't talking to you, mind your business then.* The meaning of the word is the same, but the doors lock from the other side now.

Jay Rock, in Black Hippy, "BET Cypher 2013" (2013)

• •

What is more serious than a poem? A heart attack, sure. Justice. Revolution. Infrastructure, soybean futures. Action! A poem is a poem, by some judgments, because it does not act. Because it is resolutely inert, entitled and impractical, useful precisely in its lack of utility. It looks at a bird, leaves a note about some plums. It is a species of thought, says Howard Nemerov, with which nothing else can be done.

• •

"I'm not into poetry," mutters Lil Wayne in a scene from the 2009 documentary *The Carter* where a journalist asks him to comment on the influence of jazz on his poetry, moments before calling off the interview and waiting in sullen silence for the journalist to leave the room. "This interview is with a rapper."

• •

All rap is lyrical if you define the word narrowly enough. Even Lil Jon brays *words*. Whatever else you might choose to say about the many arresting qualities of "Get Low," though—that it rhymes *panty line* with *calm down*, for instance—you wouldn't call it lyrical in the conventional sense. It's not lovingly wrought and languorously beautiful, not a nacreous oasis of inutility. It doesn't sigh with sweet secrecy, doesn't drape over the beat. Rakim *drapes*. Nas, Biggie, Lauryn Hill, they drape. Complexly, ornately. You could replace their voices with saxophone bleats and they'd still sound *meaningful*.

To the window / To the wall / Til the sweat drip down my balls / Til all these bitches crawl

Lil Jon & The East Side Boyz, "Get Low" (2002)

But a lot of rap—a lot of great rap, at that—is ugly and slap-dash. A lot of it is a grim box-checking exercise in come-hither-ing and wealth-signaling and anti-opp posturing and perfunctory exhortations to grind quantifiably harder. A lot of it is, in point of fact, *pure* utility. By this logic, the only thing that makes anyone think to call it poetry is the fact that it rhymes.

• •

Rhyme has no beef with or baggage about utility. Rhyme does things. It builds, in the Five Percenter sense. Chants rhyme. Lies sound truer when they rhyme. *Liar liar combustible pants.* Rhyme, per the title of an Ice-T album, a pun on *crime* that ultimately proves its own point, *pays*. In full or by any means. Not so for poets, except on payday, and we know how that ends. Rakim talks way more about rhyme on *Paid in Full* than he does about poetry—indeed, takes it *more serious.*

Are chants poetry? There are unpoetic rhymes and there are unrhymed poems and there is poetry that can move your feet, but perhaps as soon as it does it ceases to be real poetry.

Rhymes are poetically kept and alphabetically stepped / Put in an order to proceed with momentum except / I say one rhyme out of order, a longer rhyme shorter / Or pause— but don't stop the tape recorder

"My Melody"

• •

Category as a weapon.

• •

Unlike *serious rap*, what we in the West call *real poetry* isn't in the eye of the beholder, not really. Real poetry is an institution, in that it's been present for millennia and in that it has an intimate rela-tionship with power. In the U.S., poetry's economy and terminol-ogy and valuation have long been and mostly still are, in a word, white. Real poetry in the U.S. is a canon, a syllabus, Shakespeare and *Beowulf* and the Psalms. Wallace Stevens walking to work at the insurance office. Black poetry is part of the lineage too, native poetry, Chinese poetry, Persian poetry, but we call those by their

Dat baby don't look like me like me

Shawty Putt, "Dat Baby" (2008)

names, with the prefix and not without ceremony. Real poetry is just *poetry*.

"'Real' (viz. academic) U.S. poetry," David Foster Wallace wrote in 1990,

a world no less insular than rap, no less strange or stringent about vocab, manner, and the contexts it works off, has today become so inbred and (against its professed wishes) inaccessible that it just doesn't get to share its creative products with more than a couple thousand fanatical, sandal-shod readers, doesn't get to move or inform more than a fraction of that readership (most of the moved being poets themselves), doesn't generate revenue for much of anyone save the universities to whom the best Ph.D. poets rent their names and time... and *especially* does not inspire a whole culture's youth to try to follow in its Connecticut-catalogue brogan's prints.

It's marginal, is what he's saying. *Academic* as in irrelevant. Real American Poetry (no Five Percenter) has made strides coloring itself in, but it's almost stifling how acutely the description above still captures something about American whiteness.

• •

"While literary poetry often follows highly regularized forms— a sonnet, a villanelle, a ballad stanza—rap is rarely so formally explicit, favoring instead those structures drawn naturally from oral expression," Adam Bradley writes in *Book of Rhymes: The Poetics of Hip Hop*. Later: "This is poetic freedom rappers didn't inherit; they created it for themselves out of the need for expressive range and the desire for verbal ingenuity."

You do the 'rithmetic, me do the language arts

Andre 3000, in Outkast, "A Day in the Life of Benjamin André (Incomplete)" (2003)

"Whenever I have been confronted by a powerful poetic expression," Alexs Pate writes in *In the Heart of the Beat: The Poetry of Rap*, "neither my first nor second response is 'Where did this poet learn how to do this?'"

The condescension casually calcified in the conversation claiming rap for poetry, positing that Homer or Shakespeare or T. S. Eliot was the original MC, or Bob Dylan or Johnny Cash or Henry V or Art Carney or Dr. Seuss. Frank Gehry reminiscing about the time he asked Jay-Z who the first rapper was, then mailed him a recording of James Joyce reading from *Finnegans Wake*. Saul Bellow wondering aloud who the Tolstoy of the Zulus was.

Ralph Wiley: "*Tolstoy* is the Tolstoy of the Zulus."

• •

Poetry, writes Audre Lorde, is not a luxury.

Poetry is the language of imagination, says KRS-One: **Poetry is a form of positive creation.**

in Boogie Down Productions, "Poetry" (1987)

It is unspeakably difficult, writes Jelani Cobb, to be a poet in a language that is hostile to your existence.

Poetry, that's a part of me, says Nas—and then **retardedly bop**, two words with such pleasing mouthfeel they might as well be Edward Lear.

"Memory Lane (Sittin' in da Park)" (1994)

"In a society where public education, particularly for young black children, is woeful, it would be quite foolish to say that some systematic process is at work which yields knowledgeable and craft-conscious poets," writes Pate. "Yet, through some cultural osmosis, mimeticism, and instinct, scores of young people have emerged using all of the traditional and nontraditional poetical conventions of the English language."

Sleep him, he could argue with the fishes / No retreat and never no surrender

Kevin Gates, "Tattoo Session" (2015)

"A rap is a form of a poem," says Fredro Starr of Onyx, a four-person embodied scowl from Queens whose first album was called *Bacdafucup*. "I love poetry and I love English—that was one of my best subjects—and I guess it transcended into rapping."

Rap, writes Bradley, simply replaces the lyre with two turntables and a digital sampler.

Even N.W.A called themselves poets when it suited them.

Now get it from the underground poet / I live it, I see it, and I write it because I know it

••

Hip-hop, writes Rachel Kaadzi Ghansah, is black America's repurposing of the poem.

••

Rap, written or oral, is a performance of performative talk, a Schrödinger's cat superposed between expression and action. Same for poetry, but differently. Maybe their having this in common is the root of the mesmerizingly odd way people repudiate one or the other, or sometimes both.

Lil Wayne again: "When you use the pen and the pad, you're reading. When you're reading something, man, you're paying attention to what you're reading instead of what you're doing."

••

Why not flip the script and call poetry a kind of rap? Rap contains among its multitudes love poems and war poems and epistles and mock heroics—*She rollin' I'm holdin' my scrotum and posin'*—and perfect lapidary confections of sound and sense—*Rolls Royce umbrella I'm hoping it rain*—just as it contains fantasy and horror and reportage and idealism and blasphemy and shit-talk and seriousness. *My pussy wrote a thesis on colonialism.* It is rhyme with an agenda, means given an end, and sometimes the end is rhyme. *I just wanna be high as a plane baby I just wanna be high as the rain.* It is poem and blackbird. Thought with which nothing else can be done, coupled with action and purpose and breath.

Kendrick Lamar, "Backseat Freestyle" (2012)

(Lil Baby &) 42 Dugg, "Grace" (2020)

Young Thug, in DJ Holiday, "Everyday" (2015)

WRITING/NOT WRITING

I wasn't born last night
I know these hoes ain't right
But you was blowin' up her phone last night
But she ain't have her ringer nor her ring on last night

Lil Wayne, in Chris Brown, "Loyal" (2014)

• •

"NO EVIDENCE," says Lil Wayne, in another scene from *The Carter*, when a journalist asks about his famous practice of recording raps without writing them down first. He says it with this gleam in his eye, the look of someone dropping some extremely freaky realness on you concerning crop circles and alien replicants and also, as it turns out, being right. It is also admittedly the look of someone who has logged a lot of time by this point in the film sipping lean and puffing on blunts and fucking with interviewers basically for sport. (About ten years earlier, he told *Murder Dog* magazine he just kept all his lyrics in his head because "I ain't got no drug habits to wipe it out.") Back in 2009, in the same interview where he tells *GQ* that "nothing that's written is to be believed"—including the Bible, excepting "the damn dictionary"—he offers another explanation: "You could read what's on the paper, right? So basically anybody that could read could recite it. That takes something away from it." That was also the year he hit the lab and recorded a thirty-five-minute auto-da-fé of all the lyrics he'd previously collected in various notebooks. It's called "10,000 Bars" and it doesn't sound meaningfully different from his other work, which is to say it is both deeply unfocused and generally awesome. Nearly the first thing you hear him say is "S-Q-A-D."

Plenty of rappers do write their lyrics down, of course. *Looked at the pad and pencil and jotted what I feel.* But some noticeably big names don't, or don't always: Biggie, Kanye, Roxanne Shanté, T.I. It's no longer uncommon to hear of people cutting out that step altogether, going into the booth and unloading song after song from some wired hybrid of memory and improvisation. Some of them, when asked, give slightly less puzzling accounts than Wayne's: they talk about spontaneity, about living in the moment, about preserving the texture and inflection and delivery that first popped into their heads. "When I write lyrics down on paper, it doesn't allow me to play with the flow like I like to do," Big Sean tells *Vanity Fair*. They talk about necessity: Jay-Z—who dreamed up the first verse of "99 Problems" in the studio after thirty minutes of what Rick Rubin describes as "kind of humming"—says he picked up the habit while hustling, training himself to keep rhymes in a drawer of his brain because there was no time to write anything down. (You also see rappers returning to physical writing while serving prison sentences: another link in the pen–*pen* chain.) Schoolly D says he learned from James Brown to write down only one word to remind himself of what he meant to say. Young Thug, according to the Atlanta producer Dun Deal, draws "weird signs and shapes" and brings them into the booth with him: "One day I went in there and looked at it and said, 'You didn't write any words down.' He looked at me and said: 'I don't need no words.'"

Something, I feel dimly, is at stake here. I'd be less preoccupied if these were rappers spitting simplistic in-the-park-after-dark doggerel; with all love and respect to Jeezy, it doesn't tease

---

I write my lyrics on parking tickets and summons to the court / I scribbled this on an application for county support / I practice this like a sport, met Donald Trump and he froze up / Standing on his Bentley, yelling "Pimps down, hoes up"

Boots Riley, in The Coup, "Ghetto Manifesto" (2001)

Who's the nicest, life or lifeless, on these mic devices / And I don't write this, I just mic this, I will it to happen / One-take Hov, I'm real at this rappin'

"Pump It Up (freestyle)" (2003)

I looked and I said, "No ma'am"

220

my brain to learn that he doesn't write out *his* rhymes. But we're talking about the authors of raps that are consistently complex and dexterous and sensitive to something more than just sound, more even than just meaning—something I can't help thinking resembles the shapes of the words themselves. Wayne's witticisms can be howlingly dumb and his punchlines the lowest-hanging fruit, but overwhelmingly often he raps like someone who can turn on and off a faucet connected directly to this massive dematerialized archive of rhymes and cadences and tropes and trains of thought that is language in its pure kinetic form. And even if he chooses to use that ability mostly to make death threats and dick jokes, he still brings to them a practically mathematical kind of elegance and intricacy, like that ingenious little specimen of rhetorical cuckoldry above, **her ringer nor her ring on.** *Nor*! He still sometimes rhymes like he's *looking* at a piece of paper he bought into the booth but failing to read it correctly through a haze of weed smoke, or like he's folding random text-to-speech mishaps into the rhymes themselves. It's just that at no point, apparently, did he bother to *write* any of it. *No evidence.*

No evidence! I should explain that I depend on evidence, the written kind, to have any kind of sustainable relationship with my own thoughts. I don't think about committing the words passing through my head to text so much as I do it involuntarily; words tend to appear before me peripherally, like phosphenes, as a byproduct of my hearing them. For me, even as sound, speech *is* text, and if I don't capture it I usually lose it forever. So it's not that I'm jealous, although I am jealous. It's not that I don't respect the knack, because I recognize it as the confluence of multiple oral traditions, from toasting to the blues to narratives passed among slaves who weren't allowed to learn to read or write. I know about the unwritten transmission of Homeric verse, the ambulatory composition of Wallace Stevens and Jacques Roubaud, rappers memorizing lines to spit at block parties rather than recording studios, Jay-Z humming

Now it's blue blood in my veins so you know what I came fo' / Born in a world goin' where they told me I cain't go / In my lane, though, I'm in the same boat as Usain Bolt / Get ahead by any means so the head's what I aim fo'

Big Sean, "No Favors" (2017)

Lookin' for the one? Well bitch you lookin' at the one / I'm the best yet and yet my best is yet to come / 'Cause I've been looking for somebody, not just any fucking body / Don't make me catch a body, that's for any and everybody

in DJ Khaled, "I'm the One" (2017)

Ran up the stairs, to the top floor / Opened up a door there. Guess who I saw there? / Dave, the dope fiend, shootin' dope / Who didn't know the meanin' of water nor soap

Slick Rick, "Children's Story" (1989)

Got paper like a fax machine, it's asineen / Damn, I mean asinine, I'm Dapper Dan / And after mine there will be nine / Damn, I mean there will be none

Lil Wayne, "You Ain't Got Nuthin'" (2008)

Check my swag, I travel like sound, dog / You play hard and I'm gravel like ground, dog / I'm underground, call me groundhog / Lay down laws, call the ground law

Lil Wayne, "BM J.R." (2004)

to himself all day on the corner or for half an hour in the booth. It's not that I judge it: I don't *comprehend* it. It is an elsewhere to me.

Now, there's plenty about Wayne that I don't comprehend, and I'm still quite certain he's a genius. This seems hopeful to me, even, the precarious pleasure of an excellence that can't be explained or taxonomized or domesticated. But the pleasure comes with its own new vertigo, its own rabbit hole, another set of questions about what I thought I could take for granted. If these songs were never written down, can they be said to have been *written* at all? Are they even songs? Are they organized and stable units of authorship and art and meaning, or just someone leaving the faucet running for a few minutes at a time? How can I assume like standards, assume I know what's good about any of this, when Wayne doesn't trust anything he reads? If he's speaking and I'm reading—and again, I'm more or less reading even when I'm listening—are we even really using the same language?

So much depends, in the way I process rappers' work, on my being able think about them as *writers*: as deliberate positers of image and argument, as stylists and wits and careful choosers of words. Understanding that writing is only one kind of composition, alongside painting and choreography and beer-can sculpture, alongside oral-formulaic traditions that don't necessarily leave a trace, is one of those things that's disturbing and liberating at once. Perhaps writing is a kind of composition the way text is a kind of evidence, the way poetry is a kind of rap. And perhaps assuming the compatibility and interoperability of these multiple modes is, in a certain sense, dangerous.

WHAT YOU HEAR IS NOT A TEXT

I can't help the poor if I'm one of them
So I got rich and gave back to me that's the win-win

Jay-Z, *"Moment of Clarity" (2003)*

• •

OVER THE YEARS I've rewound these lines enough, literally and figuratively, to imprint their timbre and cadence on my brain. I've memorized the lockstep way the words unspool over the beat like a zipper zipping down slowly, tooth by tooth. I've logged Jay's nearly unaccountable pronunciation of *poor* and the weird emphasis he puts on *back*. But I've never managed to visualize how the second half of the couplet is punctuated. Depending on whether you put the caesura before or after *to me*, the sentiment could be the smirking boast of a ruthless street entrepreneur—

So I got rich and gave back to me. That's the win-win.

—or, on the contrary, a statement of magnanimity such as we might imagine a captain of industry including in his prepared remarks at a function honoring his charity work:

So I got rich and gave back. To me, that's the win-win.

Both are plausible from a historical perspective, 2003 being roughly when Jay began trying on the role of reformed drug kingpin-cum-benevolent wealthy person. And of course you could rightly argue that the line isn't *punctuated* at all, since it's not written but spoken, and since Jay claims he's been composing in his head almost exclusively since 1996. Nonetheless, *Decoded* rules in favor of the second interpretation, the Good Samaritan one. (Jay basically gives the captain-of-industry speech later in the book anyway, right after the part where he hangs out with Bono.)

And yet I just... don't *buy* it. It's not that I believe the book is wrong, in the sense that an intern mistranscribed the lyric and Jay signed off in haste because he was late for a sweater fitting or something. It's that I believe the other, darker way of hearing the lyric—*I got rich and gave back to me*—is the more colorful and compelling one, the *realer* one, like how God is sort of a dullard in *Paradise Lost* and you end up rooting for Satan. I believe the *literally authoritative* reading suggested in *Decoded* simply isn't the best sense to be made of those words. (One chapter in the book is called "The Voice in Your Head Is Right.")

For the record, this is not my only quibble. What the book transcribes as *thing ain't lie*, at the beginning of the second verse in "Public Service Announcement," I refuse to not hear as *Sing ain't lie*, which is also what Biggie says in "Somebody's Gotta Die" after a former neighbor—*my nigga Sing, he used to sling on the sixteenth floor*—accurately tips him off to the whereabouts of the guy who just killed Biggie's friend C-Rock. But this one I do prefer to believe was the error of an inattentive lackey.

• •

Despite the enviable suavity with which I've obviously carried it off, presenting the lyrics in this book *in this book* has required an

So I got rich and gave back / To me that's the win-win

Thing ain't lie / I done came through the block in everything that's fly
(2003)

Sing ain't lie / There's Jason with his back to me, talking to his faculty
(1997)

224

enormous number of decisions, starting with the intractable choice between *if you're into getting rubbed* and *if ya into gettin' rubbed.* Is *lobsterhead* one word or two? Does AZ say *that's why we puff la* or *that's why we puff lye*? Is it a violation to reinsert, for the sake of clarity and/or fidelity to standard written English, the apostrophe-*s* black English often elides from possessives? How much *G* do you need to hear to swap out the apostrophe in *speakin' my language*? Do you transcribe a hashtag rap line with an actual hashtag, and what happens when you don't? What do you do with a passage that's not only in a different language but also in a different alphabet? Perhaps you're encountering some of these lyrics for the first time, perhaps you're replaying them in your inner ear as you read; either way, I'm inflecting them, semantically, subtly or not so subtly. There's literally no way around it. *I never heard it like that*, whether said with the delight of someone who's just unlocked a double entendre or with the peevishness of yours truly grousing about putative mistranscriptions, means you're still untangling the wires between hearing and seeing. Like a friend of mine who for several years thought the Notorious B.I.G. song "Gimme the Loot" was called "Gimme the Lute," with the attendant mental image of Biggie, agitated and out of breath, chasing woodland sprites around.

Adam Bradley and Andrew DuBois, in their editors' introduction to the 2010 Yale *Anthology of Rap*:

Hide the rest of the yams in my auntie's house

"Two thumbs up!"
—Ebert and Roeper

Two thumbs up Ebert and Roeper

> Those who wish to transcribe a song face the immediate challenge of comprehension: Can you decipher all the words? Particularly for rap, can you comprehend the slang? Next is the challenge of orthography: How do you represent the distinctive sound and accent of someone's speech? Do you resort to deliberate misspellings to capture, for instance, the difference between the artist saying "singin" rather than "singing"? The final matter for transcription is one of form: Where do you break the line? What are the basic structures upon which rap songs are forged?

They don't call me Big for
{nothing, nutting} / All of a sudden

Jay-Z, in Rick Ross, "3 Kings"
(2012)

These are but a few of the banana peels strewn along the path between a recorded rap song and the text of same. It's all but impossible to elegantly represent the homophones and duplicitous pronunciations and off-kilter emphases that power rap's this-but-not-*this* misdirection, at least without bleeding them dry on the page. There's a careful logical ambiguity to the way some litanies cascade through time—*Banksy; bitches; Basquiat*—that can be compromised irrevocably by overzealous punctuation. *Banksy, bitches! Basquiat!* There are rappers who have entire nonverbal vocabularies of grunts and cackles and chirrs that are as semantically rich yet phonetically undistillable as the slurry *wazz-zups* of those late-nineties Budweiser spots. There are songs, early ones in particular, that vary from release to release, even from recording to packaging, in lyrical detail or verse order or the spelling of names and titles that are often deliberately nonstandard to begin with. *I'm the S to the P double O-N-Y*, says Spoonie Gee on his first single, "Spoonin Rap," whose printed label lists him as Spoonin Gee.

None of which even broaches the weird dimension of literalism and judgment and hierarchical superciliousness hovering over the enterprise of transcription into standard written English, especially when there's a subtext of racial "translation" at play. Here's how the black satirist Fran Ross pillories it in her 1974 novel *Oreo*, a wryly colorized retelling of the Theseus myth:

From time to time, her dialogue will be rendered in ordinary English, which Louise does not speak. To do full justice to her speech would require a ladder of footnotes and glosses, a tic of apostrophes (aphaeresis, hyphaeresis, apocope), and a Louise-ese/English dictionary of phonetic spellings. A compromise has been struck. Since Louise can work miracles of compression through syncope, it is only fair that a few such condensations be shared with the reader. However, the substitution of an apostrophe for every dropped *g*, missing *r*, and absent *t* would be tantamount to *tic douloureux* of movable type. To avoid this, some sentences in Louise-ese have been disguised so that they are indistinguishable from English. In other cases, guides to pronunciation and/or variant spellings are given parenthetically whenever absolutely

226

necessary to preserve the flavor and integrity of the Louise-ese or, antithetically, translations are provided for relict English words, phrases, or sentences that survive her mangle-mouth.

Legion, in short, are the obstacles confronting the would-be transcriber of an oral form as fluid and unruly and indomitably alive as rap. Sometimes there are correct answers, sometimes there are none, sometimes it depends on the voice in your head. The fact is always obvious much too late, to paraphrase Salinger, but the most singular difference between text and speech is that text is a solid and speech a liquid. We freeze rap at our own risk.

• •

So why do it? At first the question seems frivolous, so self-evident are its various answers; then it seems sort of rhetorical, existential even, so slyly does it evoke bigger ideas around art and access and time and meaning. Consider, though, how rapidly our everyday interactions with the mechanics of language are evolving. Consider those studies suggesting that a majority of American college students perceive terminal periods in chat and text messages as emotionally aggressive. That Oxford's Word of the Year in 2015 was an emoji. That there are significant gradients of meaning, whether or not you have the patience to parse them, between *LOL* and *lol* and *haha* and *ha ha*. Consider that we have no reliable way of knowing whether what we call *standard written English* will look, in twenty years, much less a hundred, more like this paragraph or like the last SMS you received from a teenager. Consider that one of the biggest pop hits of the past decade was a song called "XO Tour Llif3," by a rapper whose name you have to say out loud to get.

And then consider that, as hip-hop vernacular continues to leach into the public linguistic water supply, the round trips it makes between speech and text—whichever it originates as—will span ever greater and more elaborate distances. Which means that

I be that nigga with the ice on me / If it cost less than twenty it don't look right on me

B.G., "Bling Bling" (1999)

more and more people will regularly first encounter rap's language divorced from its native musical context, like whatever percentage of Europeans have heard Nicolas Sarkozy described by pundits as *le président bling-bling* but not the Big Tymers song "Bling Bling." Which means in turn that one day, not all that far in the future, how a rap looks on the page or screen or T-shirt or tea towel may contribute as much to its influence, or its susceptibility to dismissal—to whether it scans as the work of patient wordsmiths or unlettered thugs, of philanthropists or gangsters—as how it sounds.

ON POSSESSION

Hi haters, I'm back off hiatus
I feel just like you—I mean, even I hate us

Kanye West, in Consequence, "Grammy Family" (2006)

● ●

THERE HAS LONG been, to my mind, a palpable sense in which the majority of Kanye West's lyrics are neither written nor spoken but hewn from enormous slabs of expensive mineral and plated in some kind of rare foreign gold.

● ●

If asked to give a practical rationale for transcribing rap lyrics once they've already been spoken—the "why do it?" raised above—I imagine most people would frame it in terms of comprehension, as Bradley and DuBois do in their *Anthology of Rap* introduction. "Just as a mechanic might take apart an engine in order to understand how its constituent parts fit together," they reason, we write rap lyrics down in order to consider them more intimately, to annotate and analyze and argue about them. To behold how a carefully wrought word machine transcends the sum of its parts. We choose text as our tool because it allows us to handle and re-parse and

229

cross-reference the words and their connections in a way speech doesn't: it makes them more material, easier to manipulate and share, almost graspable.

		Hi		haters					
I'm back			off	hiatus	I		feel	just	like	you
I mean		even	I	hate	us.				

Naturally, the pursuit of graspability can be at odds with the very slipperiness that made a line alive and worthy of a second look to begin with, the enchantment that lives in that fleeting moment before a swarm of potential meanings resolves into a stable double or triple entendre. This boast from the iconically jewel-teethed Houston rapper Paul Wall—

Say cheese and show my fronts:
It's more {carrots, carats} than Bugs Bunny's lunch

"Sittin' Sidewayz"
(2005)

Livin' life without fear / Puttin'
five carrots in my baby girl ear

The Notorious B.I.G., *"Juicy"*
(1994)

—is far from the state of the art in misdirective wordplay, but it still requires a delicate kind of simultaneity to work properly: you have to hear both *carats* and *carrots* at once, oscillating between their identical sounds and distinct meanings. Seeing both words together, as above, short-circuits the effect; seeing only one of them isn't any better, because each discrete word is only half of what the machine needs to function. The sound *kerət* needs to be able to "luxuriate in the chaos of ambiguity," as Henry Louis Gates, Jr., puts it, and text rarely cooperates with speech that way. (Nor speech with text—it's unclear whether *minute* is a unit of time or a synonym for *tiny*, but only until you hear it out loud.) No matter how carefully it's done, transcription always risks creating a short-circuited facsimile of comprehension, pinning an open sound to a single entendre, foreclosing all the other options that aren't not also there.

But the complexity is also what makes transcription so alluring. I said before that I tend to see words when I hear them: if you were to visualize the mental workspace where they appear, you would find page after hysterically cluttered page of experiments subjecting them to variable spelling, punctuation, font, size, spacing, line weight. You would see, as I do, phrases of every origin—song lyrics, movie dialogue, ad copy, overheard conversational fragments—transcribed and transposed into as many hypothetical contexts as I can conjure. Soviet propaganda posters, church marquees, love-letter valedictions, *New Yorker* cartoon captions, Bollywood subtitles, band names, yearbook quotes, tombstone inscriptions, all-caps white overlays on photographs of suggestively writhing housecats. *Draw me like one of your French girls. Oh you fancy huh. Bling bling!*

In my experience, the satisfaction that comes from getting a match, pinning down a snug textual fit for this or that phrase, is not like the simple relief of finishing your taxes or locating your car in an airport parking lot. It's not binary, doesn't get extinguished once the task is done. It's not a satisfaction that fizzles out; on the contrary, it expands, burrows, becomes a stone in the pocket that feels worth sharing. All the more so, perhaps, because the fit isn't objective: because ultimately it says more about the experimenter than it does about the specimen.

Hi, haters! I'm back off hiatus. I feel just like u—I mean, even I hate us!

Perhaps we would do better to think of the transcriber's purpose less in terms of comprehension and more like the reader's "purpose," such as it is, in underlining a passage or dog-earing a page or copying a sentence into a commonplace book. That is, maybe we should think about it as a kind of purposelessness too. There is a desire behind those readerly habits to understand the material, to explain it, to solve it—*this would be a good place to scratch*—but it's secondary to a vaguer, more instrumental drive to possess something in or of or about the language itself. To still have a place to go after you've purchased the album, learned the lyrics, seen the concert and hung up the poster. Perhaps transcribing rap is simply the best way to grasp it; perhaps—it wouldn't surprise me to learn this of myself, in any case—we're driven to grasp it above all because we have, in text, a tool that's so beguilingly imperfect for the job.

A preliminary definition, then: to possess a piece of language is to make sense of it—literally to fabricate its sense, above and beyond the one conferred on it by its native context. To put it to use in your own reality, to model where and how it is most truthfully or invigoratingly applicable to your experience of the world. Each transcription I deem correct—where I don't just get the words right but get the signifiers around the words right too, where all the cues chunk into place like slot-machine sevens—is a singular experimental demonstration of how the world looks, sounds, *means* to me and me alone.

Hi haters

I'm back
off hiatus

    I feel
    just like
    you I

mean even
I hate

us.

Thing is, it doesn't want to remain for me alone. It wants to spread outward, as urgently and tenaciously as the first time I heard

I'm the motherfucking king like Oedipus and wasn't content to merely hear it. Greg Tate's description of this is impeccable, if awfully vivid: "The mordant wit hiphop likes to show off with these days not only makes it our most quotable pulp, but the only one whose exegesis requires ballistics. The dope measure of a new jack lyric is whether it blows into the ear like a dum-dum bullet, indelibly stains the brain, and frequently exits the victim's mouth in the form of a conversation piece."

One of my favorite things to do on Genius is look at a recent song where so far only a few users have stopped by to annotate, generally not very persuasively, one line here, another there. What their commentary lacks in subtlety—and it runs the gamut from "trout in this context means vagina" to "The term is a derivative of the previously used slang, 'I'm ghost,' meaning that, like a ghost, the speaker will disappear. In 1990, Patrick Swayze starred in the movie 'Ghost' with Demi Moore which obviously changed many rappers lives" to "NIGGA SHE A BABOON, ITS SELF EXPLANATORY"—it almost always makes up for in the way it evinces that same need to riff on the words, to hype-man them, to pseudo-publicly rub your scent on them. Even the barest idea of an audience, another user's transient attention, lends the work a little thrill of promise. Why transcribe a text, or paraphrase it, or explain it, or make a map of a neighborhood or a genome, if you're going to keep it to yourself?

All of my diamonds is wet like a typhoon / Bitch my diamonds on monsoon / Ho, I got water like bathrooms / Big booty bitch, she a baboon

SahBabii, "Watery" (2018)

hi haters i'm back
off hiatus. just like you,
even i hate us

Once you get beyond comprehension, that is, beyond the basic housekeeping of opening up phrases that are idiomatically foreign or words that are literally unintelligible, transcription and the critical tasks that accompany it can function as a means of individuation, the way variations on a familiar cliché can individuate a rapper. An account like *Decoded* can be the beginning of a conversation about alternate readings, not a ruling that definitively snuffs them out. What's pertinent is not what the author or speaker intended but how we hear and read the words, how we inhabit them and vice versa. We can set down the particular sense they make to us and leave it somewhere for others to read, puzzle over, react to, pick up and carry onward—inscribing in those words, at best, a tiny index of the way they have possessed us.

• •

Some years, I imagine, there will be flames shooting out at rhythmically determined intervals from the serifs of HI HATERS; other years, depending on how Kanye's career evolves, the letters will be lit from within by hundreds of small spherical bulbs. Sometimes there will be a comma—HI, HATERS—sometimes more aggressively experimental punctuation, sometimes none. Only the words, such as they are, will remain the same.

ON POSSESSION WITH INTENT TO SELL

Cash rules everything around me

Method Man, in Wu-Tang Clan, "C.R.E.A.M." (1993)

• •

HOT CHEETOS AND TAKIS. *Sippin' on some sizzurp.* Beamer Benz
or Bentley. Narcotraficante. *Drive it like you stole it. Rumpole
of the Bailey. Subaru Impreza*, for some reason. *Daniel Levin
Becker*. There are cadences that are like monkey bars. *Rhythm
is a dancer. Zipper, snaps, and buttons.* Melodies like ornaments, syntax that signifies. I can't tell you how many times I've
falsettoed a triviality with the right number of syllables—*That
quiche was porous*, say, or *Raccoons are brazen!*—to the tune
of Bell Biv DeVoe's *That girl is poison.* I have idly rewritten
entire Notorious B.I.G. songs to be about desserts: in hindsight,
they read like Action Bronson songs without the poetical spark.
There are some Young Jeezy lyrics I cannot hear without imagining them spoken by an earnestly overmotivated construction
foreman. When Kendrick Lamar's ghost chorus of prerecorded
selves repeats *ya bish* as a micro-refrain in "Money Trees," I picture it as a punctuation mark, a finger-snap, a hood ornament,
a slight angle-tweak to the brim of a snapback baseball cap. A

*You never thought shortbread
would make it this far / Now I'm
eating lime pie, watching time fly
/ Time to get weighed, blew up
like the World Trade*

*Hot sauce all in our Top Ramen,
ya bish (ya bish, ya bish) / Park
the car then we start rhymin', ya
bish (ya bish, ya bish)*

(2012)

235

skillful flip off a diving board, with splash. These are stones in my pocket that I stroke absently, rosary together and worry to a shine to distract myself or keep myself company. That's what possession looks like for me. I don't do it instrumentally or analytically; I do it reflexively, incessantly, and with great joy.

At ya-bish.com, you will find an instance-by-instance close-reading of "the polysemic term 'ya bish'" as it shape-shifts throughout "Money Trees," the site having been created partly in defense of the song and simultaneous protest against a *Village Voice* editorial that condemned it for its casual bandying of the B-word. You can also buy a T-shirt that says *Ya Bish* in fat, laid-back cursive, white on red on a white background. Or you could. That T-shirt is sold out as I write this, but never fear, you can buy ten others elsewhere on the internet that say the same thing, differently. You can buy a *ya bish* tank top, a *ya bish* tote bag, a *ya bish* coffee mug, a *ya bish* iPhone case, a *ya bish* spiral-bound notebook, a *ya bish* wall clock, a *ya bish*-patterned pencil skirt. You can download multiple images styled like that British WWII poster that flooded memespace sixty years after the fact, should your purposes call for one—though, again, I suspect the existence of these items has less to do with purpose, commercial or otherwise, than with that communicable satisfaction of making things from the words rattling around in your brain. "We decided to take the phrase 'Ya Bish' and do what we do best as designers," explain the creators of ya-bish.com: "play."

There's *so much* play out there. So many materialization games that begin where the rap ends, that recycle and riff on lyrics in the form of lo-res jpegs or print-on-demand clothing or beer cozies or what you will. A T-shirt that says CRUISIN DOWN THE STREET IN MY 64 above a Photoshopped Eazy-E awkwardly astride a Nintendo 64 console. A onesie that says IT'S ALL GOOD BABY BABY over a black-and-white line drawing of Biggie in

KEEP
CALM

YA
BISH

236

Versace sunglasses and a Coogi sweater. Any number of products that say ROLLIN' WITH MY HOMIES—next to a tricycle, next to a wheelchair symbol, next to three sushi rolls, a twenty-sided die, a rolling pin and some gingerbread men. STRAIGHT OUTTA AZKABAN, STRAIGHT OUTTA AMSTERDAM, STRAIGHT OUTTA KINDERGARTEN. And so on.

This stuff is not always good, not always funny, not even frequently worthy of its source material. But quality and tastefulness aren't the point of play. Play doesn't have to be positive, or reverent, or done in the best interest of the thing being played with—consider the politically contemptible but rhetorically artful *blue lives matter*—to be play, at least to somebody. When you think about it, this is the same way language moves and evolves and propagates itself within rap—this chain of repetition and revision and perversion, from a fragment in a rhyme book to a line in a song to an allusion in someone else's song to a sample in another to a hook in still another. Rakim wondering *how could I get some dead presidents*, Nas repeating *I'm out for dead presidents to represent me*, Jay-Z sampling Nas and calling the song "Dead Presidents." (Rakim once described his early writing style as thinking of "slogans that somebody would want to put on the side of their car.") So it seems brittle on some level, hair-splitting, to argue that the divergent course the same lyrics can take, from a line in a song to a book title to a hat to a hashtag to a crossword puzzle clue to a cartoon overdub video, is any less legitimate a kind of play. Play is play. But is it fair to call it signifying?

So yeah, I sampled your voice, you was using it wrong / You made it a hot line, I made it a hot song
Jay-Z, "Takeover" (2001)
"The World Is Yours" (1994)

Let's make it so free and the bars so hard / That it ain't one goshdarn part you can't tweet
Chance the Rapper, in Kanye West, "Ultralight Beam" (2016)

Miniature-golf enthusiast's credo (26 letters): I LIKE BIG PUTTS AND I CANNOT LIE
Paranoid gardener's lament (18): THESE HOES AIN'T LOYAL
Renaissance Faire supervisor to underperforming musician (12):

I intuitively understand this proliferating cottage industry around language exported from rap, recognize in it my own

237

fidgety habits of possession—and at the same time I don't trust it. I contain the generative impulse of the maker and the eye-rolling skepticism of the hater. Am I entitled, as any old internet rando, to use and denature lyrics in this way? But also: am I entitled to be offended by such wanton intermingling of media and registers and styles of discourse, by the T-shirtification of rap's semiotic technologies? What business is it of mine whether MC Hammer sees any of the profit from a coffee mug sold on Etsy that says *I am unable to quit as I am currently too legit*? What happens to language abstracted from authorship and made into something as apparently "traditional" as "Auld Lang Syne"? Is there a limit to the good that can come from our sharing it? What happens to signifying as a strategy of escape when it's not just decoded but openly and joyously commodified?

Language, writes Russell Potter,

changes hands so often that the image it bears loses all recognition, and yet perhaps it is precisely in this vernacular (re)circulation of words that hip-hop culture, like other African-American artforms before it, has its greatest impact. Anonymous, and yet continually shifting in connotative significance; used again and again but never used up, appropriated, deformed, returned, discarded—language is perhaps the only particle small enough to fit every crack in the system.

Inner-city black kids, writes Jason Tanz,

seeking a modicum of respect and financial security, created a point of entry into the commercial world that had ignored them for so long. We white kids, drawn to the implicit escape that their music and lifestyles represented, bought it. Hip-hop is where we meet, we on our way out of the system, they on their way in. Is hip-hop a door that swings open between our two cultures, letting us mix freely with each other, or is it a revolving door, endlessly spinning, allowing us to pass in opposite directions without ever actually touching?

Materials, writes Questlove, of The Roots,

> have a tensile strength, which is a measurement of the maximum stress that they can withstand before failing or breaking. That can happen as a result of violence, but it can also happen as a result of indifference, or craven commercialism, or thoughtless rhetoric, or thoughtless anything else, for that matter. Hip-hop can be stretched in a way that exceeds its tensile strength. Don't think that there's not a point of no return.

Wu-Tang's "C.R.E.A.M." is a brick wall covered in spray-painted gossip, a grammar workbook printed on post-consumer pulp, a goofy Five Percenter backronym that happened to land in a dope song—seriously, imagine it to the tune of "I've Been Working on the Railroad" instead—and become a statement iconic enough to both affirm and eclipse itself. *Cash rules everything around music*, says Future. *Cash rules everything except me*, says the Canadian rapper Saukrates. *Cash ruins everything around me*, I grumble to myself when I'm feeling spiteful about self-employment tax or YouTube rap video censorship or gentrification in neighborhoods where I'm not directly responsible for it. CATS RULE EVERYTHING AROUND ME, says a shirt you could at one point buy from a website called Rap T-Shirts for White People. Cookies Rule Everything Around Me, proclaims the name of a chain of ice cream shops in California, which people just call C.R.E.A.M., I think. I've never been able to bring myself to go, though I can't explain convincingly why not.

"Sorry" (2017)

"Rollin'" (1999)

I'm pretty sure it's wrong for me to begrudge these contagious bits of language the long strange lives they go on to lead in a wealth of contexts and colors and shapes, the attention and goodwill and money they may or may not accrue back to the people who coined them. Wrong or at least unnecessary. Generous as it is as an ethos, rap has been a culture industry inscribed intimately and enthusiastically under cash's rule since before I was born.

These words didn't become commodities when someone thought to print them on a T-shirt; they became commodities when someone rapped them into a microphone in exchange for real or cultural or social or sexual capital. Just because I'm loath to part with the stones in my pocket doesn't mean they're not products, doesn't mean they're immune from the undertow of capitalism. Still. For no one's sake but my own, something in me hopes there's a difference, one that really matters, between possession and possession with intent to sell.

SIGNIFYING ORNAMENTS

I spell it how the fucks I want

Pusha T, in Clipse, "Big Dreams" (2008)

• •

PUSHA T INTERJECTS this one sound a lot. It's most recognizably a noise of disgust—you can picture his head turning almost involuntarily when he makes it—but it's also somehow triumphant, the way "disgusting" can be a compliment. Sometimes it's really just an announcement of presence, an evocative logo-noise like Rick Ross's husky seal bark or Jadakiss's enervated hyena laugh. There's a Clipse song called "Eghck" circulating online, one that doesn't appear on any official release that you can pay money for, and the title plainly refers to the sound in question, which Pusha makes four times in the first twenty seconds as if to dispel any lingering doubts. But *eghck* is a poor approximation of how the sound actually sounds. The consonant cluster checks out, but there's no way the vowel is just a single E. I've seen it spelled other ways, including *yechk, eeyuck, euaghk,* and *yuuuugk,* that last one from Pusha himself, though he admits he uses other spellings too. "*I spell it... like, either Y-U-U-G-H or just U-U-G-H,*" he says in a video annotation on Rap Genius, eyes fixed in the upper middle distance,

Niggas hear the yeughck and they know it's me

in Clipse, "Hello New World" (2006)

241

a smile playing faintly on his lips. "But it's usually Y-U-U-G-H. I gotta look at my rap book."

Rollies and Pashas done drove me crazy / I can't even pronounce nothin'—pass that Versacey!

(2004)

Another thing Pusha does from time to time is playact a kind of underclass simplemindedness, the kind Kanye does in "All Falls Down" where he goes out of his way to mispronounce *Versace*. For instance, on a song with Fabolous, Pusha thinks out loud:

Yacht-Masters at the yacht party
Sittin' at the dock is a drop 'rari
That's pole position with a joystick
That's push-button, that's like Atari   *"Life Is So Exciting" (2012)*

It's quite possible that he's explaining this to me like *I'm* the simpleton—and it's true, I did have to look up Yacht-Master, which turns out to be a make of Rolex that retails around twenty-five grand—but then elsewhere he'll say something like ***Fiberglas, Ferrari leather,***

in Future, "Move That Dope"
(2014)

and designer shit that I misspells, followed by his trademark disgust-noise. It would be a terrible pity, by the way, if the Brooklyn rapper Desiigner never sampled that line.

Here's another turn of the screw: Pusha and his brother Malice, once the other half of Clipse, run a designer line of their own, a "progressive streetwear" brand that's spelled Play Cloths and pronounced "play clothes." (It made and sold a campaign T-shirt for Hillary Clinton at one point.) It's not immediately clear why someone who not only writes his lyrics down in a rap book but takes the time to spell out his expectoratory ad-libs would greenlight this, but Pusha gives an almost obscenely crafty explanation it in the chorus of the mixtape track "Big Dreams," simultaneously hyping the brand and modeling how to say it:

Stop searching for the Es 'cause the Os is long
I spell it how the fucks I want
Stop searching for the Es 'cause the Os is long
Now go and put your Play Cloths on

An O is, in certain company, an ounce of cocaine, and Pusha is assuring us that these are not in short supply, that they are in fact *long* as Georgia might be long on peaches after a prodigious harvest, the way money might be *long like train smoke* or *long like a tube sock.* Long like a mess of commas. Non-sartorial revenue streams are in full effect, we are given to understand, so the founders of Play Cloths can say and spell its name however they please. The *yueghck* is implied. It's playing dumb as a classic signifying parry, all play and no dumbness.

Like Krispy Kreme I was cooking them Os

• •

The Ebonics kerfuffle of the late nineties, rooted in panic at the prospect of a few schools in Oakland using black English as a language of instruction, put a name and a cause to the apparently deathless misconception that black English is unsophisticated, unruly, unmoored, that it has "no right or wrong expressions, no consistent spellings or pronunciations and no discernible rules," to quote a jocular 1996 *Washington Post* op-ed by William Raspberry. Black English is in fact a highly conventional set of exceptions to so-called standard English, and the "anything goes" fallacy, as linguists John and Russell Rickford call it, is crucially wrong—but you have to think of the strategic opportunities afforded by not going out of your way to correct it. Deliberately misspelling or mispronouncing or misusing words in order to produce a particular semiotic effect—what Kevin Young calls "a machining, rejiggering, and at times rejection of English"—is its own with-us-or-against-us sorting mechanism, a way of separating those who can appreciate the nuance from those who mistake it for carelessness or illiteracy. What Pusha is doing with those open-ended vowels is characteristically subtle and resourceful language play, but making it look unconsidered and obstinate to the hasty observer—that's the shrewdest kind of tricksterism. "Ornaments," writes John Jeremiah Sullivan, "can signify."

Calling her a crab is just a figure of speech

Thus 2Pac, and Outkast and Xzibit and Whodini and Ma$e, and Eyedea and Eminem and 3OH!3 and SPVCXGHXZTPVRPP (pronounced and sometimes spelled SpaceGhostPurpp). Thus Desiigner and Bhad Bhabie. Thus Onyx's *Bacdafucup*, home to such orthographic abattoirs as "Bichasbootleguz," "Stik 'n' Muve," and—my favorite for its apparent helplessness but to spell one word properly—"Blac Vagina Finda." Thus Jay-Z removing the hyphen from his name in 2013 and reinstating it in 2017. Thus Ice Cube naming an album *AmeriKKKa's Most Wanted*, his point all the more piquant, all the more credible, because the country's name doesn't sound any different. Thus the variant stylings of *signifying*, each with its own careful reasoning. "Spelling, like finding meaning, is often a creative endeavor," writes Felicia Miyakawa in *Five Percenter Rap*. This isn't phonetic decay, as Young puts it, but rather the fruit of close attention to how words look and feel, not just how they sound, not just what they mean.

Greg Tate on graffiti futurist and sometime musician Rammelzee:

Asked why he spelled Ikonoklast with a "k" when he named his practice of armored graffiti writing "Ikonoklast Panzerism" (after the tank), Zee said: "Because the letter 'c' in its formation is an incomplete cipher: 60 degrees are missing. A 'k' is a formation based on the loki of it; a certain kind of science based on the knowledge of formation mechanics…"

And Del the Funky Homosapien, explaining to an interviewer in 2009 the circumstances under which he went by "Del tha Funkeé Homosapien" for the better part of his career:

That was something the record company thought was aesthetically better. Shit, I know how to spell. I just didn't care at the time. I was like, "I'm putting a record out! Call me whatever the fuck you want." They probably thought they were being hip.

"Those who first wrote 'phat' diverged from standard English as a direct result of their awareness of standard English," write John Baugh and Geneva Smitherman: "the divergence was not by chance linguistic error."

Gretchen McCulloch puts it more succinctly: "No one who writes 'u' does it because they're unaware that 'you' is an option."

The idea that everything fits, or at least that it could—which doubles as a generous encapsulation of the semantic mechanics of Supreme Mathematics—is not the same as the idea that anything goes. Building, showing and proving—these are ideas of language as actively *doing*, not just through its referents but through the extraordinary toolkit of levers and signifiers that is the written word. Try to say Gucci Mane's name without succumbing to an Alabama twang; try to say Fetty Wap's with patrician diction. Try spelling "Ty Dolla $ign" over the phone, and godspeed to you in your endeavor. To manipulate such tools as ingeniously as Pusha does and still ruffle the feathers of those intent on seeing black English as a sign of chaos and corruption—as "the dialect of the pimp, the idiom of the gang-banger and the street thug, the jargon of the public-school dropout, a form of pidgin English indicative of African-American failures"—is an impious power play worthy of the trickster deity, carried off with the high intelligence it takes to successfully pantomime ignorance.

I'm coming after you like the letter V

OUTSIDER ART

And all the people always know me for my comedy
I make you laugh I make you giggle ha ha hee hee hee
I graduated from hip-hop university

Biz Markie, *"Studda Step"* (1996)

• •

THE FIRST GANGSTER rap track ever recorded, most scorekeepers agree, is a hissy, reverb-drenched blast of chilled air from 1985 called "P.S.K. What Does It Mean?" It's got all the fixtures you find in 50 Cent's "In Da Club"—sex, drugs, fancy cars, ambient menace—and threads a classic day-in-the-hood narrative through them without ever actually explaining what P.S.K. stands for. It's the song Ice-T, whose "6 in the Mornin'" is routinely cited as the watershed moment in gangster rap, says made him want to become a rapper.

The song's author, the slickly menacing Philadelphia mainstay Schoolly D, is also, recall, the first and so far as I know the only rapper to devote an entire song to the signifying monkey legend. That the same person brought "P.S.K." and "Signifying Rapper" into the hip-hop narrative is not, I don't think, a coincidence. Gangster rap is the genre's final and most fitting embodiment of

246

the signifying monkey's spirit: his nihilistic itch to get into a fight, his baiting and name-calling and voice-throwing, his weaponized inconsistencies—*Say it wrong, we fuck you up*—and apparent lack of qualms with being punished by a system that refuses to stop taking him at his literal word. Played thoughtfully, the gangster rapper is every bit as witty and unpredictable, every bit as doomed-or-not-depending-on-who's-telling-the-story, as the beleaguered but scrappy Esu-Elegbara.

Before the gangster, though, rap's primary agent of flux and mutability was the clown. The slobbering caperer, the winking joke-butt, the wild card. Think of Ol' Dirty Bastard piling his wife and three of his thirteen kids into a limo to go cash a welfare check. Think of the Beastie Boys circa *Licensed to Ill*, swearing adenoidal devotion to White Castle and Brass Monkey. Think of Humpty Hump, Shock G behind a novelty nose so big it literally obscured his identity. Think of Kool A.D. and Heems spending a whole song drunk-dialing each other from a labyrinth of corporate fast-food oases. Think of Flavor Flav, all basehead whine and hectoring *Yeeeeeahhh bwoyeeeee*, clock around his neck to let suckers know what time it was, whom Greg Tate once called "a surefire professor of ign'ance whose mismatch with the main-man derails the tradition of cult-nat loudmouths who don't know how to laugh at themselves." And think of the indispensable Long Island goofball Biz Markie, "the clown prince of hip-hop," who could rhyme really deftly when he felt like it but mostly favored a loping, declamatory waddle-flow that showed no regard for stress or scansion or filling bars with an even distribution of syllables. He rapped in a unique patter—"slurry but sly," says Dan Charnas—about boogers and bad breath and broken hearts, sang with a sense of melody roughly analogous to Pusha T's disdain for correctly spelling luxury brands. On "Studda Step" he leverages a stylized stutter into a hypnotic record-skipping effect—Nicki Minaj would also do this later on—and the whole thing

I look funny / But yo, I'm making money

in Digital Underground, "The Humpty Dance" (1990)

But if you listen to me / The diabolical energetical B / The I-Z-mizza-mizza-A-R-K-I-E / I'm tryna give you H-E-L-P

"The Dragon" (1989)

sounds not inadvertently sloppy but the opposite: like something patiently, masterfully wrought to sound boorish.

Like Lil Wayne, surely rap's greatest confluence of gangster and clown, Biz often seemed bigger than language: it's difficult to imagine anything he couldn't credibly, incredibly say. I don't know how or why he chose to make a career of this persona, and for me that's part of it too: the perfect inscrutability of the clown, the crazy-like-a-foxness. How do you laugh with a clown, anyway? (Asking for real, never been to a circus.) How do you make it understood that you understand that it's all a self-conscious spectacle of buffoonery, that he's only playing at playing himself? Is it possible to sing along with Biz's lavishly detuned Freddie Scott hook on "Just a Friend," or better yet with his delirious caterwaul all over Elton John's "Bennie and the Jets," without implicitly casting him as some kind of outsider artist?

A lot of the rap I'm drawn to has at least the appearance of being *outsider art* in the ordinary sense: a practice performed without ceremony or ambition by someone uninterested in discussing its mechanics or meaning or place in a cultural tradition. Lil Wayne refusing to be in the same room as a guy who's just indirectly called him a poet. But rap is an art that deliberately, conspicuously creates insides and outsides, *yous* and *Is*, and for all my love, all my attention, I'm no insider. Being an outsider doesn't dampen my love, but it does awaken a sense of liability around how I express it. I've lost untold hours to fretting over the difficulty of demonstrating that I'm in on the joke without making it seem like I believe rap *is* the joke, because I've just seen it too often: even the most earnest and well-meant gesture of co-signing the point can come across as a full-throated attempt to miss it.

There are plenty of books about hip-hop that rub me the wrong way, but one of my top three bêtes noires has to be *Understand Rap: Explanations of Confusing Rap Lyrics You & Your Grandma Can Understand*, a novelty title by William Buckholz—as I recall, I bought it in a museum gift shop—whose conceit is that it glosses

Eh-eh-eh-eh-eh, that is my talk / You can tell I'm from LI, NJ and New York / I got I got the smarts like Dr. Zhivago / I talk more bull than the team of Chicago

"Studda Step"

248

more or less memorable quips like Paul Wall's *Say cheese and show my fronts / It's more carrots than Bugs Bunny's lunch* in a sort of fuddy-duddy robo-English that doesn't actually engage why the lines in question might be worth dwelling on:

> Direct your focus toward my anterior incisor and cuspid teeth, which are most visible when my mouth opens, and pay no attention to the molars and bicuspids, which may be easily visible. As you can see, the weight of the diamonds inset into my decorative mouthpiece is a larger number than the quantity of vegetables a cartoon rabbit would eat during his midday meal.

"While at times humorous because of the contrast between the artists' language and the language of the author," Buckholz writes at the beginning, "the intention of this book is not to poke fun at rap music." I take him at his word, but I still wonder: how different would the book look if that *were* its intention? Do you think the Snacks and Shit guys annotating "ridiculous rap lyrics" because they sounded stupid or gross or whatever thought of themselves as working in poor faith, as *poking fun at rap music*? My issue isn't that anyone would experiment with these waggish détournements, quite the opposite: I too share the compulsion, as much as I might resent the majority of the executions it yields. By that logic, though, what's to stop you from reading the same ungracious motivations into what I'm doing here, no matter how insistently I assure you of my goodwill and solemn respect? You see the rub. I've judged too many strangers myself to trust that my own intent will map faithfully to the resulting effect.

Art crisis, am I right? Well, so goes the world. Irreconcilable multitudes and all that. Bad faith is everywhere, good faith too. Sometimes—okay, a lot of the time—bad faith sells better than good; sometimes cynics and opportunists are more talented than adepts and zealots. I wish I got to tell you which one I am, but that's not how it works. This isn't what the crisis is, but it does make it sting a little more: knowing that being possessive of and particular about and devoted to rap doesn't mean that I'm—

And that's the hole in the sentence I've been staring down for the better part of a decade. Here is the lacuna. (Pay no attention to the molars and bicuspids!) It's not that it's something I can't reach, but that I can't even articulate what I'm reaching for: the adjective that encapsulates how I should *be* toward rap, the value I have to offer it in return for all it gives me, the thing I want so badly to earn even if it means disparaging other devotees in my quest to get there. Respectful, maybe. Appropriate. Pious. Accepted, welcome, deserving. Worthy.

For what it's worth, I've come to believe that it makes no difference to the clown what I'm laughing at. That my approval and comprehension are, and always were, beside the point; that being made fun of is part of the art. That his willingness to be misunderstood, whether naively or maliciously, is inseparable from his genius. *They say I look and sound funny but I don't be caring*, says Biz in "Nobody Beats the Biz," just after the line sampled in the hook of "Studda Step":

I rock the Latin Quarter, Rooftop, Union Square and
Roseland, the Heartthrob, Madison Square Garden
Even rocked the World's Fair at Javits Center. Pardon
the way that I be talking about the places I be rocking
I love to perform for the people that be clocking   *(1988)*

And it's true: you can tell he loves it. You take him at his word. Whether it's careful or careless, whether he's sweating or smirking, there remains this unmistakable story-spinning gift, this spellbinding charisma, this irresistibly cool anti-cool that oozes from his every line, the subtly measured and the flagrantly mistimed, the needlessly spelled out, the terribly silly. Or is it the terribly lazy? I suppose it makes no difference to me either. Perhaps, as Camus didn't say,

I arrived in front of the dormitory
/ Please can you tell me where is
door three?

"Just a Friend" (1989)

250

we must imagine the clown content to entertain. Ennobled by it, even. Imagine his joy no less authentic, no less real, than his hidden mastery, his inner self-possession, his secret seriousness. Greg Tate: "Like hiphop needs me to prove it has a brain."

ON IRONY

This is fucking awesome

Macklemore (& Ryan Lewis), "Thrift Shop" (2012)

• •

AFTER MACKLEMORE AND his producer, Ryan Lewis, won the 2013 Grammy for Best Rap Album, Macklemore sent a text message to Kendrick Lamar—whose excellent *good kid, m.A.A.d city* had consequently not won the 2013 Grammy for Best Rap Album—to say he regretted the outcome. *I wanted you to win. You should have*, he wrote. *It's weird and sucks that I robbed you.* (Macklemore's album was called *The Heist*.) The trouble started afterward, when he posted a screenshot of the message on Instagram, a gesture Drake—the internet-savviest rapper for a healthy chunk of the 2010s and no slouch in the self-aggrandizement department himself—called "wack as fuck." Macklemore, who is white, was roundly lambasted for a few news cycles, less for "muscling into a historically black genre, essentially uninvited, and taking its laurel," as Jon Caramanica put it, than for the very public crocodile tears. Nobody called him out for using two spaces after each period in a text message, which honestly, to me, is the most scandalous thing about the whole incident.

I had no dog in this fight—I think Kanye should have won that Grammy for *Yeezus*—and I have no beef with Macklemore, who I think is robustly talented and politically *comme il faut* and admirably self-scrutinizing about his place as a best-selling white artist in a historically black genre. (I also applaud his decision to truncate his original name, Professor Macklemore.) His two songs about white privilege, "White Privilege" and "White Privilege II," parse the whole existential conundrum as equitably and soul-searchingly as I think anyone could reasonably ask. I don't find him too earnest or too soulful, nor do I suspect him of angling for drive-by thug cred when he, say, uses *come-up*—which usually refers to something obtained by armed robbery—to talk about a righteous bargain on a secondhand coat. I'm miles away from being the guy he should be worried about offending, but I don't find him offensive.

Still, I don't think it's out of line to find his breakout hit "Thrift Shop," with its barely-sub subtext of triumphant appropriation, a little queasily on the nose. It's a perfectly jubilant song about hanging out and trying to be fly, but you can't tell me someone who has released two non-consecutive songs about white privilege didn't see the unsavory reading: that it's the fate of secondhand clothing, not unlike that of hip-hop, not unlike that of most historically black art forms, to be bought for pennies on the dollar by white tourists and ironists wholly indifferent to whom they used to belong to and what they once meant to those people. To be carried off, thrown in the wash, used to cobble together a vague personal style. I have spent years of my life wearing thrift-store clothes in essentially this way; for a time in high school I had a powder-blue T-shirt that said EXTRA SPECIAL GRANDMA in flowery block capitals and I couldn't tell you even now what category of pleasure I derived from owning and wearing it. Thing is, from the outside it's indistinguishable. You can find a shirt or a dress or a pair of boots and love it, want with all your heart to possess and inhabit it, think *This is fucking awesome* in the gravest sincerity, and still appear, to an observer, to be no less

Hip-hop started off on a block I've never been to / To counteract a struggle that I've never even been through / If I think I understand just because I flow too / That means I'm not keeping it true, nope

"*White Privilege*" (2005)

I'm gonna pop some tags / Only got twenty dollars in my pocket / I'm huntin', lookin' for a come-up / This is fucking awesome

"*Thrift Shop*"

crass and predatory than some douche who thinks tuxedo shirts or boat pants are funny because they're so lame.

I believe Macklemore *means it*, is what I'm saying, and I'm not just saying it because in this extended metaphor he could very easily be me. I believe he comes to hip-hop from a place of love and excitement, even if it's the excitement of the parvenu, someone who can't know the real story of the thing he pulls off the rack and tries on and finds fits him, suits him, becomes him. I believe he's eager to learn, willing to do the work, committed to making his come-up a net-positive transaction. And yet nothing about believing all of that diminishes or displaces my underlying fear: that maybe, to an onlooker inclined to withhold the benefit of the doubt, for good reasons or petty ones or something in between—like, say, an ill-advised public gesture of private apology—maybe *meaning it* means nothing.

What vertigo, reader, to think I'll never be sure you understand and accept my affection for the rhymes I've been rewinding and quoting to you, my esteem for their creators, my respect for the trajectories that brought them to this present. This preoccupies me so much more than any doubts as to what you may think of my own words, my own ideas, because I know where those originated, can remember more or less when I snatched them off the shelf and tried them on for the first time. And if I'm afraid of using these lyrics irresponsibly, unworthily, then maybe on some level it's because I can't be completely certain that some part of me isn't making fun of them too.

• •

This is, I think, an uncertainty greatly perpetuated in the last few decades by the word *awesome*, which has been rubbed so flat that instead of resulting from thoughtful critical engagement—like, say, Macklemore's songs about white privilege—it's come to signify its absence. Its replacement, at best, by an affinity that is shallow and noncommittal and cheap. Seth Price:

It was no longer necessary to deem a piece interesting, provocative, weird, or complex, and it was almost incomprehensible to hate something because you liked it, or like it because it unsettled you, or any of the other ambivalent and twisted ways that people wrestled with the intersection of feelings and aesthetics. You almost didn't need words anymore: it was enough to say, "That painting is *awesome*," just as you'd say, "This spaghetti is *awesome*."

The problem with this kind of aesthetic category is like the problem with judging artistic merit by commercial success: it bestows a corrupted sense of value on things. It asks us to inflate that which is awesome but not actually *good*—like the *Fresh Prince* theme or "Baby Got Back" or Pen & Pixel album art—not because we can't articulate what good is, but because we don't care.

I sympathize with the diagnostic definition of irony, advanced around the turn of the century by people like Jedediah Purdy in the face of what they perceived as a generational epidemic thereof, as a form of inoculation from meaning it. A reflex to put everything between finger quotes; an aversion to believing in anything, especially belief itself. I genuinely remember experiencing coming of age into this cultural moment, and it's not a coincidence either that the kid whose wardrobe was mostly thrift shop–sourced was also the kid for whom bemused detachment was the most natural, or the least precarious-feeling, stance to adopt toward the world. It seems to me beyond the pale to conclude that irony is why white kids love hip-hop, to borrow the title of a book by Bakari Kitwana, but I don't think it's wrong to call it primarily a white affliction. "While being a hipster means that you're always looking to the past for some quaint discovery to re-purpose," Carvell Wallace writes, "being black means that you look to the past and think, *Damn, my ass would have been lynched.*"

But it also seems to me that a tradition that has room for the blistering irony of teenage Tyler, the Creator and the captivatingly impenetrable motivational-speakerism of DJ Khaled *and* the

I'm awesome / And I fuck dolphins
Tyler, the Creator, "Tron Cat" (2011)

255

plummy earnestness of party guests like Macklemore, all at once, is strong enough and generous enough to reflect and reward whatever brand of sincerity you project onto it. You can appreciate it ironically, and you can appreciate it for its own irony, and you can appreciate it for the escape it provides from irony: great rap, I think, speaks to all of these drives at the same time.

When you look closely, so many of English's words for excellence invoke the status of unreality. *Awesome*, like *incredible* and *unbelievable* and *fantastic*, is how we once described that which was astonishing and unascertainable, that which was mighty and bewitching and asked nothing from us. It's still, somewhere, how we make sense of that which is cooler than we are. Awe can lead to detachment and disengagement for multiple reasons, not least among them fear of the difficult and unpredictable things we might find within if we abandon ourselves to it. But it doesn't have to. It can also lead—and this is the sense in which I trust that Macklemore means it—to a patient, reverent reckoning with its object's power and mystery, irrespective of retail price and cultural cachet. Arrived at piously or flippantly, used with irony or with wide-eyed sincerity, the word ultimately leads us back to a kind of love that doesn't require complete understanding.

What's normal to us is an illusion to them

DUMB LOVE

Yo! Microphone check 1-2 what is this
The five-foot assassin with the roughneck business
I float like gravity, never had a cavity
Got more rhymes than the Winans got family

Phife Dawg, in A Tribe Called Quest, "Buggin' Out" (1991)

• •

PHIFE DAWG MADE great first impressions. He would show
up on the track, usually second, with these improbably fly throat-
clearings, these extravagantly hokey topic sentences. *I'm not your*
average MC with the Joe Schmoe flow / If you don't know me by now you'll
never know, he says on "We Can Get Down." *Now here's a funky*   (1993)
introduction of how nice I am, he says on "Check the Rhime": *Tell*
your mother tell your father send a telegram. His soundcheck above,   (1991)
in the opening bars of "Buggin' Out," doesn't accomplish anything
Wonder Mike didn't do twelve years before at the top of "Rapper's
Delight," down to the winking hey-is-this-thing-on. Yet it feels far-   *Now what you hear is not a test /*
ther out by light years, evolved over screwy millennia. It's savant   *I'm rappin' to the beat*
and juvenile, oblique and frontal, utterly fresh and totally corny.
Under no authority I can identify, it makes shortness of stature and
a good dental history and a gossipy zinger about a Detroit gospel

257

dynasty—and, later, an endorsement of New Balance sneakers—sound *so fucking cool*. It's so fly it's weightless. It's so all over the place it contains elsewheres within itself.

Is this a case for why it's good or for why it's awesome? I find myself wondering things like this a lot when I try to size up my fondness for A Tribe Called Quest. Their music is a sort of universal solvent, never the wrong thing to put on, Phife's coarse leftfield rhymes pairing beautifully with Q-Tip's unflappable smooveness, the whole thing buoyed by a fluent fusion of earthy instrumentation and golden-era boom-bap. It's expansive but hospitable, strange without being inaccessible. It fills every crack. Which leaves, perhaps, a shortage of oxygen with which to talk about it. *I float like gravity, never had a cavity* is an exquisitely tilted eight-word cosmos, but I find I don't have much of analytical value to add to it. My mental workspace is curiously blank. Even when, a few lines later, Phife talks about how much soda he drinks, and then an album later he calls himself *a funky diabetic*, and in 2016 he dies from diabetes-related complications. What does that tell me? Something about candor, something about groundedness, something about not over-reaching and taking inspiration from what's closest at hand? It is both too much and not enough for my reasoning brain to process. Q-Tip sounds cool as hell when he says

I never half-step 'cause I'm not a half-stepper / Drink a lot of soda so they call me Dr. Pepper
"Buggin' Out"

Just like Ringling Brothers, I'll daze and astound
Captivate the mass 'cause the prose is profound
We do it for the strong, we do it for the meek
Boom it and you boom it and you boom it in your Jeep

"Jazz (We've Got)" (1991)

but I can't tell you how it operates, what it signifies or signifies on, whether the circus it conjures is arch entertainment-industry commentary or just a first-thought reverie that wandered a little afield of the point. Is it a happy accident or a master stroke, and if the latter then a master stroke of what, exactly? What's profound about

258

boom it in your Jeep? How does Tip get away with calling it *prose*? Isn't *astounding* just another bedfellow of *awesome*, another word for the hypnotic pull of an attraction that won't explain itself?

Tribe were a little silly, a little unpredictable, the type to follow a savant disquisition on the merits and perils of the N-word with a line like **My style is kinda phat, reminiscent of a whale.** But their next-level magnetism, forever scrambling my analytical faculties and impervious to my critical scratching, isn't silliness. It's a kind of good I have no category for, never knowingly opted into. I can't break it down, can't find its seams, can't reconstruct the precise effort that went into it. It *doesn't sweat.* I'm describing cool again, aren't I? That tractor beam that invites me in only to keep me at arm's length, that enigmatic *x*-factor that keeps the sum of the facts from adding up to complete understanding. I'll stop short of saying I love A Tribe Called Quest *because* I don't know why I like them, but only just. That dynamic is there, an irreducible part of their hold on me—not the reason, but part of the texture. My love is dumber than the thing it loves. Inexplicability is somehow its essence.

Q-Tip, in "Sucka Nigga" (1993)

Q-Tip, telling Brian Coleman about "Check the Rhime":

> I don't really know why we spelled *rhyme* like we did [*laughs*]. I just liked fucking up words, doing lowercase and uppercase where they didn't belong. I also take full responsibility for making up the word *vivrant* [*laughs*].

Puzzles aren't cool—not classically, anyway—but coolness, I often think, is a puzzle. An instability, a challenge. Isn't that what we're pursuing, that elusive and self-evident answer, when we transcribe and annotate and sloganize, when we try to possess a little piece of a rap song? I don't just mean mapping an oblique De La Soul rhyme scheme or footnoting every reference in a Das Racist song or plotting occurrences of the *My watch cost more than your house* trope on a map of the American South. I mean trying somehow to *solve* how and why this breezy meta-talk, this pattering into

She ride 'cause her testament has been day one / A nigga got trust 'cause she been day one / Day one's done, build a fam Bruce Lee / So we K-I-S the BS goodbye

Trugoy, in Handsome Boy Modeling School, "If It Wasn't for You" (2004)

259

the microphone just to see if it's plugged in, keeps me in such thrall. For like fifteen years I thought Raekwon was saying *I kick it like a night flight* in "Wu-Tang: 7th Chamber," when it's actually—I finally caved and looked it up on Genius—*I kick it like a Nike flight.* Which makes way more sense, even without the expected second syllable in *Nike*—and yet the whole time I had it wrong I got this little rush of associative pleasure whenever I boarded a red-eye, and the whole time I was so sure I was just one element shy of the life-enriching solution to a riddle. But naturally it's the riddle that's enriching, not the solution: the missing piece and the coolness reinforce each other in infinite regress. I don't know why I like it, and I like it because I don't know why.

(1993)

Mark Costello, on walking home with David Foster Wallace after rap concerts in Boston in the summer of 1989: "Dave's question on those walks was always the essential one: 'So—did that show *suck*? Or was it kind of crazy, great, and free?'"

Do you like the garments that we wear?

Phife Dawg, in "Can I Kick It?" (1990)

"They was wearing some real questionable type shit, but people didn't look at them as weirdos," says Black Thought from The Roots in the 2011 documentary *Beats, Rhymes & Life*, recalling Tribe's early look, described by Q-Tip as *daishikied out*. "They looked at them like the Miles Davis of hip-hop-type shit, like, 'Oh, okay, they just know about some shit that we're obviously not up on.'"

Here's that other shit that y'all ain't discovered yet

Rock and roll to the beat of the funk fuzz

Wipe your feet really good on the rhythm rug

Q-Tip, in "Can I Kick It?"

Glenn Collins, quoting Will Smith in the *New York Times* in 1988: "The Fresh Prince believes that white and middle-class audiences are being drawn to the raw energy of authentic rap. 'They see that we're into something they don't understand, they've got to know what it is, and that's why we've sold a million records.'"

Here is something you can't understand

Phife Dawg, in "Electric Relaxation" (1993)

Let me hit it from the back, girl, I won't catch a hernia
Bust off on your couch, now you got Seaman's Furniture

At the end of the same article, Collins quotes Yale historian Robert Farris Thompson, who "maintains that rap will remain a moving target": "'Once America thinks it has got it right, rap will have moved on,' he said. He added, 'I wouldn't be surprised if rap is going into the 21st century.'"

Q-Tip, in "What?" (1991)

What is a Glock if you don't have a clip?
What's a lollipop without the Good Ship?

All the discrete and interwoven pattern recognitions in this book, assembled with joy and leaving me no closer to a unified theory of how it all fits together, seem to me to be proof of rap's multitudes, its dynamism, its knack for illuminating a bigger picture by obscuring many smaller ones. This is what the best art does, and I think it's also why we play with puzzles. It's not about the completed image, but about the slow, oddly suspenseful progress we make toward resolution and completeness—otherwise we'd just look at the picture on the box the puzzle comes in, right? There is so much in the world that is at least provisionally more awesome, more arresting, more puzzling than good. The endlessly deferred promise of understanding, being in the dark and working ever toward the light, just might be what makes the whole thing, impossibly, float.

Music-orientated so when hip-hop was originated / Fitted like pieces of puzzles—complicated

(Eric B. &) Rakim, "Microphone Fiend" (1988)

CRITICISM AND CATEGORIES

He's a big bad wolf in your neighborhood
Not bad meaning bad but bad meaning good

DMC, *in Run-DMC, "Peter Piper" (1986)*

• •

BUT, HARD AS it is for me to wrap my head around, comprehension isn't everything. "Nothing I understand haunts me," writes Mary Ruefle. "Only the things I do not understand have that power over me." As much as I relish the satisfaction of a solution, instantaneous or hard-won, there will always be puzzle pieces I can't place, lacunae I can't fill. There will always be lyrics that no amount of rewinding will explain or disarm, lines that I'll run through each test in my little intellectual battery and that will fail every single one, whereupon I'll take grim stock of the results and conclude that I need new tests. Lines whose merit I can't substantiate—lines, even, that should by all available accounts be bad—but that I know in my ear and my heart and my brain, in that order, are good.

Of course, these qualities sit on a Mobius strip. Mutability and flux. I think a lot about Run-DMC's iconic three-word value-toggle, ***bad meaning good***, how casual it sounded and how ready the world was to follow suit and flip that most fundamental set of

I'm just barely getting started, you already upset / Got a tiger as a pet, I just took him to the vrrwwww

T-Wayne, *"Nasty Freestyle" (2015)*

Bitch I'm cooler than a cooler / Big shouts out to my jeweler

Chief Keef, *"Hallelujah" (2012)*

You 'bout that evil?

Juvenile, *"Solja Rag" (1997)*

262

poles. I think about the halo of admiration that's hovered ever since over words like *wicked* and *phat* and *dumb* and *funky* and *foul* and "'stupid' (terrific)," about how *treacherous*, per David Toop in 1983, "definitely has a positive connotation." I think about the aspirational wingspan of *thug* and *pimp* and *killa*, inside rap and increasingly beyond it, how Fabolous can take Destiny's Child's **trifling good-for-nothing type of brother** and turn it into a boast, how the Geto Boys can outright call the president a gangster and make it obvious that it's a compliment. I think about how the foulest ritual-ized insult exchange in the black vernacular tradition is sometimes called *good talk*, and how the Mandinka expression for "it is very good," *a ka nyi ko-jugu*, translates literally to "it is good badly."

On this continuum, what good are my tests? I consider myself a critic, vocationally and spiritually, but how am I supposed to speak from a position of authority when my good and my bad keep shift-ing and inverting and bleeding together? How do I judge a work by the standard of its intended goals if I can't assume that its creator's values about legal or social or artistic or linguistic norms—even about whether the written word is to be trusted—are consistent with mine? How do I judge something cooler than I am? Do cool and good always overlap?

Maybe it doesn't matter. Maybe authority is beside the point. Given the choice, I prefer to think of the critic less as an arbiter of taste than as a kind of performative interpreter, someone who tries to understand a work and succeeds or fails in a candid and illumi-nating way. Someone who works to extract meaning from it but also radiates his own back in, who finds affinities and symmetries that didn't exist moments before. Someone who has patiently culti-vated that literacy, that specialized knowledge—the art of knowing the hidden roads that go from poem to poem, as Howard Nemerov defines criticism—but is also at all times learning by getting lost. Someone whose authority, perhaps, is little more than his need to possess the words that haunt him and set them down precisely as he

Dart specialist, new Cappadonna get treacherous / I rock tracks like a necklace
Cappadonna, "Slang Editorial" (1998)

To all you Republicans that helped me win / I'd sincerely like to thank ya / 'Cause now I got the world swingin' from my nuts / Damn it feels good to be a gangsta
J. Prince, in Geto Boys, "Damn It Feels Good to Be a Gangsta" (1992)

He better call Becky with the good hair

Got the world going wild 'cause my style so prolific / Me and my dogs so close we cable-knitted
Remy Banks, in Da$h, "4:50 AM" (2015)

Allow me to pause and hit the Mork / Nanu nanu
Bahamadia, "Wordplay" (1996)

You for surely a pawn / Read my story in Psalms
A-Mafia, "My Boy" (2015)

hears them, his willingness to be sung by the song for a while and report back not whether the song is good but how and why it sings.

One of the truly magical things about rap, as sociology and as art, is its capacity to contain enormous literal bad without succumbing to it. It makes space for violence and misogyny and venality and alienation and hatred, not to mention the historical conditions those things reflect and magnify, while itself remaining fundamentally generative, generous, true, real. It doesn't valorize the bad by promoting it, as the most frequent and least intelligent denunciations insist; it valorizes the bad by complicating it, by inventing new categories in which it might eventually find a kind of redemption. Bad like the big bad wolf. Bad like the big bad faggot. Bad like a bad motherfucker. Bad like a bad bitch. *Damn it feels good to be a gangsta. Swear it oughta be a crime just to feel this good.*

Critics love categories. I love categories. To be totally honest, I consider myself a critic largely out of a desire to valorize my love of categories. Give me your -cores, your -waves, your alt-s and -gazes yearning to be post-. Categories can be dangerous too, reductive and dehumanizing: categorical thinking can be racist, or rather racist thinking is categorical in an idiotic way. This is true of blind reverence as much as it is of blind dismissal and disdain—of the view that all rappers are magical language fairies whose exploits are beyond earthly reproach no less than the view that all rappers are violent thugs who should be locked away forever. But it is something humbling, something restorative, to watch as rap takes the easy inherited categories, starting with *good* and *bad*, and atomizes them into something as complex and contradictory and shapeshifting as the world itself.

Maybe the job of the critic, then, is simply to keep track of those categories as they split apart, to help strip them of their explanatory force. I can recognize good in the sense of exemplary and bad in the sense of incompetent, but who can't? Criticism, says George Santayana, is an investigation of what the work is good *for*. Maybe the job of the critic is to challenge the face value of the old binary poles, to set an example by publicly being a little bit bored with that which is simply good, and a little bit haunted by that which is still in the process—by transgressive means, antisocial means, *bad* means—of becoming it.

So come give me a hug if you're into getting rubbed

A LARGER ENGLISH

I been a champion, happy as I ever been
Lampin' in the Hamptons like "What the fuck is a hammock?"
The chef up in the kitchen like "What the fuck is a sammich?"
I'm like, "We gotta find middle ground, we need balance"

Lil Wayne, "Stilletos" (2005)

• •

Lampin' in the Hamptons like "What the fuck is a hammock?"

OKAY, FOR STARTERS, that second line. Say it out loud. If that doesn't do anything, listen to how Wayne says it, the way his emphases become their own miniature breakbeat, using the stressed internal rhymes like a kick drum and the monosyllables in between like a snare. These eleven words were an itch to scratch, an urge to repeat and write down and tinker, long before I had a chapter to name after them. For a long time, like MON CONCEPT VIENT D'AILLEURS on the side of that always-parked truck in Paris, it was just the words floating in isolation. But then I zoomed back out to the whole thought and found a depth I'd been missing. Sometimes you get lucky with the lyrics that choose to make you rewind them.

Only a fool would look to Lil Wayne for guidance on how to be compassionately engaged and community-minded. He's not going to phone bank with you or boycott Amazon on behalf of your local indie

266

bookstore or decline to drop some coiled genius on a track because it's on a Chris Brown album; like that of writer and that of poet, morally upstanding guy is a role he seems profoundly uninterested in playing. But every so often, as in this vignette from a two-minute afterthought of a track on his first *Dedication* mixtape, he happens to nail the zeitgeist right to the wall. Intentionally or not, this moment of mutual misunderstanding and mismatched class appurtenances is a wonderful distillation of the different experiences of the world conveyed by different, sometimes barely compatible Englishes.

What might balance and middle ground require? Perhaps it's what H. Samy Alim calls linguistic equanimity, the political and social equality of languages and vernaculars accepted as distinct. (Remember the liberal uproar about the SAT's verbal bias against inner-city students who didn't know what the hell a *regatta* was?) Perhaps, conversely, it's what John McWhorter calls a larger English: a space where there's no difference in official value or respectability between what is currently standard discourse and what remains, in more ways than we tend to admit, criminal slang. (Remember the conservative uproar about President Obama inviting Common— *Common!*—to perform at the White House?) Perhaps it's more structures in which we reward the authors of novel figurations of reality and elaborate rhetorical risk-takings with more than just album streams and profiles in *The FADER*, in which we praise them for their resourceful and self-conscious language play rather than grousing about their assaults on proper English or misinterpreting their words to perpetuate an agenda of predatory criminalization. Perhaps it's a space where we talk to each other less about our differences and more about what we share, even if it's just love for the same song, a space where it can be felt as true that we—a genuine civic *we*—are speaking and listening to the same words.

It seems melodramatic, in a world with a VC-funded lyric annotation platform and an Ivy League anthology of rap and more college courses each passing semester dedicated to engaging hip-hop

Swagger just dumb, call it Sarah Palin / If you niggas fly then I must be parasailin' / We are not the same, I'm a motherfucking alien

Lil Wayne, "No Ceilings (Pop That)" (2009)

via institutionally sanctioned methods, to argue that we're not at least beginning to make that space. But we don't live there yet.

Kevin Young:

As the stilted Ebonics debate of the 1990s pointed out, we Americans still conceive that there is such a thing as proper English (and just who speaks this? newscasters? politicians? British people? Presumably whoever is speaking, or posing the question); that dialects of all stripes are lesser forms, evolved out of lack of intelligence, rather than need; and an especially unshakable view that black vernacular in particular is a broken, mutilated, ahistorical, insufficient, pidgin English. At our peril we ignore the fact that black vernacular, like the blues, both has a form and performs.

> The Ebonics debate was almost three decades ago, and there was a time when reviving it in order to frame America's race sickness as a question of linguistics might have felt trumped up. But the era of Trumpism has re-exposed some deep wounds that testify to the arbitrariness and arrogance of power, the deafness and invulnerability of ignorance, the baffling impossibility of agreeing on a statement as brutally simple and self-evident as *Black lives matter*. They show how legitimately scary a lack of middle ground can be. Language is how we work toward consensus reality, and if we can't agree on reality, on realness, on the simple mechanics of meaning without misdirection or doublespeak, what hope is there for any other kind of consensus?
>
> Toni Morrison:

It's terrible to think that a child with five different present tenses comes to school to be faced with books that are less than his own language. And then to be told things about his language, which is him, that are sometimes permanently damaging. He may never know the etymology of Africanisms in his language, not even know that "hip" is a real word or that "the dozens" meant something. This is a really cruel fallout of racism.

Rap is not coterminous with the black American experience; I have no doubt that the interval between the first time I wrote these words and the moment you're reading them will only have proven this further. But rap cuts across both blackness and Americanness in a way that's visible, audible, present in the present. Its use of language—the way it both is and isn't capital-E English—is what makes it illuminating, what makes it irresistible, and what makes it frightening.

James Baldwin:

> No true account, really, of black life can be held, can be contained in the American vocabulary. As it is, the only way that you can deal with it is by doing great violence to the assumptions on which the vocabulary is based.

The poet John Agard is from British Guiana, not the United States, and his poem "Listen Mr Oxford Don" preceded the first rap song by a decade, but it has everything to say about the loop of history in which we're still stuck:

> Me not no Oxford don
> me a simple immigrant
> from Clapham Common
> I didn't graduate
> I immigrate
>
> But listen Mr Oxford don
> I'm a man on de run
> and a man on de run
> is a dangerous one
>
> I ent have no gun
> I ent have no knife
> but mugging de Queen's English
> is the story of my life

I don't need no axe
to split/ up yu syntax
I don't need no hammer
to mash/ up yu grammar

I warning you Mr Oxford don
I'm a wanted man
and a wanted man
is a dangerous one

Dem accuse me of assault
on de Oxford dictionary/
imagine a concise peaceful man like me/
dem want me serve time
for inciting rhyme to riot
but I tekking it quiet
down here in Clapham Common

I'm not a violent man Mr. Oxford don
I only armed wit mih human breath
but human breath
is a dangerous weapon

So mek dem send one big word after me
I ent serving no jail sentence
I slashing suffix in self-defence
I bashing future wit present tense
and if necessary

I making de Queen's English accessory/ to my offence

I believe with every fiber of my being that rap is meant not to assault or undermine the American vocabulary but to expand it, open it to include the fringe, the nonstandard, the improper. If that sounds like an echo of the *huddled masses yearning to breathe free* in the Emma Lazarus poem inscribed on a bronze plaque inside the Statue of Liberty, I mean it to. Hip-hop's language space has room enough for ironists and zealots, philanthropists and thugs, people who say *lugubrious* and people who say *on fleek*. It is as close as I know, in its pluralism and diversity and inclusiveness, to an actual working model of the American democratic experiment.

DMC, eulogizing Run-DMC's DJ, Jam Master Jay, gunned down at age thirty-seven in a recording studio in Queens:

> He was the personification, the embodiment of hip-hop. He had love for the strong, he had love for the weak. He treated all people alike and to him no man was better than the next man. Jam Master Jay hung out with the homies and he also hung out with the nerds. He did everything a so-called hip-hopper was supposed to do. He loved our music.

I'm not so naive as to think balance and middle ground will exist in my lifetime. I know it's utopian to think that love is enough, that rap is enough, that language and music and human breath are enough—that any of these things can change a world where Eric Garner says *Don't touch me please* and *I can't breathe*, eleven times, in plain standard English, and is still choked to death by five police officers. These things are not enough, and that is heartbreaking. But I have to believe they're something. A start. If nothing else, speaking the same language is part of what it means and what it takes to agree on what you want, a sandwich or a job or liberation, whatever it turns out to be, whenever we get there.

He gets better 'cause he knows he hasta

A chokehold is a yoke

You would rather have a Lexus or justice? / A dream or some substance? / A Beamer, a necklace, or freedom?

dead prez, "Hip Hop" (2000)

WITNESS

Party and bullshit and party and bullshit and
Party and bullshit and party and bullshit and

BIG, *"Party and Bullshit" (1993)*

• •

FIRST IT WAS a warning. Clamorous, foreboding, cynical. The Last Poets' proto-rap number "When the Revolution Comes," released in 1970, is a fantasy of change, a prophecy of a new order that won't spare the weak or the distracted or the complacent. *Transit cops will be crushed by trains after losing their guns and blood will run through the streets of Harlem drowning anything without substance when the revolution comes,* it says. *White death will froth the walls of museums and churches, breaking the lies that enslaved our mothers when the revolution comes.* But it's a tautology, not a timeline: the revolution will come when the revolution comes. And until then, the poem ends, *you know and I know niggas will party and bullshit and party and bullshit and party and bullshit and party and bullshit and party...*
   Some might even die before the revolution comes.
   Biggie's very first gesture on record—before his debut album, *Ready to Die,* came out; before he even settled on the Notorious B.I.G. as a stage name—was to appropriate that doomsaying outro

272

and repeat it over and over, like a mantra, on the hook to his first single. It's the most nihilistic act of signifying I've ever heard. By the early nineties the revolution had not come: crack had come instead, and Biggie was still halfway embroiled in selling it. At least one of the Last Poets' predictions had come true, though, revolution or not—*guns and rifles will be taking the place of poems and essays*—and it set the tone perfectly for his career, the four years he got to shine impossibly bright before death came and called that album title's bluff.

"Party and Bullshit" doesn't critique or revise "When the Revolution Comes" so much as opt out: enjoy your revolution, gentlemen, I'll be out here hustling, living for the moment. But it's an extraordinary song. It's dexterous and funny and sublimely light, its intricately nested rhymes propelled forward by sheer momentum, and it's as rewarding a first glimpse of a character in his milieu as "In Da Club" was for 50 Cent. Biggie doesn't talk about selling drugs, but we learn everything else from watching him at work and at play: rolling blunts, toting guns, hitting skins, politicking. Sing, who would show up again in "Somebody's Gotta Die," makes an appearance. It's all there. Nothing is out of place. And at the end of all three verses, each one an announcement of a phenomenal lyrical talent at the very outset of its promise—and one of which cuts out for eight perfectly timed bars while a brawl erupts and subsides—comes the naggingly simplistic hook: *All we wanna do is bullshit, and party, and bullshit, and party, and bullshit.* That *bullshit* comes first doesn't seem to bother anyone. It's a loop, a canon, an endless cycle.

Alongside the ready-to-die nihilism for which Biggie became first a spokesman and then a martyr, that hook does something tricky. It taps into rap's deep-rooted tension between talking and doing, between seriousness and triviality, between cutting loose and planning the revolution. The words *party* and *bullshit* have split personalities of their own, holding the traces of all the political parties that have come and gone and the bullshit they swore to

It don't take nothing but fronting for me to start somethin' / Bugging and bucking at niggas like I was duck huntin'

"Party and Bullshit"

See my man Sing that I knew from the projects / Said he had beef, asked me if I had my piece / Sure do, two .22s in my shoes

"Party and Bullshit"

eradicate, all the parties people have thrown to relax and bullshit away their cares. They carry those histories with them, even as at face value they evince the desire to forget, because that's what words do. They bear witness. They remember. And so the Last Poets are somewhere at this party too, maybe scowling in disapproval, maybe one generation more wasted than everyone else in the house.

The notion that speech is a lesser form of endeavor than action is an alluring one, and the energy rap culture derives from it is crucial. But it's also a red herring. Talking is, has always been, a species of doing: a talking drum, a protest chant, a whisper network. It's a place to start the revolution, or to gather while you wait a few more years for it to arrive. It's its own kind of revolution as well. *Black lives matter* didn't come about for twenty-five more years—and so many more deaths, by gun and rifle and transit cop—but its rhetorical power reaches back through time, because that's also what words do. The slogan is now a global movement, and even as "Party and Bullshit" says it's false, the fact of the song—the fact that the song is still here, singing us—argues persuasively for its truth.

Tradition keeps bearing this out. At a time when so much feels fast and ephemeral, rap invests language with life and depth; at a time when black death is still rhetorically and politically cheap, rap builds meaning that lasts by evolving and morphing and regenerating itself, forgetting nothing, signifying everything. Rhyme, semantic drift, quotation, sampling: these are ways of stopping time. That they happen to be good ways to pass time as well—or, sure, to kill it—is not a miracle or an accident but a gift. It's the product of ingenuity and passion, hard work and generosity. "The long life of a people can use their fugitivity, their grief, their history for good," writes Rachel Kaadzi Ghansah. "This isn't magic, this is how it was, and how it will always be. This is how we keep our doors open."

Howard Nemerov:

> It is part of the power of a poem to generate meanings from what may originally be meaningless. Perhaps what I am thinking of as rightness in language is this abstract power, or power gained from being very abstract—the power to handle a great many situations at once, the power of poetry to be somewhat more like a mind than a thought. These apparently trivial examples of things that one repeats to oneself rather as though they were talismans, are they not after all the stuff and substance itself of poetry, and more visibly so for not being so cluttered with meanings that we can't see the things for themselves? After all, delight itself may mean nothing. Love may mean nothing. The world appears to have every prospect of never meaning anything again. But love and delight and, so far, the world remain.

As does rap. May it ever be thus. It is recreation and it is revolution, but at base and at best it's a lot of dudes and some ladies passing the time by talking flyly, beautifully, with great urgency and great frivolity, about this and that. About sex and death, past and future, hopes and fears. About fights and rights and parties and bullshit. About nothing and everything, the answer to a question that also isn't.

SOURCES

So MANY THREADS went into this book that it's daunting to try to gather them all back up, but here goes. Not cited here, for the most part, are the many fragments of commentary and hearsay and armchair scholarship trawled from the middle depths of the internet; I mean in particular user-contributed Genius annotations, Wikipedia articles, and Urban Dictionary definitions. A few music columns or blogs—online, naturally—deserve special mention as regular sources of raw material: Tom Breihan's "Status Ain't Hood" in the *Village Voice* and later at Stereogum; the multiply authored "Rap-Up" column at *Passion of the Weiss*; Noz's *Cocaine Blunts and Hip-Hop Tapes* and *Tumblin Erb*; and *2DopeBoyz*, *The Martorialist*, *Dirty Glove Bastard*, and on and on. *The Rub*'s "History of Hip Hop" mix series was a precious resource as well. The assignment of sources to chapters is in many cases approximate; some of the books, essays, and films cited below were influential to my thinking somewhere along the way, even if no direct traces thereof remain in the final product.

RHETORICAL QUESTIONS
Davey D, "Interview w/ 50 Cent," 2003. See www.daveyd.com/interview50centpt2.html.

ON COOL
Regina Bradley, "Contextualizing Hip Hop Sonic Cool Pose in Late Twentieth- and Twenty-first-Century Rap Music." *Current Musicology* 93, 2012.

Trey Ellis, "The New Black Aesthetic." *Callaloo* 38, 1989.

Henry Louis Gates, Jr., *The Signifying Monkey: A Theory of African-American Literary Criticism*. Oxford University Press, 1988.

Michael P. Jeffries, *Thug Life: Race, Gender, and the Meaning of Hip-Hop*. University of Chicago Press, 2011.

Robin D. G. Kelley, *Yo Mama's DisFUNKtional!: Fighting the Culture Wars in Urban America*. Beacon Press, 1997.

Questlove, "How Hip-Hop Failed Black America." *Vulture*, April 22 to May 27, 2014.

Cornel West, "Black Culture and Postmodernism," in Barbara Kruger and Phil Mariani, eds., *Remaking History*. Bay Press, 1989.

ON ME
Adam Bradley and Andrew DuBois, eds., *The Anthology of Rap*. Yale University Press, 2010.

Adam Krims, *Rap Music and the Poetics of Identity*. Cambridge University Press, 2000.

Adam Mansbach, *Angry Black White Boy*. Crown, 2005.

Jason Tanz, *Other People's Property: A Shadow History of Hip-Hop in White America*. Bloomsbury, 2007.

William Upski Wimsatt, *Bomb the Suburbs*. Subway & Elevated Press, 1994.

SERIOUS RAP
Dan Charnas, *The Big Payback: The History of the Business of Hip-Hop*. New American Library, 2010.

Nelson George, *Hip Hop America*. Penguin, 1998.

Kenji Jasper and Ytasha Womack, eds., *Beats, Rhymes & Life: What We Love and Hate About Hip-Hop*. Crown, 2007.

Sacha Jenkins, Elliott Wilson, Jeff Mao, Gabriel Alvarez, and Brent Rollins, *Ego Trip's Book of Rap Lists*. St. Martin's Press, 1999.

John McWhorter, *All About the Beat: Why Hip-Hop Can't Save Black America*. Avery, 2008.

Tricia Rose, "Never Trust a Big Butt and a Smile," in Murray Forman and Mark Andrew Neal, eds., *That's the Joint! The Hip-Hop Studies Reader*. Routledge, 2004.

David Foster Wallace and Mark Costello, *Signifying Rappers: Rap and Race in the Urban Present*. Ecco, 1990; reissue, Back Bay Books, 2013.

S. Craig Watkins, *Hip Hop Matters: Politics, Pop Culture, and the Struggle for the Soul of a Movement*. Beacon Press, 2005.

WORD MACHINES
Jaswinder Bolina, *Of Color*. McSweeney's, 2020.

Adam Bradley, *Book of Rhymes: The Poetics of Hip-Hop*. Basic Civitas, 2009.

Kevin Young, *The Grey Album: On the Blackness of Blackness*. Graywolf, 2012.

SLANG EVOLUTION & SLANG AND SLIPPERINESS
H. Samy Alim, *Roc the Mic Right: The Language of Hip Hop Culture*. Routledge, 2006.

Paul Beatty, *Slumberland*. Bloomsbury, 2008.

Janette Beckman, *Rap: Portraits and Lyrics of a Generation of Black Rockers*. St. Martin's Press, 1991.

Jonathan Bonanno, "Return of the Dragon." *The Source*, March 2000.

Regina Bradley, "Getting Off at the 13th Floor: Rap Genius and Archiving 21st Century Black Cultural Memory." *Journal of Ethnic Literature* 4, 2014.

Glenn Collins, "Rap Music, Brash and Swaggering, Enters Mainstream." *New York Times*, August 29, 1988.

Jay-Z with Dream Hampton, *Decoded*. Spiegel & Grau, 2010.

Matt Jost, "For the Record: RapGenius.com Stole My S#!t," May 15, 2015. See www.rapreviews.com/special/jost-fortherecord-may15.html.

Jesse McCarthy, "Notes on Trap." *n+1* 32, 2018.

Claudia Mitchell-Kernan, "Signifying and Marking: Two Afro-American Speech Acts," in John J. Gumperz and Dell Hymes, eds., *Directions in Linguistics: The Ethnography of Communication*. Holt, Rinehart and Winston, 1972.

Alexs Pate, *In the Heart of the Beat: The Poetry of Rap*. Scarecrow Press, 2010.

John Russell Rickford and Russell John Rickford, *Spoken Soul: The Story of Black English*. Wiley, 2000.

Geneva Smitherman, *Talkin and Testifyin: The Language of Black America*. Wayne State University Press, 1986.

Peter Spirer, *Rhyme & Reason*. City Block Productions, 1997.

Lawrence Stanley, ed., *Rap: The Lyrics: The Words to Rap's Greatest Hits*. Penguin, 1992.

Lois Stavsky, I. E. Mozeson, and Dani Reyes Mozeson, *A 2 Z: The Book of Rap & Hip-Hop Slang*. Boulevard, 1995.

Alonzo Westbrook, *Hip Hoptionary: The Dictionary of Hip Hop Terminology*. Harlem Moon, 2002.

ON RHYME

Bradley, *Book of Rhymes*.

David Caplan, *Rhyme's Challenge: Hip Hop, Poetry, and Contemporary Rhyming Culture*. Oxford University Press, 2014.

Anderson Cooper, Eminem interview. *60 Minutes*, October 2010.

Matthew S. McGlone and Jessica Tofighbakhsh, "Birds of a Feather Flock Conjointly (?): Rhyme as Reason in Aphorisms." *Psychological Science* 11 (5), 2000.

Smitherman, *Talkin and Testifyin*.

Matthew Zapruder, *Why Poetry*. Ecco, 2018.

ON REGISTER

William Jelani Cobb, *To the Break of Dawn: A Freestyle on the Hip Hop Aesthetic*. NYU Press, 2008.

Jeff Chang, *Can't Stop Won't Stop: A History of the Hip-Hop Generation*. Picador, 2005.

Matt Daniels, "The Largest Vocabulary in Hip-Hop." *The Pudding*, February 2017. See pudding.cool/projects/vocabulary/index.html.

HAUNTED ROOTS

Dan Chiasson, "Color Codes." *New Yorker*, October 20, 2014.

Hua Hsu, "What Normalization Means." *New Yorker*, November 13, 2016.

Cord Jefferson, "Kanye West and His 'Thirty White Bitches.'" *The Awl*, June 25, 2013.

Claudia Rankine, *Citizen*. Graywolf Press, 2014.

Rickford and Rickford, *Spoken Soul*.

CODE AND CONTRABAND

Frederick Douglass, *Narrative of the Life of Frederick Douglass, an American Slave*. 1845.

Rita Dove, "Canary," in *Grace Notes*. W. W. Norton & Company, 1989.

W. E. B. Du Bois, *The Souls of Black Folk*. 1903.

Henry Louis Gates, Jr., "Criticism in the Jungle," in Henry Louis Gates, Jr., ed., *Black Literature and Literary Theory*. Routledge, 1984.

Jay-Z, *Decoded*.

Cheryl Keyes, *Rap Music and Street Consciousness*. University of Illinois Press, 2002.

Erik Nielson, "'Can't C Me': Surveillance and Rap Music." *Journal of Black Studies* 40 (6), 2009.

Imani Perry, *Prophets of the Hood: Politics and Poetics in Hip Hop*. Duke University Press, 2004.

Smitherman, *Talkin and Testifyin*.

Snacks and Shit. See snacksandshit.typepad.com.

Greg Tate, *Flyboy in the Buttermilk: Essays on Contemporary America*. Fireside, 1992.

Young, *The Grey Album*.

INTELLIGENCES

Du Bois, *The Souls of Black Folk*.

Jeff Chang, *We Gon' Be Alright: Notes on Race and Resegregation*. Picador, 2016.

Brian Cross, *It's Not About a Salary... Rap, Race + Resistance in Los Angeles*. Verso, 1993.

William Empson, *Seven Types of Ambiguity*. New Directions, 1966.

Nikki Giovanni, "Ego-Tripping (there may be a reason why)," in *My House*. William Morrow, 1974.

Ice-T, *Something from Nothing: The Art of Rap*. JollyGood Films, 2012.

Jay-Z, *Decoded*.

Krims, *Rap Music and the Poetics of Identity*.

Audre Lorde, "The Master's Tools Will Never Dismantle the Master's House," in *Sister Outsider: Essays and Speeches*. Crossing Press, 2007.

Emily Lordi, *The Meaning of Soul: Black Music and Resilience Since the 1960s*. Duke University Press, 2020.

Wallace Stevens, "Man Carrying Thing," in *The Collected Poems of Wallace Stevens*. Knopf, 1954.

Zapruder, *Why Poetry*.

POWER PLAY

Bradley, *Book of Rhymes*.

F. Scott Fitzgerald, *The Great Gatsby*. 1925.

Henry Louis Gates, Jr., "The 'Blackness of Blackness': A Critique of the Sign and the Signifying Monkey." *Critical Inquiry* 9 (4), 1983.

Gates, *The Signifying Monkey*.

Charles Holdefer, "'Shaving Cream' and Other Mind Rhymes." *Antioch Review* 67 (1), 2009.

Douglas Martin, "Rudy Ray Moore, 81, a Precursor of Rap, Dies." *New York Times*, October 22, 2008.

Adam Sexton, ed., *Rap on Rap: Straight-Up Talk on Hiphop Culture*. Delta, 1995.

Elijah Wald, *The Dozens: A History of Rap's Mama*. Oxford University Press, 2012.

WORD AS BOND

Ernest Allen, Jr., "Making the Strong Survive: The Contours and Contradictions of Message Rap," in William Eric Perkins, ed., *Droppin' Science: Critical Essays on Rap Music and Hip Hop Culture*. Temple University Press, 1996.

Jenkins et al., *Ego Trip's Book of Rap Lists.*

Michael Muhammad Knight, *The Five Percenters: Islam, Hip-Hop and the Gods of New York.* Oneworld Publications, 2008.

Michael Muhammad Knight, *Why I Am a Five Percenter.* Tarcher Perigee, 2011.

Krims, *Rap Music and the Poetics of Identity.*

Felicia M. Miyakawa, *Five Percenter Rap: God Hop's Music, Message, and Black Muslim Mission.* Indiana University Press, 2005.

Ben Westhoff, *Original Gangstas: Tupac Shakur, Dr. Dre, Eazy-E, Ice Cube, and the Birth of West Coast Rap.* Hachette, 2016.

ANTI-SIMILE

V. S. Ramachandran, *The Tell-Tale Brain: A Neuroscientist's Quest for What Makes Us Human.* W. W. Norton & Company, 2011.

ECONOMY AND TIME

Allison P. Davis, "Regular, Degular, Shmegular Girl from the Bronx." *New York*, November 13, 2017.

Gates, *The Signifying Monkey.*

Young, *The Grey Album.*

SIGNIFYING CHAINS

Cobb, *To the Break of Dawn.*

Roy Christopher, *Dead Precedents: How Hip-Hop Defines the Future.* Repeater Books, 2019.

Gates, *The Signifying Monkey.*

Fredric Jameson, *Postmodernism, or, the Cultural Logic of Late Capitalism.* Duke University Press, 1991.

Howard Nemerov, *Figures of Thought: Speculations on the Meaning of Poetry and Other Essays.* Godine, 1978.

RECYCLING

Jorge Luis Borges, "Pierre Menard, Author of the *Quixote*," in *Collected Fictions*, tr. Andrew Hurley. Penguin, 1999.

Bradley, *Book of Rhymes.*

Russell Potter, *Spectacular Vernaculars: Hip-Hop and the Politics of Postmodernism.* SUNY Press, 1995.

ELECTIVE CHRONOLOGY

Pierre Bayard, *Le Plagiat par anticipation.* Editions de Minuit, 2013.

Steve Erickson, *These Dreams of You.* Europa Editions, 2012.

Potter, *Spectacular Vernaculars.*

Tricia Rose, *Black Noise: Rap Music and Black Culture in Contemporary America.* Wesleyan University Press, 1994.

Young, *The Grey Album.*

ANCESTOR WORSHIP

Potter, *Spectacular Vernaculars.*

WRITING/BITING

Jay-Z, *Decoded.*

Jenkins et al., *Ego Trip's Book of Rap Lists*.

Ariel Schneller, "Jay-Z 'recycling' Biggie's rhymes: biting, allusion, unaware, or public domain?" *Genius*, January 23, 2010.

Reeves Weideman, "Conversation Piece." *New Yorker*, November 22, 2010.

"Ice-T Calls Out Jay-Z Fans over Ownership of 99 Problems," ArtisanNewsService, August 5, 2014.

"Ice-T Talks New Body Count Album, Jay-Z's Remake of '99 Problems' & Much More," Radio.com, July 7, 2014.

AGGRAVATED QUOTATION

Brian Coleman, *Check the Technique: Liner Notes for Hip-Hop Junkies*. Villard, 2007.

William Eric Perkins, "The Rap Attack: An Introduction" in Perkins, ed., *Droppin' Science*.

Westhoff, *Original Gangstas*.

HYPERLINKS

Robert Christgau, "Who's That? Brooown!" *Barnes & Noble Review*, December 26, 2012.

Zapruder, *Why Poetry*.

ON CLICHÉ

Gérard Genette, *Palimpsests: Literature in the Second Degree*, tr. Channa Newman and Claude Doubinsky. University of Nebraska Press, 1997.

Jenkins et al., *Ego Trip's Book of Rap Lists*.

Mary Ruefle, *Madness, Rack & Honey: Collected Lectures*. Wave Books, 2012.

Tate, *Flyboy in the Buttermilk*.

Ben Westhoff, *Dirty South: OutKast, Lil Wayne, Soulja Boy, and the Southern Rappers Who Reinvented Hip-Hop*. Chicago Review Press, 2011.

Young, *The Grey Album*.

WHO WORE IT BETTER?

Bradley, *Book of Rhymes*.

Tom Breihan, "Jay Z Would Like to Remind You That He Can Rap." *Stereogum*, June 8, 2016.

Genette, *Palimpsests*.

DENIABLE PLAUSIBILITY

Ernest Baker, "Drake in Real Life." *Complex*, April 17, 2015.

Rachel Kaadzi Ghansah, "Her Eyes Were Watching the Stars: How Missy Elliott Became an Icon." *Elle*, May 15, 2017.

ON FIRST PERSON

Hanif Abdurraqib, *They Can't Kill Us Until They Kill Us*. Two Dollar Radio, 2017.

Roland Barthes, *Mythologies*. Le Seuil, 1957.

Chang, *Can't Stop Won't Stop*.

Coleman, *Check the Technique*.

Robert Christgau, Consumer Guide review of *Da Drought 3*, 2007. See www.robertchristgau.com.

Jeremy Gordon, "Is Everything Wrestling?" *New York Times*, May 27, 2016.

Curtis Hanson, *8 Mile*. Imagine Entertainment, 2002.

Kathy Iandoli, *God Save the Queens: The Essential History of Women in Hip-Hop*. Harper Collins, 2019.

Jenkins et al., *Ego Trip's Book of Rap Lists*.

Robin D. G. Kelley, "Kickin' Reality, Kickin' Ballistics: Gangsta Rap and Postindustrial Los Angeles," in Perkins, ed., *Droppin' Science*.

Kelley, *Yo' Mama's DysFUNKtional!*

Katja Lee, "Reconsidering Rap's 'I': Eminem's Autobiographical Postures and the Construction of Identity Authenticity." *Canadian Review of American Studies* 38 (3), 2008.

Spirer, *Rhyme & Reason*.

Jia Tolentino, "The Year We Played Ourselves." *New Yorker*, December 5, 2016.

Young, *The Grey Album*.

TRUTH AND CONSEQUENCE

Abdurraqib, *They Can't Kill Us Until They Kill Us*.

Bradley, *Book of Rhymes*.

Coleman, *Check the Technique*.

Jimmy Fallon, Ice Cube interview on *Late Night with Jimmy Fallon*, January 15, 2014.

Rick Famuyiwa, *Dope*. Significant Productions, 2015.

Jasper and Womack, eds., *Beats, Rhymes & Life*.

Jeffries, *Thug Life*.

Michael Larnell, *Roxanne Roxanne*. Netflix, 2017.

Lee, "Reconsidering Rap's 'I.'"

Richard Lowe and Martin Torgoff, *Planet Rock: The Story of Hip-Hop and the Crack Generation*. Prodigious Media, 2011.

Perry, *Prophets of the Hood*.

Potter, *Spectacular Vernaculars*.

Edwin Ortiz, "Donovan Strain Shares His Analysis of Figuring Out the Exact Day Ice Cube Was Talking About on 'It Was a Good Day.'" *Complex*, January 20, 2014.

Eithne Quinn, *Nuthin' but a "G" Thang: The Culture and Commerce of Gangsta Rap*. Columbia University Press, 2004.

Tricia Rose, *Hip-Hop Wars: What We Talk About When We Talk About Hip-Hop—And Why It Matters*. Civitas, 2008.

Steve Stoute, *The Tanning of America: How Hip-Hop Created a Culture That Rewrote the Rules of the New Economy*. Avery, 2012.

Donovan Strain, "I Found Ice Cubes 'Good Day.'" Murk Avenue, January 27, 2012. See murkavenue.tumblr.com/post/16553509655/i-found-ice-cubes-good-day.

Stephen Lester Thompson, "Knowwhatumsayin'? How Hip-Hop Lyrics Mean," in Derrick Darby and Tommie Shelby, eds., *Hip Hop and Philosophy: Rhyme 2 Reason*. Open Court, 2005.

David Toop, *Rap Attack: African Jive to New York Hip Hop*. South End Press, 1985.

Young, *The Grey Album*.

CRIMINAL SLANG

David B. Caruso, "More Rap Lyrics Showing Up in Court." *Washington Post*, December 21, 2006.

Charnas, *The Big Payback*.

Mike Corbera, *Eminem AKA*. Xenon Pictures, 2004.

Andrea L. Dennis, "Poetic (In)Justice? Rap Music Lyrics as Art, Life, and Criminal Evidence." *Columbia Journal of Law & the Arts* 31 (1), 2007.

Gilad Edelman, "Killer Mike's Supreme Court Brief." *New Yorker*, December 28, 2015.

Stuart P. Fischoff, "Gangsta' Rap and a Murder in Bakersfield." *Journal of Applied Social Psychology* 29 (4), 1999.

Gates, *The Signifying Monkey*.

Jack Hamilton, "Rhyme and Punishment." *Slate*, March 31, 2014.

Charis E. Kubrin and Erik Nielson, "Rap on Trial." *Race and Justice* 4 (3), 2014.

Jay-Z, *Decoded*.

Lee, "Reconsidering Rap's 'I.'"

Sam Lefebvre, "Rap's Poetic License: Revoked." *East Bay Express*, April 29, 2015.

Adam Liptak, "Hip-Hop Artists Give the Supreme Court a Primer on Rap Music." *New York Times*, March 6, 2019.

Joëlle Anne Moreno, "What Happens When Dirty Harry Becomes an (Expert) Witness for the Prosecution?" *Tulane Law Review* 79 (1), 2004.

Leon Neyfakh, "Eric Garner. Michael Brown. Bobby Shmurda." *Slate*, February 3, 2015.

Erik Nielson and Michael Render, "Rap's Poetic (In)justice: Flashback." *USA Today*, November 28, 2014.

Erik Nielson and Andrea L. Dennis, *Rap on Trial: Race, Lyrics, and Guilt in America*. New Press, 2019.

Perry, *Prophets of the Hood*.

Tricia Rose, "Rap Music and the Demonization of Black Males," in Thelma Golden, ed., *Black Male: Representations of Masculinity in Contemporary American Art*. Whitney Museum of Art, 1994.

Toop, *Rap Attack*.

Brianna Younger, "The Controversial Use of Rap Lyrics as Evidence." *New Yorker*, September 20, 2019.

SELLING WORK

"Makonnen addresses his sexuality and shades OG Maco!" Hot 97, December 9, 2014. See www.youtube.com/watch?v=spdmtEF4gnM.

Bradley, *Book of Rhymes*.

Coleman, *Check the Technique*.

Thomas LeClair, "'The Language Must Not Sweat.'" *New Republic*, March 21, 1981.

Rose, *Hip-Hop Wars*.

Shea Serrano, *The Rap Year Book: The Most Important Rap Song from Every Year Since 1979, Discussed, Debated, and Deconstructed*. Abrams Image, 2015.

Tate, *Flyboy in the Buttermilk*.

Young, *The Grey Album*.

ON VALUES

Joan Morgan, *When Chickenheads Come Home to Roost: My Life as a Hip-Hop Feminist*. Simon & Schuster, 1999.

Questlove, "How Hip-Hop Failed Black America."

ON THE B-WORD

Joe Coscarelli, "The Story of 'Mo Bamba': How a SoundCloud Rap Track Goes Viral." *New York Times*, September 4, 2018.

Ana Marie Cox, "Ice Cube Might Have Dinner with the President." *New York Times*, August 9, 2015.

Ashon T. Crawley, *The Lonely Letters*. Duke University Press, 2020.

Ava DuVernay, *My Mic Sounds Nice: The Truth About Women and Hip Hop*. Forward Movement, 2010.

Pierre Evil, *Gangsta Rap. Dr. Dre, Snoop Dogg, 2Pac et les autres*. Le mot et le reste, 2018.

Chinaka Hodge, *Dated Emcees*. City Lights Publishing, 2016.

Iandoli, *God Save the Queens*.

Joan Morgan, "Hip-Hop Feminist," in Forman and Neal, eds., *That's the Joint!*

Joan Morgan, "The Nigga Ya Hate to Love," in Sexton, ed., *Rap on Rap*.

Morgan, *When Chickenheads Come Home to Roost*.

Mark Anthony Neal, "I'll Be Nina Simone Defecating on Your Microphone: Hip-Hop and Gender," in Forman and Neal, eds., *That's the Joint!*

Conan O'Brien, Snoop Dogg interview on *Late Night with Conan O'Brien*, March 3, 2004.

Pate, *In the Heart of the Beat*.

Quinn, *Nuthin' but a 'G' Thang*.

Brian Robbins, *The Show*. Savoy Pictures, 1995.

Tracy Sharpley Denean-Whiting, *Pimps Up, Ho's Down: Hip Hop's Hold on Young Black Women*. NYU Press, 2008.

David Sheff, "The *Playboy* Interview with Snoop Doggy Dogg." *Playboy*, October 1, 1995.

Hanif Willis-Abdurraqib, "In Defense of 'Trap Queen' as Our Generation's Greatest Love Song." *Seven Scribes*, June 5, 2015.

Young, *The Grey Album*.

ON THE N-WORD

Abdurraqib, *They Can't Kill Us Until They Kill Us*.

Mark Blackwell, "Niggaz4Dinner." *Spin*, September 1991.

Jeff Chang, *Who We Be: A Cultural History of Race in Post–Civil Rights America*. Picador, 2016.

Ta-Nehisi Coates, "In Defense of a Loaded Word." *New York Times*, November 23, 2013.

Jesse Dylan, *How High*. Jersey Films, 2001.

Jonathan Gold, "Twenty-seven years later, N.W.A still rubs a raw spot," *Los Angeles Times*, September 5, 2015.

Ben Horowitz, "The Past and Future of Systems Management." Andreessen Horowitz, March 12, 2015. See www.a16z.com/2015/03/12/the-past-and-future-of-systems-management.

Lauren Michele Jackson, *White Negroes: When Cornrows Were in Vogue… and Other Thoughts on Cultural Appropriation*. Beacon Press, 2020.

Tim Mohr, "Cornel West Talks Rhymes and Race." *Playboy*, November 2007.

Perry, *Prophets of the Hood*.

Tanz, *Other People's Property*.

Jonah Weiner, "'Niggas,' in Practice." *Slate*, June 12, 2012.

Westhoff, *Original Gangstas*.

Damon Young, *What Doesn't Kill You Makes You Blacker: A Memoir in Essays*. Ecco, 2018.

Young, *The Grey Album*.

ON WHITE PEOPLE

Hilton Als, *White Girls*. McSweeney's, 2013.

Eula Biss, "White Debt." *New York Times*, December 2, 2015.

Ta-Nehisi Coates, *Between the World and Me*. One World, 2015.

Robin D'Angelo, "White Fragility." *International Journal of Critical Pedagogy* 3 (3), 2011.

Mickey Hess, *A Guest in the House of Hip-Hop: How Rap Music Taught a Kid from Kentucky What a White Ally Should Be*. Ig Publishing, 2018.

bell hooks, "Interview." *Spin*, April 1993.

Potter, *Spectacular Vernaculars*.

Rose, *Hip-Hop Wars*.

Tanz, *Other People's Property*.

Carvell Wallace, "On Kendrick Lamar and Black Humanity." *Pitchfork*, March 19, 2015.

Greg Tate, ed. *Everything but the Burden: What White People Are Taking from Black Culture*. Crown, 2003.

ON SECOND PERSON

Questlove, "How Hip-Hop Failed Black America."

IS RAP POETRY?

Houston Baker, *Black Studies, Rap, and the Academy*. University of Chicago Press, 1995.

Bradley, *Book of Rhymes*.

Cobb, *To the Break of Dawn*.

Paul Edwards, *How to Rap: The Art and Science of the Hip-Hop MC*. Chicago Review Press, 2009.

Ghansah, "Her Eyes Were Watching the Stars."

Audre Lorde, "Poetry Is Not a Luxury." *Chrysalis: A Magazine of Female Culture*, 1977.

Adam Bhala Lough, *The Carter*. QD3 Entertainment, 2009.

Nemerov, *Figures of Thought*.

Pate, *In the Heart of the Beat*.

Wallace and Costello, *Signifying Rappers*.

Young, *The Grey Album*.

Zapruder, *Why Poetry*.

WRITING/NOT WRITING

Black Dog Bone and Paul Stewart, eds., *Murder Dog: The Interviews, Volume 1*. Over the Edge Publishing, 2015.

Devin Friedman, "Lil Wayne: The Uncut Q&A." *GQ*, January 13, 2009.

Jayson Greene, "Chaos Theory: The Glorious Unpredictability of Young Thug." *Pitchfork*, September 28, 2015.

Iandoli, *God Save the Queens*.

Lough, *The Carter*.

Kia Makarechi, "Big Sean Collapsed in Tears When His Album Was Released." *Vanity Fair*, March 2, 2015.

WHAT YOU HEAR IS NOT A TEXT

Bradley and DuBois, eds., *The Anthology of Rap*.

Jay-Z, *Decoded*.

Gretchen McCulloch, *Because Internet: Understanding the New Rules of Language*. Riverhead, 2019.

Fran Ross, *Oreo*, reprint edition. New Directions, 2015.

Young, *The Grey Album*.

ON POSSESSION

Bradley and DuBois, eds., *The Anthology of Rap*.

Tate, *Flyboy in the Buttermilk*.

ON POSSESSION WITH INTENT TO SELL

Jeffries, *Thug Life.*

Phillip Mlynar, "Kendrick Lamar Wants Us All to Say 'Bitch.'" *Village Voice*, November 1, 2012.

Potter, *Spectacular Vernaculars.*

Tanz, *Other People's Property.*

Questlove, "How Hip-Hop Failed Black America."

SIGNIFYING ORNAMENTS

John Baugh and Geneva Smitherman, "Linguistic emancipation in global perspective," in H. Samy Alim and John Baugh, eds., *Talkin Black Talk: Language, Education, and Social Change*, 2007

Baker, *Black Studies, Rap, and the Academy.*

Chris Martins, "Del the Funky Homosapien." *AV Club*, May 12, 2009.

McCulloch, *Because Internet.*

Miyakawa, *Five Percenter Rap.*

Geoff Nunberg, "Standard Issue," in *The Way We Talk Now*. Houghton Mifflin, 2001.

Warren Olivo, "Phat Lines: Spelling Conventions in Rap Music." *Written Language & Literacy* 4 (1), 2001.

Rickford and Rickford, *Spoken Soul.*

John Jeremiah Sullivan, "In Memoriam: Lil Peep," *GQ*, January 28, 2018.

Tate, *Flyboy in the Buttermilk.*

Young, *The Grey Album.*

OUTSIDER ART

William Buckholz, *Understand Rap: Explanations of Confusing Rap Lyrics You & Your Grandma Can Understand*. Abrams Image, 2010.

Charnas, *The Big Payback.*

Cross, *It's Not About a Salary.*

Tate, *Flyboy in the Buttermilk.*

ON IRONY

Nitsuh Abebe, "The Rules of the Game: A Fuller Thought on J. Hopper and Vampire Weekend." *A Grammar*, January 29, 2010. See agrammar.tumblr.com/post/359990238/the-rules-of-the-game-a-fuller-thought-on-j.

Jon Caramanica, "Finding a Place in the Hip-Hop Ecosystem." *New York Times*, January 27, 2014.

Bakari Kitwana, *Why White Kids Love Hip-Hop: Wankstas, Wiggers, Wannabes, and the New Reality of Race in America*. Civitas, 2005.

Seth Price, *Fuck Seth Price*. Leopard Press, 2015.

Jedediah Purdy, *For Common Things: Irony, Trust, and Commitment in America Today*. Vintage, 2000.

Carvell Wallace, "Being a Hipster Is Not Compatible with Being Black." *Vice*, December 17, 2015.

DUMB LOVE

Coleman, *Check the Technique.*

Collins, "Rap Music, Brash and Swaggering, Enters Mainstream."

Michael Rapaport, *Beats, Rhymes & Life: The Travels of A Tribe Called Quest*. Sony Pictures Classics, 2011.

Tanz, *Other People's Property.*

Wallace and Costello, *Signifying Rappers.*

CRITICISM AND CATEGORIES

Guy Davenport, *Every Force Evolves a Form*. North Point Press, 1987.

Jeffries, *Thug Life*.

Nemerov, *Figures of Thought*.

Quinn, *Nuthin' but a 'G' Thang*.

Rickford and Rickford, *Spoken Soul*.

Ruefle, *Madness, Rack & Honey*.

George Santayana, "Reason in Art," in *Reason in Art: The Life of Reason*. Dover, 1982.

Smitherman, *Talkin and Testifyin*.

Toop, *Rap Attack*.

A LARGER ENGLISH

John Agard, *Alternative Anthem*. Bloodaxe Books, 2009.

Alim, *Roc the Mic Right*.

James Baldwin, *The Last Interview and Other Conversations*. Melville House, 2014.

Charnas, *The Big Payback*.

LeClair, "'The Language Must Not Sweat.'"

John McWhorter, *Talking Back, Talking Black: Truths About America's Lingua Franca*. Bellevue Literary Press, 2017.

Young, *The Grey Album*.

WITNESS

Jeff Alessandrelli, *The Man on High: Essays on Skateboarding, Hip-Hop, Poetry and the Notorious B.I.G.* Squint Books, 2018.

Rachel Kaadzi Ghansah, "A Most American Terrorist: The Making of Dylann Roof." *GQ*, August 21, 2017.

Nemerov, *Figures of Thought*.

David Roth, "Guru: Hard-Earned." *The Awl*, April 22, 2010.

RIGHTS AND PERMISSIONS

THE QUOTATIONS IN *What's Good* are strictly for the purposes of scholarship and criticism. The vast majority of these are *de minimus* uses covered under the doctrine of fair use as codified in Title 17 of the United States Code, section 107 of the Copyright Act of 1976.[1] In certain cases where it was necessary to quote a more substantial excerpt of a copyrighted work, the author has sought and obtained permission from the relevant copyright holders. Those permissions appear below. In a very small number of cases, no rights administrators were found. Any copyright holder who believes there is an erroneous attribution or omission may contact the author c/o City Lights Publishers.

---

1 See https://www.copyright.gov/title17/92chap1.html#107.

LYRICS

293

OTHER

The poem by John Agard, "Listen Mr Oxford Don," is from his collection *Alternative Anthem: Selected Poems with Live DVD* (Bloodaxe Books, 2009). *Reproduced with permission of Bloodaxe Books.* www.bloodaxebooks.com

ACKNOWLEDGMENTS

• •

I HOPE IT GOES without saying that I'm deeply, ecstatically grateful to all of the artists and scholars whose work is quoted or evoked in the preceding pages. Just in case: thank you for everything you do.

For believing in this project early on, and for the high standard to which you patiently held it throughout its development, thank you to Garrett Caples and to the rest of the team at and around City Lights: Gerilyn Attebery, Elaine Katzenberger, Peter Maravelis, Stacey Lewis, Chris Carosi, Emma Hager, Jeff Mellin, and Michael Young.

For attentive and generous readings of some or all of the manuscript in early or late iterations, thank you to Adam Bradley, Brandon Bussolini, Martin Glazier, Arielle Harrison, Hua Hsu, Casey Jarman, Michelle Kuo, Rami Levin, Maureen Miller, Ismail Muhammad, Ethan Nosowsky, Ian Port, Jeremy Schmidt, Ross Simonini, Ethan Watters, Anna Wiener, Andi Winnette, Colin Winnette, Albert Wu, and Etay Zwick. Thanks also to Mauro Javier Cardenas, Anisse Gross, Anthony Ha, Rachel Khong, Alice Sola Kim, Reese Kwon, Greg Larson, Caille Millner, Tony Tulathimutte, Vauhini Vara, Esme Weijun Wang, and Annie Julia Wyman.

For publishing-world guidance, thanks to Anna Stein, Jacqueline Ko, Taylor Sperry, Melissa Flashman, and Robert Guinsler. For time, space, and other material considerations, thanks to Paul Aleman Jr., Michael Becker and Mary Baim, Anne Fadiman, Pat and Ira Potovsky, Nicole Smith, and MacDowell. For enthusiasm, encouragement, and other practical and spiritual assistance, thanks to Hanif Abdurraqib, Luca Balbo, Valérie Beaudouin, Catherine Brobeck, Jeff Chang, Dale Conour, Michael Dawson, Jeremy Galen, Rashawn Griffin, Melissa Holub, Brad Johnson, Jim and Mindy Kearns, Tom La Farge, Abigail Lance-De Vos, James David Lee, Andrew Leland, Jonathan Lethem, Kate Levy, Daniel Medin, Warren Motte, Niela Orr, Jean-Jacques Poucel, Clara Sankey, Shawn Setaro, David Shields, Will Toussaint, Wendy Walker, Alex Wipperfürth, Matthew Zapruder, and Ilan Zechory.

For a lifetime's worth of listening companionship and conversation, which whether you intended it or not helped make me a better critic, thank you to Brandon Bussolini, Ben Chung, Martin Glazier, Niko Koppel, and Chris Zamiar. Thanks also, on similar grounds, to Rob Bales, Andy Barrett, David Becker, Jonathan Becker, Hayden Bennett, Eduardo Berti, Satya Bhabha, Rishi Bhat, Aparna Chandrasekhar, Brian Christian, Kristin Cox, Thomas Crowley, Elliot Epstein, Peter Feigenbaum, Frédéric Forte, Clark Freeman, Veronica Scott Esposito, Gordon Faylor, Hannah Frank, Colin Gilford, KC Gleason, Elizabeth Gumport, Rick Harrison, Otis Hart, Catherine Herdlick, Nina Holbrook, Sam Hunt, Josh Izenberg, Josh Joseph, Jason Kirk, Rachel Khong, Naomi Leibowitz, Nik Lund, Patrick Masterson, Ian Monk, Nathaniel Motte, Aaron Peck, Ian Port, Dylan Posa, Nicolas Richard, Ehsan Sadeghi, Rod Sanjabi, Andy Schneider, Elaine Schwartz, Ian Sherman, Jessica Siegler, Richard Siegler, Gabe Smedresman, Elaine Schwartz, Alec Tabak, Jeff Treviño, Daoud Tyler-Ameen, Shontina Vernon, Chris Weingarten, Brandon and Bryce Wilner, Colin Winnette, and Mark Yoshizumi. I've tried my best to make this book feel as rich and rewarding as talking to you.

For literally all of the above, and everything else, thank you to Kristina Kearns. You are good.

ABOUT THE AUTHOR

• •

DANIEL LEVIN BECKER is a critic, editor, and translator from Chicago. An early contributing editor to Rap Genius, he has written about music for *The Believer*, NPR, *SF Weekly*, and Dusted Magazine, among others. His first book, *Many Subtle Channels*, recounts his induction into the French literary collective Oulipo.